ACCIDENT OR SUICIDE?

ACCIDENT

→ OR ←

SUICIDE?

Destruction by Automobile

By

NORMAN TABACHNICK, M.D., Editor

and

JOHN GUSSEN, M.D.
ROBERT E. LITMAN, M.D.
MICHAEL L. PECK, Ph.D.
NORMAN TIBER, Ph.D.
CARL I. WOLD, Ph.D.

Accident Research Program
Suicide Prevention Center
Los Angeles, California

CHARLES C THOMAS • PUBLISHER
Springfield • Illinois • U.S.A.

Published and Distributed Throughout the World by
CHARLES C THOMAS • PUBLISHER
Bannerstone House
301-327 East Lawrence Avenue, Springfield, Illinois, U.S.A.

© *1973, by* CHARLES C THOMAS • PUBLISHER
ISBN 0-398-02819-2
Library of Congress Catalog Card Number: 73-2870

*With THOMAS BOOKS careful attention is given to all details of
manufacturing and design. It is the Publisher's desire to present books that are
satisfactory as to their physical qualities and artistic possibilities and
appropriate for their particular use. THOMAS BOOKS will be true to those
laws of quality that assure a good name and good will.*

Library of Congress Cataloging in Publication Data
Accident or suicide?

1. Suicide. 2. Crash injuries. I. Tabachnick, Norman. II. Gussen, John. [DNLM:
1. Accidents, Traffic. 2. Psychoanalytic interpretation. 3. Suicide. WA 275 A171
1973].
RC574.A24   616.8'5844   73-2870
ISBN 0-398-02819-2

Printed in the United States of America
AA-1

For our wives and children

CONTRIBUTORS

John Gussen, M.D.
Clinical Professor of Psychiatry, University of Southern California; Senior Research Psychiatrist, Los Angeles Suicide Prevention Center; Faculty Southern California Psychoanalytic Institute; Senior Attending Staff, Cedars Sinai Medical Center.

Robert E. Litman, M.D.
Chief Psychiatrist, Suicide Prevention Center and Institute for Studies of Self-Destructive Behaviors; Training and Supervising Analyst, Southern California Psychoanalytic Institute, Los Angeles, California; Chief Psychiatric Consultant and Deputy Coroner, Los Angeles County Medical Examiner-Coroner's Office.

Michael Peck, Ph.D.
Director of Narcotics and Drug Abuse Rehabilitation Program, Suicide Prevention Center, Inc.; Assistant Clinical Professor, U.S.C. Medical School: Diplomate in Clinical Psychology, American Board of Professional Psychology.

Norman Tabachnick, M.D.
Clinical Professor of Psychiatry, University of Southern California; Training Analyst and Co-Director of Research Division of the Southern California Psychoanalytic Institute; Associate Chief Psychiatrist at the Los Angeles Suicide Prevention Center.

Norman Tiber, Ph.D.
Associate Professor of Psychiatry and Psychology, University of Southern California; Director of Psychology Internship Training Program at the Los Angeles County University of Southern California Medical Center.

Carl Wold, Ph.D.
Associate Clinical Professor of Psychiatry (Psychology), U.S.C. Medical School; Director of Research and Chief Psychologist, Suicide Prevention Center, Inc.

INTRODUCTION

The Social Problem

IN 1970, 54,800 PEOPLE in the United States of America lost their lives in automobile "accidents." An additional two million were disabled for a period of more than one day. The amount of reported property damage due to automobile accident was 13 billion, 600 million dollars.[1]

These facts only outline the devastation which is done to the human race by "accident." Add to them the psychological distress that follows death or injury (more people than just the victim are involved), the fears and restrictions (both physical and mental), and the loss of productive capacity which often follows accident, and the problem becomes greater. Then consider that the automobile is the modality for only one type of accident and begin listing the others—industrial, home, recreational, and many more.

Clearly, then, the person who concerns himself with the cause and prevention of accidents has locked horns with an important social ill.

Suicide in Accident

This book revolves around a specific theory of the etiology of accident—namely, that in many, perhaps even most accidents, suicide or suicide-like factors are in evidence. As we shall presently relate, intuitions which many people have had suggest this etiology; a number of psychological theorists have reasoned why and how such a situation could be true; and finally certain scientific works support the proposition.

For a number of reasons, it seems likely that not all "accidents" are suicide attempts. Although there are undoubtedly some suicides which are subsequently called *accident*, the number is probably small. Since accidents seem to be linked to so many forces, the possibility that a single one would explain all accidents seems remote. Yet, in amassing evidence about this theory, two important possibilities exist. One is that a significant number of "accidents" belong to a sub-group which is, in fact, suicidal. The second possibility is that there may be some important similarities in the psychology of "suicidal" and "accidental" people, and that these similarities are, to some degree, responsible for the occurrence of accidents.

Piqued by these possibilities, a group of Los Angeles psychoanalysts and psychologists* began research in 1964. A number of studies led to the formulation of a large-scale investigation which was started in 1968 and completed in 1971. This book presents the results of these studies and integrates them with other relevant work.

Social Use of the Concept "Accident"

What in the world *is* an accident? When we began our work, such a question did not even occur to us—we believed we knew. However, we have come to see that in our day, *accident* means different things to different people. This diversity reflects different theories of the causation of events. These causative theories in turn are partly based on the state of knowledge in different periods of history and partly based on man's psychological makeup.

In today's world, accident is commonly thought of as occurring "by chance" or "for no specific reason" or "as an act of God." To some degree, these designations reflect ignorance. In the past, much less was known about the causation of accidents than is known today. It is understandable that with this lack of knowledge, people might think that in fact there were *no* answers to the riddle of accident. Also, to deal with sudden dramatic and overwhelming events by ascribing them to the influence of supernatural forces is by no means unusual. Many nontechnological societies explain a great deal in this way, and we also know that in previous periods of history among "western civilizations," such explanations were common. Indeed, explana-

---

* From the Los Angeles Suicide Prevention Center and the Southern California Psychoanalytic Institute.

tions of this type still occur today in "modern" societies. Moreover, there are certain socio-psychological reasons which, in addition to explaining the unknown, act to produce "divine" or "by chance" theories of accident.

People are often shocked by the sudden and profound effects of accident—death, great injury to their loved ones, catastrophic property loss. At such times, intense feelings of guilt and responsibility are mobilized. These feelings are severely uncomfortable and must be dissipated in some way. To attribute the cause of the catastrophe to divine or chance forces becomes possible, and the possibility is enhanced since, in many cases, the "causes" are indeed not known.

Another reason why "chance" or "divine" theories of accident persist may be found in man's attraction to chance-taking behavior. Of course, not all people or peoples possess this, and there is a great deal of variation in it from person to person. But some nations seem to have more of it. American (USA) history and social psychology reflect a strong trend toward being adventurous and daring. That is how "the West was won," and we are a people who traditionally think of ourselves as facing some frontier—some new great challenge. Such a nation does not want to be tied down unnecessarily (with safety precautions, for example). It also believes that taking a chance means taking risks, and when you take risks, you can get hurt. Indeed, the scars of your accidents are tributes to your daring and thus are valuable. It fits into this way of facing and conquering the problems of life to think of accidents as unavoidable.

Definition of Accident

The above discussion suggests that *accident* may be associated with a number of values and thus have several meanings and definitions. We must try to make our particular understanding of it explicit.

There are three components to the type of accident we concern ourselves with in this book. We shall list them as follows:

1. *An accident is an event associated with a significant personal or social loss.* There are many events called *accidents* which do

not result in loss. An accidental slip of the tongue may not even produce embarrassment. An accidental meeting with a friend may bring about pleasure, etc. However, we are interested in those accidents following which a person or group of persons experience that something important—life, well-being or property —has been taken from them.

2. *An accident involves a transfer of physical (or chemical, or thermal, or electrical) energy between two separate reservoirs of energy.* This uncomfortably technical statement tells in specific terms *how* the loss occurs. What it means is that people and inanimate objects can be damaged or destroyed when something without much resilience hits them with great force or when something very hot or highly charged with electrical energy comes into contact with them.

3. *An accident is unplanned and mostly unanticipated.* Although there are "reasons" why accidents happen, they are not completely or at all known to the victims.

This general attribute must obviously be modified, however, if some accidents are suicides. In such cases, the event would *seem to be unplanned and unanticipated to the outside observer.* (If this observer would believe the event to be a suicide attempt, he would call it that and not an "accident.") However, research would establish that the victim knew very well what would happen. In this case, we would have a suicide masquerading as an accident.

If, in some accidents, there are operative factors similar to suicide, these may still fit the "unplanned and unanticipated" part of our definition. In these situations, even though the person may be depressed, thinking of death, even thinking of suicide, if he were not actually planning suicide, then his accident would still be unplanned and unanticipated by him.

Now let us return to the part of the definition which says "mostly unanticipated." In some situations, there may be presentiments of accidents, feelings that something tragic may be occurring soon. These are similar to the feelings of impending doom that occur in some depressed and/or suicidal people. However, in the true accident (one that is not a masked suicide), the presentiments of mishap are not linked to a specific time and place. And indeed the person is usually not *sure* that something dangerous will happen. This is what we mean when we say "mostly unanticipated."

Multi Factorial Causation of Accidents

Our research concerns itself with a few related and circumscribed concepts. We believe that to look into the suicidal nature of man may tell something valuable about accidents in general, or some groups of accidents. But it is important to say immediately that accidents may result from the interaction of many forces (not only psychological ones) and that the multi-factorial approach to understanding accident is important if one is truly to understand it. (Such a precaution to the reader and to the researcher becomes particularly significant in our age of specialized scientific knowledge. Otherwise, each scientist tends to "explain" accident in terms of his special background. But this would be short-sighted, since accident is connected not only with psychology but with engineering, meteorology, physical health, sociology and many other areas which touch human existence.)

We deal in our researches mainly with automobile accidents, and so to illustrate the multi-factorial causation of these, let us set forth the by now classical tripartite approach to research in automobile mishap.[2]

One might divide all possible causes of auto accident into three main categories: (1) those reflecting the environment in which the automobile moves; (2) those having to do with the automobile itself; and (3) those dealing with the driver.

In the first category, *the environment,* such factors as the weather, the quality of the surface over which the vehicle travels, the absence or presence and type of traffic regulating devices, and the traffic patterns in which the vehicles move are a few of the significant issues.

In considering *the automobile,* one focuses on the intactness of the brakes and steering mechanism, the kind of vision afforded to the driver, the visibility of the vehicle in terms of other drivers, and other factors.

In terms of *the driver* of the automobile, one would have to consider his knowledge of the characteristics of the vehicle, his knowledge of the roadways, traffic patterns, and other characteristics of the path which he traverses, his physical health and, last but not least, a number of psychological attributes. Here one would ask: How alert is the driver? Does he have a characteristic driving pattern (cautious or impulsive)? Is he able to be flexible in terms of his response to shifts in traffic and possible hazards? And finally, does he have suicidal or self-destructive trends? It is to these last factors that we shall devote the most careful study in the pages of this book.

Research Methods and Problems in Our Study

In our work, we used psychological and psychoanalytic techniques and methods. As we proceeded, there were a number of problems, both practical and theoretical, which confronted us. For example, there were problems of utilizing psychoanalytic theory and technique in a study in which rather specific data were sought. The essence of the psychoanalytic interview is that the subject has freedom in determining what he speaks of and how he speaks of it. Indeed, it is by observing his characteristic way of choosing subjects and methods that the psychoanalyst is enabled to draw inferences. If one abridges this freedom, can one obtain valuable psychoanalytic data?

Another problem was posed by the possibility of the psychoanalyst interviewers having preconceived biases about the hypotheses of the study. First of all, did they have such biases? Secondly, if they did, did the biases influence the material they elicited or their interpretations of that material? In many psychoanalytic researches, it has been assumed that the psychoanalyst can be objective about his own biases and thus prevent them from disturbing his work. Indeed, one purpose of psychoanalytic training is to prepare him specifically to work in this way. We did not assume that our interviewers would be objective about their biases; we, however, attempted to evaluate them. We subsequently used the results of this evaluation in reaching an understanding of our research data.

There were other problems of method which we encountered in this research. Some we attempted to deal with, and some we could only note down for the benefit of future exploration in this field.

Thus, this book has two purposes. One is to evaluate the presence and significance of suicide-like factors in automobile accident and to apply that understanding to the general issues of the causes and prevention of accident. The second is to present our thought about the resolution of certain problems of psychological and psychoanalytic research method.

N.T.

REFERENCES

1. Automobile Club of Southern California: 1970 Statistics.
2. McFarland, R. A.: *The Epidemiology of Motor Vehicle Accidents, JAMA,* pp. 180-289, 1962.

ACKNOWLEDGMENTS

Iᴛ ɪꜱ ɴᴏᴡ ᴏᴜʀ ᴘʟᴇᴀꜱᴜʀᴇ to identify the many people who directly and indirectly helped in the performance of the work which led to this book. The major portion of this research was supported by MH Grant No. 15510. This grant was awarded and administered by The Center for Studies of Suicide Prevention of the National Institute of Mental Health. The two Heads of this section during the period that this work was done were Edwin Shneidman, Ph.D., and Harvey Resnik, M.D. Both of them, as well as many other members of their staff, gave us support, encouragement and many kinds of practical help during the years of the study.

Our work had its main center and coordination at the Los Angeles Suicide Prevention Center. All of the authors are members of the regular or consulting staff of the Center. It is a place where there are people who radiate enthusiasm, support and love. That general atmosphere was very important for the sustenance of our effort which extended over several years. In addition to that good atmosphere, we wish to thank the many members of the SPC staff who contributed time and thought and effort to helping us in various ways.

A second center of activity for this research was The Southern California Psychoanalytic Institute. Much of the thinking and research evaluation which led to and which stemmed from our research took place at the Institute. We were fortunate to have a specific seminar devoted to the goals of our work.

In addition to the support and help of various members of the Institute staff, 15 psychoanalysts who were members of that special seminar participated actively in various phases of clinical investigation and evaluation. They were Marshall Cherkas, M.D., August Kasper, M.D., Irving Matzner, M.D., Leonard Nevis, M.D., Marvin Osman, M.D., Louis Paul, M.D., Ernest Pullman, M.D., Howard Ross, M.D., Melvin Schwartz, M.D., Steven

Schwartz, M.D., Robert Sokol, M.D., Bernard Sosner, M.D., Fred
Sturm, M.D., James Weishaus, M.D., and Burton Wixon, M.D.
Two psychoanalytically trained psychologists also assisted in this
phase of the work. They were Elaine Caruth, Ph.D., and Joel
Shor, Ph.D.

A most important third center of activity in this research project was the Los Angeles County-USC Medical Center. This is the
largest general hospital in the Los Angeles area. It was on the
wards of this hospital that we found and interviewed those people who were the subjects in our study. We wish to thank them
for their participation in what often was a difficult and arduous
task. We are also grateful for the help given by various members
of the staff of the Medical Center. From the administration of
the hospital, the ward physicians, nurses and clerks, we received
the most interested and complete cooperation.

Three of the staff at the Suicide Prevention Center made special contributions to our work. David Klugman, M.S.W., worked
for several years on this project and helped it in a number of
ways both administratively and in terms of thinking through
some of its problems. Celeste Dorsey was a full-time secretary,
a part-time administrator and always lent charm and enthusiasm
to her work. Judith Davis, A.A., was our administrator, chief
secretary, scientific colleague and good friend. Our study seemed
to us a very complicated one at times. We were doing literally
dozens of things simultaneously. Machinery had to be set up to
implement procedures and it was necessary to see that the procedures were completed. Records had to be kept, timetables set up
and many other things accomplished. All these tasks we came to
see could be trusted to Judy. She did them admirably, managed
to keep in good spirits through it all, and helped us to persevere.

Finally, we see our work as one small effort among that of the
many people in the past, present and future who have been or
will be involved in research about accident, suicide, self-destruction and man's mind. We want to acknowledge our gratitude to
those whose findings and thinking we leaned upon and to say to
those who will come after us, "May you have as good and excit-
ing a time as we did."

CONTENTS

Part Four

THE IMPLICATIONS

ACCIDENT OR SUICIDE?

PART ONE

→ THE APPROACH ←

Chapter 1

SELF-DESTRUCTIVE FACTORS IN ACCIDENT

The Development of the Concept

Summary

Much research touches on possible self-destructive psychological factors in the production of accident. Although only a fraction of this research has been specifically conducted along psychoanalytic lines, it is possible to conceptualize all of it within a psychoanalytic framework. This we attempt to do here, utilizing the psychoanalytic adaptational approach. This approach deals with the relationship of human beings to their environment and takes into account all of the possible factors which affect that interrelationship. There are many environmental factors which may be pertinent, and there are also a number of factors within the individual which should be taken into account. When the bulk of past research and thinking is classified, it is found that the problem of production of accident, in terms of possible self-destructive psychological factors, may be approached from three main viewpoints:

1. Motivation. *A number of formulations center around the concept of a death instinct or a motivationally self-destructive force within the individual. Some studies have focused on direct manifestations of this instinct or force, whereas others have evaluated suicidal and depressive factors within accident victims.*

A number of additional motivations have been postulated and researched. These include erotic trends, self-expiatory feelings, unacceptable urges to dispose of no longer useful tools, and desires to deal in an acceptable way with the anxieties and threats of new responsibility.

2. Action Orientation. *A second group of formulations cen-*

5

*ters around an hypothesized action orientation of accident vic-
tims. It is asserted that these individuals tend to be active, emotional, non-intellectual and unconcerned with social responsibility. It has furthermore been postulated that certain individuals
are "accident-prone," that is, that they tend to have accidents repeatedly as a way of dealing with anxiety-provoking life situations.*

*Some theorists have postulated hyperactivity or hyperpassivity
of certain ego apparatuses. These malfunctions may decrease
the normal life-preservative activities of the ego and thus lead,
through a variety of mechanisms, to accident.*

3. Alcohol. *Alcohol is the single factor most significantly
linked to accident (especially automobile accident). It is felt
that alcohol leads to accidents because of its toxic effect upon
the neurophysiological apparatuses which normally provide vigilance against accident hazards. However, it is also possible that
increased intake of alcohol is merely one symptom of a disturbed psychological state and that accident occurrence is highly
linked to this disturbed state. It is possible that those individuals
designated as "chronic alcoholics" are members of the group
with the disturbed psychology. Finally, it is possible that alcohol
exerts its influence by a combination and mutual potentiation of
the two factors listed above.*

SELF-DESTRUCTION has been identified—sometimes in a direct
way, sometimes less directly—as a significant factor in accident in many writings. In this chapter, we will locate those references and evaluate them. This evaluation provides the rationale for our specific research.

Our theoretical approach is psychoanalytic; yet we do not con-
fine our review to psychoanalytic articles. There are two reasons
for this. First, there has not been a great deal of writing in the
"purely" psychoanalytic literature on accident, although there is
some. It is interesting and provocative, and we shall review it.
More importantly, there have been many significant contributions from non-psychoanalytic researchers and thinkers.

This situation poses no great problem for one who wishes to

formulate his ideas in the psychoanalytic manner. Although psychoanalytic therapists may utilize a specific technique, psychoanalytic theory is free to integrate data obtained in many different ways.

DEFINITION OF TERMS

At the beginning, we need some definitions. We have already defined *accident* as an unplanned and unanticipated event involving a transfer of physical, chemical, thermal or electrical energy from one object to another, and resulting in a loss. But what is *suicide?* What is *self-destruction?* And what are their relationships?

Suicide involves a specific intention on the part of the victim to kill himself. He makes a plan. He follows this plan and dies.

A suicide attempt parallels a completed suicide. However, it does not result in death. It is characterized by the addition and implementation of other motivations besides the desire to die. Indeed, the suicide attempter may have much ambivalence as to whether or not he does wish to die.

Suicide is one form of self-destruction, but self-destruction itself can be defined as the result of any force or combination of forces existing within an individual which leads to his damaging himself or losing his life. We have already spoken about the role of conscious intention in suicide. One can postulate *unconscious* intention, that is, that certain individuals have strong urges to do away with themselves. These might be motivated by a variety of issues—feelings of guilt, feelings that their time has come, feelings of wishing to move to a new existence, and others. These motivations are not necessarily conscious. Psychoanalytic theory holds that people may do things for reasons which exist outside of their awareness. So the category of *unconscious intention* is one non-suicidal route to self-destruction.

But there are others. People may be ignorant of hazards to body and life. They may choose to ignore warnings of danger. They may have a devil-may-care attitude. They may say that although a significant risk to their life exists, certain gratifications are worth the risk. (Lest we think this characteristic is present only in a small and unusual group of people, let us consider how many of us are quite willing to take the tremendous risks that are involved in driving an automobile on our dangerous highways every day of our lives.) We have touched on only a few of the routes to self-destruction which exist in present-day civilization.

It is evident that many different factors must be evaluated in understanding the term *accident*. Earlier we referred to the tripartite classification of source of accident causation (environment, vehicle, driver) which is widely utilized in accident research. This classification is an example of a widely used approach to the understanding of events which is called General Systems Theory[1] or Field Theory.[2] Its essence is that factors of many types interact to produce phenomena.

An important body of writing in psychoanalysis utilizes this approach. It is called *adaptational theory*. Its most important developer was Heinz Hartmann who, in an important monograph[3] and other works, spelled out its implications. However, Hartmann was not its originator in psychoanalysis. Freud, in his early writings, implicitly indicated that not only were there forces within the individual which must be identified in order to understand how he thinks and acts, but also these internal forces have significant relationships with different aspects of the external world. In addition to Hartmann and Freud, many other psychoanalysts have utilized and developed adaptational theory.

This review of past accident literature is framed in adaptational theory. First, some general statements concerning the theory. In essence, it deals with the relationship of man to his environment. The term *adaptational* does not mean that man needs to adapt in the sense of "conforming" to his environment, although many times this is what happens. But it is also true that many individuals try to change their world *according to some internal need*. Adaptation does not mean conforming to the environment; it is the process of relating to the environment and an evaluation of all the factors which influence this relation.

First, one must understand the environmental forces with which an individual must deal in order to survive and to gratify his goals. One must evaluate the physical aspects of the environment, the terrain, the climate, what the environment offers in terms of food, shelter and aesthetic activities. Then, social potentialities must be understood. What are the modes of living and experience that are approved and disapproved? Are free expression and impulsive activity welcomed, tolerated or frowned upon? What value is given to isolation and solitude? Is the weltanschauung a fearful paranoid one or a feeling that the world provides an abundance of everything in it, that people need not compete?

These external issues are reflected by the number and complexity of internal forces. Inside the individual, one must consider the instinctual needs and how these needs have been modified by additional forces. For example, the individual's ego which allows some activities and inhibits others modifies his instinctual goals. His superego is important, and this in at least two ways. First, he is told what he should not do. From another standpoint, his superego develops ideas of what is right and what he should strive for. Thus, we come to the individual's peculiar *values;* these influence his adaptiveness. But there are still other factors which are important.

Each individual has potentialities and limitations. He not only must understand what these imply for the present; he also may make predictions in regard to them. As an example, a person may not be learned but he may believe he has the potential to learn. This could influence him to undertake years of schooling.

It can be seen that the adaptational approach is quite complex. A number of psychoanalysts have implied that precisely because of individual variation in human beings and their adaptation, there is little to be gained in searching for common factors. Such thinkers would state that each person who gets into an accident does so through an individual and peculiar path.

We do not concur in this opinion. There is no question that our universe is complex, but in particular situations such as accidents, regularities can be found. For example, in some accidents, a common factor is ignorance of the dangerous technological effects. Consider the fact that many infants were being burned by floor heaters because of (a) their lack of knowledge of the harmful effects of these heaters, (b) their lack of ability to discriminate the source of the dangerous thermal energy, and (c) their inability to remove themselves quickly from the harmful heat. These situations were identified by research. The obvious proposals were (a) to warn parents not to put children in contact with these heaters, and (b) to induce the manufacturers to construct safeguards so that people coming in contact with heaters would not be burned.[4]

The problem in our research is not that we will not find regularities. The problem is to understand the *meanings* of the regularities so that we are in a better position to take helpful action.

A few qualifying statements about this review are in order. We have been highly selective in our choice of material. One reason for this has been practical. In the past fifty odd years, thousands of "accident" studies have been done. Many evaluations and a number of good books exist.[5, 6] We have chosen exclusively work which has a "psychological" orientation. Although we believe that many important clues to psychological processes may exist in "non-psychological" accident literature, we feel that most important psychological concepts can be found in the "psychological" work. The three broad categories of the following discussion are (1) Motivations; (2) Character Type; and (3) The Role of Alcohol.

MOTIVATIONS

In adaptational theory, a most important focus is on the motivational thrusts of the individual. These come from a number of sources. Early in psychoanalysis, certain motivational sources were postulated to be instinctual. These had to do with certain primary life preservative forces such as breathing and eating. In addition, a number of other instinctual forces not as clearly identifiable as life preservative were identified. These included aggressive or assertive thrusts and erotic and sexual ones.

Motivations come from many sources other than instincts. The ego and the superego influence the direction and trend of human activity and motivation. Some of the ego's directions have to do with defenses against instinct which come about because the direct expression of the instinctual need is dangerous or is felt to be dangerous by the individual. At other times, the ego does not act in such a "defensive" way but modifies behavior in such a way as to make the individual's goal more attainable. Likewise, the superego may act in different ways to influence the direction or character of motivational thrusts. The "realities" of the environment in which the individual exists may also modify his behavior in significant ways.

In psychoanalytic theory, a particular motivation may come from any of these sources, but as psychoanalysts actually interpret human thinking and behavior, they usually feel that any particular motivational thrust is a combination of two or more vectors operating simultaneously.

What are some of the motivational factors which have been postulated and identified as being significant in the phenomenon of "accident"?

The Death Instinct

In 1920, Sigmund Freud published *Beyond the Pleasure Principle*[7] in which he postulated the existence of a "death instinct." Alongside of those instinctual forces which strive for the preservation of human life, the attainment of satisfaction and the movement to higher unities, Freud felt that there might be an accompanying *instinctual* tendency toward the destruction of the individual. There were a number of theoretical grounds for this, of which we shall mention two.

First was the observation of a tendency toward "constancy." This meant that organisms tended, as a result of their instinctually motivated activity, to move toward a state of lesser tension. Such an observation can be made in many situations. For example, organisms exist with low states of activity, are stimulated, become more active as they deal with the stimulus, and then return to lesser states of activity. It is less certain that one can conclude as Freud did that death is the ultimate and most sought after example of relief of tension.

Second, the death instinct focuses on aggressive activities. Although there are many reasons why aggression may be manifested in living organisms (for example, as a reaction to frustration or as part of a movement toward the achievement of some goal), it was Freud's contention that much aggression is originally directed against the self and is only manifested in an outward way when this self-destructive energy is deflected to the outside.

Freud's concept of the death instinct started as a speculation, but it was one that he was fond of and he wrote about it many times after 1920. Although it has been the subject of intense controversy, and although many psychoanalysts do not believe it to have much theoretical or practical value, it demonstrates remarkable viability (if we may use the term). However, it is a concept that exists on such a level of inference and abstraction that it is difficult to devise methods of accurately establishing whether or not it actually is a valid construct.

The death instinct hypothesis has significance for the theory that some accidents might be suicidal. Freud believed that there was a strong tendency for each individual to die in his own way. Thus, even some of the life instincts could be organized to help the death instinct kill the individual. This somewhat paradoxical point can be explained in the following way. If external bearers of death came to the individual, such as diseases or lack of food, the life instincts would act in such a way as to overcome the harmful effects of these forces. (That much would be clear without the postulation of a death instinct.) However, the further thrust of Freud's thinking was that the purpose of such warding off of external dangers was to enable the individual's death instinct to kill him in its own particular way.

Such a theory would offer a likely explanation for many types of suicide. Suicide could be seen as the purest expression of the death instinct. Accident resulting in serious injury or death could be seen as a somewhat more subtle manifestation of the workings of the death instinct. Here is a quotation from Freud in a book which antedated *Beyond the Pleasure Principle* but which contains germs of the death instinct theory:

"Anyone who believes in the occurrence of half-intentional self-injury—if I may use a clumsy expression—will be prepared also to assume that in addition to consciously intentional suicide, there is such a thing as half-intentional self-destruction (self-destruction with an unconscious intention) capable of making skillful use of a threat to life and disguising it as a chance mishap. There is no need to think such self-destruction rare, for the trend to self-destruction is present, to a certain degree, in very many more human beings than those in whom it is carried out; self-injuries are, as a rule, a compromise between this instinct and the forces which are still working against it. And even where suicide actually results, the inclination to suicide would have been present for a long time before in its lesser strength, or in the form of an unconscious and suppressed trend."[8]

Karl Menninger came to similar conclusions as he evaluated a number of accidents.[9] In his article, Menninger stated, "In many of these accidents . . . illuminating instances can be shown to fulfill so specifically the unconscious tendencies of the victim that we are compelled to believe either that they represent the capitalization of some opportunity for self-destruction by the death instinct or else were in some obscure way *brought about* for this very purpose."

Now the question is, *How can this well-stated theory be demonstrated?* There are undoubtedly instances in which individuals who have strong suicidal trends die by automobile or other accidents. In some cases, it is almost certain that the accident was a suicide attempt. In others, the possibility exists that the tendency toward suicide was but one manifestation of an anxiety-laden and disorganizing tendency within the person involved. It is possible that the accident was another manifestation of this disorganizing tendency and *not* an acting-out of the self-destructive purposive trend.

What if Freud is wrong about a biological thrust toward death? Even if a death instinct does not exist, it is still possible to think of an organized self-destructive trend within certain individuals. For example, a person who feels extremely guilty about some thought or action and desperately seeks self-punishment could be said to possess such a trend. Similarly, a person who wants to get away from his present life situation and thinks of death as a mode of entering a new existence might also possess such a trend. People with such trends might highly organize their behavior in order to bring about self-destruction or death, even though they would not be acting under the influence of a death instinct as postulated by Freud.

Now we will evaluate certain data which bears on the validity of the death instinct theory as an explanatory concept in the understanding of accident. What evidence exists that certain accidents represent direct and conscious suicide attempts? The very presence of some accident-like suicides would support the possibility that there might be many other accidents which are quite similar to the "suicidal" ones but might differ in the degree of conscious awareness or conscious intention of a desire to kill oneself.

First, we would note a number of individual case reports which point strongly to accident as direct, half-conscious or unconscious suicide attempt. Here is an example:

A man of 48 had just been given an ultimatum by his mistress that he had to choose either his wife or her. He was in a depressed mood and was drinking in one of his usual haunts. While there, he discussed his problem with the bartender and a number of his cronies, giving numerous indications of the worthlessness of his life and his feeling that suicide would be the only way to settle his troubled feelings. Driving home, he had a one-car accident in which his car was completely demolished. He was not seriously injured and continued on to his home.

The next part of the story is told by his wife. She heard him enter the house, but when he did not come into the bedroom, she went looking for him. She entered the living room just in time to see him shoot himself through the head.

Impression: The "accident" was a conscious suicide attempt or was an unconscious attempt to do away with himself. When that failed, a more successful effort was made.

A number of histories which come to a similar conclusion were gathered by Moseley.[10]

There is a particular type of suicidal behavior called "Russian Roulette." In its purest form, this consists of an individual loading a revolver so that some of its chambers contain live cartridges. He spins the cylinder, aims the gun at his head, and pulls the trigger. Should the hammer fall on a live cartridge, he shoots himself and often dies.

Since an automobile is a lethal weapon (or potentially a lethal weapon), it is possible that it may be used in the acting out of a Russian Roulette fantasy. On questioning some individuals who have had serious accidents, one discovers that they have been driving erratically for some period of time. They are asked if they have been aware of this erratic trend. They answer that they have been. One then asks, "Weren't you afraid that you might get into an accident?" An answer which is on occasion received is, "I was so distraught (or worried, or feeling bad about myself) that I didn't care what would happen to me or I didn't think about the consequences, although when I think about them now, I realize how dangerous they were." Sometimes they say, "I decided to leave it up to fate."

It is clear that there are similarities between such situations and "Russian Roulette." Yet we must also keep in mind that these are retrospective constructions. They do not carry the same degree of conviction as a history of an individual pointing a gun at his head.

There are a number of additional research studies which focus on the relationship between suicide and accident. MacDonald in 1964 reported a statistical evaluation of automobile accidents causing death (of the driver or of others).[11] His conclusion was that the incidence of fatal-accident drivers in the population of psychiatric hospitals was over thirty times greater than would be expected (using the entire group of Colorado license holders as a comparison group). He further suggested that the disproportionate representation might be related to the greater risk of suicide in persons who have been in a psychiatric hospital. Although the numbers involved in this study are relatively small, the results support the hypothesis that accident may be a manifestation of suicide. What must also be considered is that there are other variables which could explain MacDonald's findings. For example, it may be that people in a state psychiatric hospital do not drive in automobiles that are as safe as those of individuals not hospitalized. This could be responsible for the increased accident rate. Until detailed statistical evaluations of this factor and many others are done, MacDonald's research presents us with an intriguing possibility but no more.

Porterfield[12] tested the hypothesis that the motor vehicle death rate followed a pattern similar to the suicide and homicide rates. The thinking behind this hypothesis was that motor vehicles are deadly weapons and that the same underlying social forces which lead to suicide and homicide may manifest themselves in the production of automobile accidents. The method utilized was the comparing of rank order of metropolitan areas in the United States according to indices of suicide, homicide, crime and motor traffic deaths. The hypothesis was supported by the correlations obtained. Porterfield concluded that "aggressive, hazardous driving is likely to be characteristic of persons similar to those who have suicidal or homicidal or both tendencies." Thus, although it is not proven that accident is the same as suicide, it is suggested that *the same type of people* are involved in both activities.

In a previous study of our research group,[13] we compared psychological characteristics of dead suicide and automobile accident victims. We found a number of similarities as well as a number of differences. The similarities were that about half of both groups had been drinking prior to their deaths. It was determined that drinking was a method which most people in both groups utilized to deal with upsetting situations in their lives. Another reaction to upset in both groups was increased motor and verbal activity. Half of both groups demonstrated impulsiveness as a character trait, and both groups tended to be conscientious and highly concerned with "good performance."

This research suggests that there may be some significant similarities between accidental and suicidal victims. However, the meaning of those similarities is uncertain. Do the similarities point to a suicidal or death-seeking trend within both groups? It is not clear that drinking is intrinsically part of a death-seeking trend. The same can be said for increased motor and verbal activity, impulsiveness and conscientiousness.

Depression

We have just discussed the relationship of suicide to the production of automobile accident. Much past research supports the linking of depression and suicide.[14, 15] If individuals involved in automobile accident actually demonstrated strong depressive tendencies, there would be indirect support for the concept that suicidal factors are operating in them. There are a few studies which bear on this issue. In comparing 15 cases of drivers killed in accidents with 15 suicides, Tabachnick et al.[13] found that one-third of the accident victims were depressed. A more recent study was conducted by Finch and Smith in Houston.[16] Much attention was paid to psychological factors and indeed, it was found that, as contrasted with a comparison group, the accident victims manifested high degrees of depression and suicidal concern. These studies, in our opinion, are suggestive. However, their methodological deficiencies make it necessary to look upon their results with some caution.

Some attention has been paid in psychoanalytic writings to a connecting link between depression and accident. It is possible that the state of relative passivity which exists in depression is manifested by a less rapid response to hazards. It is also conceivable that in the state of withdrawal that occurs in many depressive conditions, there is less attention paid to the perceptual field (so that one would not be able to note as quickly an on-coming traffic hazard). It is also possible that there is an inability or unwillingness to respond to such perceptiveness. It is as if the individual is so focused upon himself (what, in more technical psychoanalytic language, might be termed, "The individual was in a state of narcissistic withdrawal") that he has no energy left over to assess dangers of his external environment. Litman and Tabachnick[17] discussed this possibility.

Two psychologists, Barmack and Payne, presented conclusions drawn from an analysis of automobile accidents among airmen.[18] In a number of instances (they say "many"), their impression was that the psychic direction in the accident victims was passive rather than active. We quote from their work:

"We infer they were predominantly passive rather than active and that the unconscious aim of the pre-accident behavior was more often tension-reducing than self-aggressive."

We are just touching on the issue of ego processes possibly connected with automobile accident. We will return to this topic again in the section on "character type" (later in this chapter).

Additional Formulations of Freud on the "Accident" Concept

We have previously discussed certain contributions of Freud to accident theory under the heading of the death instinct. We will now list a number of Freud's ideas which come from a much earlier book, *The Psychopathology of Everyday Life*.[8] In certain ways, these ideas are less controversial than those concerning the death instinct. In the first place, the conclusions were better supported by clinical evidence. Combined with this is the fact that the level of extrapolation which leads to the conclusions is of a lesser degree than that involved in the postulation of the death instinct.

For example, in the formulations dealing with the presence of erotic trends, the significance of those trends is established by associations in the psychoanalytic hour. Such direct associations are not found in support of the death instinct. Patients do not commonly speak about a desire for death or extinction. They may often speak about a desire to rest or to be relieved of anxiety. To conclude that such comments suggest a death instinct, however, requires an additional inference (which is not necessary in examples such as the presence of erotic trends noted above).

Freud gave a number of explanations for ordinary bungled actions:

1. *Self-punishment*. This may be from guilt for some recent action, for instance, an abortion, or for some long past thought such as a wish that father would die. Nearly everyone, to some degree, has such self-punishing attitudes lying in wait ready to seize upon a suitable opportunity to gain expression.

2. *Self-sacrifice*. The injury to oneself may have the purpose of warding off greater disaster such as the loss of a loved one or castration.

3. Sometimes an accident results from *an unconscious desire to get rid of something that has depreciated.* Freud's example was an old inkstand which he broke with a clumsy movement. A modern example might be an old car. The temptation is especially strong when there is a possibility of getting something better if the depreciated possession is destroyed.

4. The purpose of an accident may be *erotic.* "When a girl falls, she falls on her back." Certain accidents rather skillfully place the victim in close connection with actual or symbolic love objects. Some persons equate a violent crash with sexual orgasm.

5. An accident may be *a means of escaping or avoiding something.* Forgetting an appointment, omitting a traffic signal or making a wrong turn may have such a motive.

The Desire to Escape

In *The Psychopathology of Everyday Life,*[8] Freud suggested that bungled actions or accidents might reflect important conflicts. Not only might the accidents reflect these conflicts, but they might represent attempts to resolve them or they might occur during the process of attempting to resolve them. These ideas were emphasized in the research of Hirschfeld and Behan.[19, 20, 21]

The Hirschfeld and Behan research centered on industrial accidents. Several hundred people who had such accidents were studied in depth. Conclusions were drawn about their psychological states and the contributions of these psychological states to both their accidents and the chronic disability which followed them. The work was clinical in nature and did not include formal control groups.

Hirschfeld and Behan concluded that many of the accident victims had been suffering from combinations of personality difficulties and troubled life situations. A typical example was a woman who lived an isolated and withdrawn life which she had been able to accept comfortably while she was married. Her husband sheltered and took care of her. However, when her husband died and it become necessary for her to be more outgoing, she began to have much difficulty.

Hirschfeld and Behan called this stage "unacceptable disability." They suggested that many people who have such *unacceptable disabilities* can resolve them by a number of mechanisms such as illness or alcoholism and, most importantly, accident. Such an accident with disability allows the victim to withdraw and yet not feel uncomfortable about it. In other words, an "unacceptable disability" is transformed by an accident into an "acceptable" one.

Similar formulations were made by our research group in two related studies.[13, 22] One of these concerned victims of automobile accidents who had died. The other dealt with survivors of accidents. Although in a relatively small number of cases, a loss preceded the accident, in a larger number of cases, a movement into new responsibility was found. These new responsibilities included getting married, moving to a new job, moving to a new location geographically, and starting graduate school. We theorized that intense anxiety was brought up by these "new responsibilities," that the individuals adopted a mode of behavior characterized by impulsiveness and erratic behavior including erratic driving, and that as a result, accidents became more possible and, in fact, did occur.

Later research and evaluation of our data made us feel that the "new responsibility" concept may have been too specific to cover all precipitating events. Although in many cases movements "upward" or to "new responsibilities" could be seen, in others losses were noted. In any event, we found it was important to evaluate the intrapersonal state of affairs. Thus, a situation might seem to an outsider to be a movement "upward" but to the involved individual, the anxiety and feeling of poor control might be experienced as a "loss" (of self-esteem, for example). We therefore amended our original concept to include the idea of any new adaptive demand.

The Need for Mastery

Next we will consider man's need to master his environment. This need has at least two correlates: One is the existential requirement, to be able to cope with certain aspects of the environment—for example, the ability to obtain food and shelter from it. In addition to this "realistic" need to survive, there is an additional need for a sense of competence. In some individuals, this need is manifested by a desire to "conquer" or "master" the environment.

The tools, implements and machines which man has fashioned have allowed him to gratify both motivations referred to. A preeminent machine of today is the automobile. It seems plausible that the automobile may be used (or misused) as a means of increasing self-esteem. The conquering of space and time and the enhancement of one's actual power through driving are the realistic aspects of this situation.

Certain adolescent drivers play a game called "Chicken." Two drivers take their cars to a deserted road. They separate, point the cars toward each other and then accelerate at full speed toward each other. The one who first swerves from the collision course is called the "chicken." This is an interesting and self-destructive way of proving oneself braver than one's competitor. The contestants flirt with a fantasy of omnipotence, using the great power of the automobile as support for the fantasy.

We are not aware of reports of actual collisions occurring in games of Chicken. However, it is possible that operating under the influence of the "chicken" philosophy, individuals shed their usual life-preserving attitudes and actions.

CHARACTER TYPE

The first part of our review focused on *motivations* and their vicissitudes. Next we turn to *character type* which emphasizes typical ways of acting or reacting which are linked to accident.

"Motivations" came from a number of sources. At times we dealt with hypothesized instinctual or "id" forces. In other formulations, the role of the ego and superego were present. We even had an opportunity to include particular types of external situations which "motivated" certain people to act in ways which were linked to accident. Similarly, in the work on character type, we can discern forces which have a variety of sources. It is apparent that certain constitutional differences may account for some of the character types which are implicated in accident. These constitutional differences may reflect themselves in peculiarities of the ego and superego. However, maturation with the opportunity for parental and other cultural forces to affect the organism may also play an important role.

The "Action" Orientation

Many accidents (automobile as well as other types) seem to be linked to hyperactivity or poorly planned activity. Are accidents caused by a particular type of person who could be called "action oriented"? He would be an individual who would use bodily movements and propulsion through space to a higher degree than others. This action orientation might be manifested as an increased penchant for action in general as well as a specific way of dealing with anxiety and conflict and of restoring self-esteem.

Two articles in the psychiatric literature supported these concepts and have acted as important stimuli to further research. Tillman and Hobbs[23] contrasted a group of 96 drivers with a record of four or more accidents with 100 accident-free individuals. The high accident group manifested difficulty with school and authority, had frequently come before the juvenile court, in adult life had had many instances of short-term employment, and tended to be "fired" quite often. The individuals in this group possessed police records (apart from traffic violations) to a greater degree than those with low accident rates. They were further marked by having a "social disregard." They were individuals who placed all emphasis on material values and who acted only with expectations of immediate satisfaction. Their driving was marked by the same tendency toward aggressiveness, impulsiveness, lack of thought for others, and disrespect for authority that was noted in their personal lives.

Similar work was reported by Conger et al.[24] Their research demonstrated that accident repeaters manifested less control over hostility and more aggression in their behavior than comparison groups. They were noted to have a personality type which at times is inclined to overdetermined acting-out behavior, either at the level of overt physical belligerence or in verbal forms.

Many subsequent studies have indicated that high accident rates are linked to more frequent traffic and non-traffic legal violations.

The most widely known and widely researched concept which speaks for an "action orientation" in individuals who have accidents is the concept of *accident proneness*. Many research studies and articles have supported and elaborated this theory. It has acquired respectability through repetition. What is not widely known but is crucial to the understanding of the *action* character type is that the accident-prone hypothesis has been severely criticized. There have been a number of re-evaluations of previous research data, follow-up studies and theoretical critiques which point to the deficiencies of this concept.

What is the accident-prone hypotheses? Essentially it states that because of factors within the personality of certain individuals, these individuals are more likely to become involved in self-destructive accidents than others. This concept can be demonstrated epidemiologically. In a specified population, a small number of people will have a large percentage of the accidents. The classic paper on this subject was written in 1919 by Greenwood and Woods.[25] It was quite cautious in its conclusions. A statistical method was used to study accidents among workers in a British munitions factory. It was found that a relatively small percentage of the workers had most of the accidents. The authors suggested there might be an unequal initial liability, that is, that some individuals were inherently more likely to have accidents. They tested out alternative hypotheses, using statistical methods, and concluded that their initial hypothesis best explained the observed facts. They were quite cautious in presenting this theory and indicated that for a number of sound experimental reasons, the studies would need to be repeated.

It was from this provocative but conservatively evaluated (by its authors) study that an immensely popular concept arose. It was later repeatedly tested and researched. Some of the popularizers in the psychiatric field were Flanders Dunbar[26] and Franz

Alexander.[27] They described persons who had multiple accidents as people who were quick, decisive, active, impulsive, independent and adventurous. They were people who made their minds up definitely and quickly and moved toward immediate rather than long-range goals. Their interest was social rather than intellectual and they tried to appear casual about emotions. Their reactions to illness were bravado, fatalism or a play for secondary gain. Immediately prior to the accident, there had been some change in a situation which threatened individual autonomy, and there was a focal conflict involving authority.

However, there are numerous criticisms of the accident-prone hypothesis which limit its applicability. A recent article by Suchman and Scherzer[28] summarizes them. The objections to the widespread utilization of the theory are statistical, methodological and theoretical.

From a statistical standpoint, the following observations and conclusions are made. In certain groups, one can find evidence to support accident proneness, that is, that a relatively small number of people have a relatively large number of the accidents. However, there is an important change in the distribution of accidents when the groups are studied over time. Although an "accident prone" group continues to exist, *its membership changes*. In year two of the study, the people in the accident-prone group are not the same as in year one. Thus, one must consider that *chance* has accounted for inclusion of many people in the accident prone group. It must also be noted that statistical correlations between present and future accidents are often low. In addition, there are a multitude of intervening factors which are often not included in the relatively crude statistical surveys upon which the conclusion of accident proneness is based.

Methodologically, the evaluation of accident proneness suffers from a number of inadequacies. Most importantly, certain individuals may be more exposed to the occurrence of dangerous mishaps than others. If such a person has an increased number of accidents, this most probably does not reflect some psychological tendency toward accident proneness but merely that he has had the higher exposure risk. Such subtle but important issues are often not considered in the experimental tests of accident proneness.

Finally, from a theoretical standpoint, there are often significant disagreements in the different studies as to the characteristics of the accident prone individual. In some cases, he is postulated to be overly timid, whereas in others, he is inclined to be aggressive. Although it is possible that there are a *number* of accident-prone personalities, when one finds different theoretical and often opposing formulations for the same syndrome, one begins to question whether such a syndrome actually exists.

In summary, although the accident-prone theory is an intriguing one, although certain theoretical possibilities exist as a sound basis for it, the critical evaluation of the research indicates that it is not as widely spread as supposed. It does remain a significant possibility, however, that certain groups of people might possess an increased tendency to have "accidents."

Over-Passivity and Over-Activity of the Ego

The studies quoted above focus on descriptive characteristics of individuals who have accidents. Those characteristics could come about in a number of ways. Several psychoanalysts have speculated on processes in the ego which may be involved in producing accidents. Rapaport is quoted by Barmack and Payne[18] as suggesting a particular type of self-destructive process. This is not suicidal but rather deals with ego autonomy. Rapaport sees ego autonomy as being an active process (active in the sense that as the ego performs its various functions through its various apparatuses, a state of activity exists). If this activity is reduced, if there is surrender of the active processes, then the organism may be in danger because usually life preservative activities have ceased.

Litman and Tabachnick[17] dealt with a number of possibilities in regard to activity and passivity of the ego. They specifically mentioned that accidents might occur as a result of over-activity of the ego, an ego which might be generating too much action or over-producing impulsive, quick reactions. Under these circumstances, individuals (for example, driving automobiles) might precipitate themselves into dangerous situations. But the exact converse is also possible. Ego apparatuses which are operating sluggishly might precipitate the individual into accidents because of "over-passivity." There is a third possibility. There may be a lack of integration between active and passive modalities of action. In a complex procedure such as driving an automobile, there are times when quick, impulsive activity may be useful, and times when exactly the contrary is called for. But there is also a need for integration between the two. Thus, sustained continuous pressure on the gas pedal may have to be augmented by speedy pressure and release of pressure on the brake pedal. If these two activities are not integrated, an accident may result.

THE ROLE OF ALCOHOL

As was pointed out previously, factors external to the personality are often linked to accident. Is alcohol one of those significant "external" factors?

It seems well established that driving ability is impaired by the ingestion of alcohol. Individual susceptibility to disintegration of driving performance varies. However, it has been established that when certain blood alcohol levels are attained, almost everyone will experience a significant diminution in his usual safe driving practices.[29]

Now a question arises. *What is the mechanism that links alcohol with accidents?* There are at least two possibilities. One is that since alcohol has been demonstrated to impair driving ability, what we are dealing with is a negative physiological side effect of man's love of drinking. A second hypothesis is possible. The drinking may be a manifestation of a disturbed psychological state. The accident may be more significantly linked to this disturbed state than to the alcohol. A third possibility combines the first two. Perhaps there is a disturbed psychological state which leads to drinking, *and* physiological effects of the alcohol potentiate the tendencies which the psychological state by itself would have to produce an automobile accident.

Selzer[30] is one of a number of researchers who have developed this hypothesis. He suggests, on the basis of some researches of his plus a review of previous literature, that many chronic drinkers may possess an "alcoholic personality," that this personality is characterized by egocentricity, omnipotence, depression, suicidal trends and chronic hostility. He believes that when the "alcoholic personality" is not drinking, these trends do not express themselves in driving behavior. Drinking, however, releases them and makes it possible for them to contribute to the production of automobile accidents.

Selzer's conclusions are supported by a comparative study of ten motor accident repeaters compared with ten individuals who did not have accidents. The accident group demonstrated poor control of hostility, less ability to tolerate emotional tension, greater dependency needs, and extremes of both egocentricity and fantasy preoccupation.[24]

A recent study of automobile accident in Houston, Texas,[16] developed data on the relationship of drinking, character and accident. In the group of accident drivers, there were 20 per cent of normal people and 76 per cent of people with personality disorders. In the comparison group, there were 88 per cent normal people and 8 per cent with personality disorder. In the accident group, the personality disorders were *alcoholic*—60 per cent, anti-social personality—24 per cent, plus various small percentages of other types of personality disorders.

At the time of the crash, 28 per cent of the fatalities had zero blood alcohol, whereas over 150 mg. per cent blood alcohol (the generally accepted legal index of intoxication) was present in 72 per cent of the fatalities. In the accident group, there were 32 per cent social drinkers and, as already indicated, 60 per cent defined as alcoholics, whereas in the control group there were 32 per cent social drinkers and only 8 per cent classified as alcoholics.

There were a number of methodological problems in the Houston study. A particularly critical eye must be directed at the control group. It is possible that since entrance into this group was on a voluntary basis, many people who would have undesirable characteristics refused to participate. Thus, the large differences between the accident and control groups might be a product of this method of selection. However, even if it proved to be true that the control group was close to the target group, the high incidence of people called "alcoholics" in the accident group is striking.

In summary, the high linkage of drinking to automobile accident is one of the most important clues to its etiology. However, this factor, whatever its ultimate relationship will be shown to be, cannot account for all accidents.

REFERENCES

1. von Bertelanffy, L.: *General Systems Theory.* New York, Braziller, 1968.
2. Lewin, K.: *Principles of Topological Psychology.* New York, McGraw-Hill Book Co., 1936.
3. Hartmann, Heinz: *Ego Psychology and the Problem of Adaptation, JAPsaA,* Monograph Series No. 1. New York, International Univ. Press, 1958.
4. Waller, Julian A.: Tic-tac-toe burns—The hazard of exposed floor-type room heaters, *New Engl J Med,* 265:1256-1257, 1961. Reprinted in *Accident Research* (Haddon, Suchman and Klein, eds.). New York, Harper and Row, 1964.
5. Haddon, William A., Edward A. Suchman and David Klein: *Accident Research.* New York, Harper and Row, 1964.
6. Roberts, H. J.: *The Causes, Ecology and Prevention of Traffic Accidents.* Springfield, Thomas, 1971
7. Freud, Sigmund: *Beyond the Pleasure Principle* in *Standard Edition of the Complete Psychological Works,* Vol. XVIII. London, Hogarth Press, Ltd., 1953-65.
8. Freud, Sigmund: *The Psychopathology of Everyday Life* in *Standard Edition of Complete Psychological Works,* Vol. VI. London, Hogarth Press, Ltd., 1953-65.
9. Menninger, K. A.: Purposive accidents as an expression of self-destructive tendencies, *Int J Psychoanal,* 17:6-15, 1935.
10. Moseley, Alfred L.: *Research on Fatal Highway Collisions,* Harvard Medical School, 1962-63.
11. MacDonald, J. M.: Suicide and homicide by automobile, *Am J Psychiat,* 121:366-370, 1964.
12. Porterfield, Austin L.: Traffic fatalities, suicide and homicide, *Amer Sociol Review,* 25:897-901, December 1960. Reprinted in *Accident Research* (Haddon, Suchman and Klein, eds.). New York, Harper and Row, 1964.
13. Tabachnick, Norman, Robert E. Litman, Marvin Osman, Warren L. Jones, Jay Cohn, August Kasper, and John Moffat: Comparative

psychiatric study of accidental and suicidal death, *Arch Gen Psychiat*, 14:60-68, Jan. 1966.

14. Beck, Aaron T.: *Depression: Clinical, Experimental and Theoretical Aspects.* New York, Hoeber Medical Division, Harper and Row, 1967.

15. Pokorny, A. D.: Suicide Rates in Various Psychiatric Disorders, *J Nerv Ment Dis*, 139:499-506, 1964.

16. Finch, John R. and James Patrick Smith: *Psychiatric and Legal Aspects of Automobile Fatalities.* Springfield, Thomas, 1970.

17. Litman, Robert E. and Norman Tabachnick: Fatal one-car accidents, *Psychoanal Q*, 36:248-259, 1967.

18. Barmack, Joseph E. and Donald E. Payne: Injury-producing private motor vehicle accidents among airmen, *Highway Research Board Bull, 285,* 1961. Reprinted in *Accident Research* (Haddon, Suchman and Klein, eds.). New York, Harper and Row, 1964.

19. Hirschfeld, Alexander H. and Robert C. Behan: The accident process. I: Etiological considerations of industrial injuries, *JAMA*, 186:193-199, Oct. 19, 1963.

20. Behan, Robert C. and Alexander H. Hirschfeld: The Accident Process. II: Toward more rational treatment of industrial injuries, *JAMA*, 186:300-306, Oct. 26, 1963.

21. Hirschfeld, Alexander H. and Robert C. Behan: The accident process. III: Disability: Acceptable and unacceptable, *JAMA*, 197:125-129, July 11, 1966.

22. Osman, Marvin P.: A psychoanalytic study of auto accident victims, *Contemp Psychoanal*, 5:62-84, 1968.

23. Tillman, W. A. and G. E. Hobbs: The accident-prone automobile driver, *Amer J Psychiatry*, 105:321-331, November 1949. Reprinted in *Accident Research* (Haddon, Suchman and Klein, eds.). New York, Harper and Row, 1964.

24. Conger, John J., Herbert S. Gaskill, Donald D. Glad, Linda Hassell, Robert V. Rainey, and William Sawrey: Psychological and psychophysiological factors in motor vehicle accidents, *JAMA*, 169:1581-1587, April 4, 1959. Reprinted in *Accident Research* (Haddon, Suchman and Klein, eds.). New York, Harper and Row, 1964.

25. Greenwood, Major and Hilda M. Woods: The incidence of industrial accidents upon individuals with special reference to multiple accidents, in *Accident Research* (Haddon, Suchman and Klein, eds.). New York, Harper and Row, 1964.

26. Dunbar, Flanders: *Psychosomatic Diagnosis.* New York, Paul B. Hoeber, Inc., 1943.

27. Alexander, Franz: The accident prone individual, Public Health Reports, 64:357-361, 1949.

28. Suchman, Edward A. and Alfred L. Scherzer: Accident proneness, in

Accident Research (Haddon, Suchman and Klein, eds.). New York, Harper and Row, 1964.

29. Cohen, John, E. J. Dearnaley, and C. E. M. Hansel: The risk taken in driving under the influence of alcohol, *Brit Med J*, pp. 1438-1442, June 21, 1958. Reprinted in *Accident Research* (Haddon, Suchman and Klein, eds.). New York, Harper and Row, 1964.

30. Selzer, Melvin L.: Personality versus intoxication as critical factor in accidents caused by alcoholic drivers, *J Nerv Ment Dis*, 4:298-303, April 1961.

Chapter 2

THE RESEARCH STRATEGY

Rationale and Critique

Summary

Psychoanalyst interviewers were used to gather the basic data in our research. They were selected because of their presumed expertise in establishing and maintaining rapport, dealing with psychological resistances, and ability to make balanced and integrated decisions regarding psychological issues.

Since psychoanalysts were the interviewers and since our hypotheses sprang from psychoanalytic theorizing, we wished to utilize many of the valuable characteristics of the psychoanalytic interviewing method. However, for a number of reasons, some practical and some theoretical, certain departures from or modifications of the "traditional" psychoanalytic method were utilized. The subjects of these interviews were different from usual psychoanalytic subjects. Furthermore there were modifications involving the setting of the interviews and important limitations in the amount of time spent with each subject.

The most important change from the usual psychoanalytic research interview was the utilization of a specific schedule of issues and questions. Each analyst was asked to complete this schedule for every research subject. We chose this procedure because it allowed us to conduct our study through the method of testing previously formulated hypotheses. This, we believed, would be better than interpreting post-interview data in a completely free manner.

We established that our method was reliable and evaluated the presence and effect of interviewer bias on the material which the interviewers reported.

Although these modifications were instituted for the purpose

31

*of producing a better type of research data, they obviously gave
rise to a total method which was different from the usual psychoanalytic one. The changes in our method may raise questions as
to the validity of the material obtained by it.*

THE RESEARCH STRATEGY we used was a blending of psychoanalytic interviewing techniques and the testing of hypotheses through gathering data on specific issues (see Appendix Section at the back of the book). Each analyst obtained data so as
to answer 205 questions. In addition, he gathered data on the incident which brought the subject into the hospital and on the
character of the subject.

PSYCHOANALYTICAL MOTIVATIONS

Why did we utilize this blend of research strategies? We felt
that psychoanalytic approaches have certain strengths and certain
weaknesses. We sought to utilize the strengths and replace the
weaknesses with improved strategies.

What values of the psychoanalytic approach did we utilize?
First, we list theoretical concepts. We chose *psychoanalytic
theory* to formulate our problem and our questions. Then we
decided *to utilize psychoanalysts as our clinical investigators,* and
we asked them to preserve many aspects of their *usual psychoanalytic clinical approach* as they gathered data.

Why did we wish psychoanalysts to do the clinical interviewing? For one reason, we were investigating psychoanalytic hypotheses, and clinicians who had familiarity with the theory
from which those hypotheses came would be an asset to our
study. More important than theoretical background, however,
was clinical skill. There were three ways in which this skill was
of value:

1. First, it made it possible for the psychoanalysts to establish
a quick rapport with the subjects and to keep it at the maximum
possible intensity during the interview.

2. Secondly, their training and experience would enable them
to deal with certain resistances to giving meaningful data or continuing the interview. Almost all psychological interviewees manifest some resistances. Fear, shame and a desire for privacy are

among the motivations for these. Actually, in addition to the usual resistances, individuals involved in accidents and individuals in a general hospital may have special resistances. Accident victims may fear that investigators represent the police or insurance companies. Other lower social class subjects may also be (rationally or otherwise) concerned about police and welfare investigations.

3. Finally, psychoanalysts should be able to monitor, evaluate and integrate interview data so as to produce well-balanced and psychologically meaningful judgments.

Because some or all of the above "values" of psychoanalysts are generally tied in with their methods of interviewing, we wanted them to use their usual methods as much as possible. However, for a number of reasons, we felt it important to modify the "usual" or "typical" psychoanalytic research approach. The chief reason for modification (which gave rise to our most important technical change) was our dissatisfaction with the method by which hypotheses are supported in the "classical" psychoanalytic research approach. To provide the rationale for this modification, we shall now discuss the traditional method of doing psychoanalytic research and then explain how our modification dealt with an important deficiency in that method.

The "Traditional" Model of Psychoanalytic Research

First, let us characterize a "traditional" model of psychoanalytic research. Such a model has never been formalized, to our knowledge. Each psychoanalytic researcher more or less indicates his methodology as he presents his data. It should furthermore be stated that in psychoanalytic research, as in other types, there are many different specific approaches used. Thus we can only give our personal impression of what the "traditional" model of psychoanalytic research is; other workers might characterize this model in different ways.

We believe that the traditional model of psychoanalytic research consists essentially of accumulating data obtained while patients are being analyzed. This method can more specifically be characterized from the following four standpoints:

1. The data consists of details of the genetic origins of the

analysand's personality and personality conflicts, and observations of his current ways of feeling, acting and psychologically
dealing with the issues of his life. It especially takes into account "transference" manifestations. Transference is a phenomenon in which the analysand reacts to current personalities involved with him (most specifically, his analyst) as if they have
the same qualities as important individuals in his past history,
such as his parents or siblings. Transference is, for the most
part, unconscious; that is, the analysand does not realize that he
reacts to people because of identifying them with past important figures. He believes that he reacts to them totally because of
their present meaning and value to him.

2. The method stresses very strongly the utilization of "free
associations." The analysand is encouraged to talk about whatever "comes to his mind." He may develop or elaborate on or relate to these concerns in any way that he wishes. The analyst di-
rects him and focuses attention on certain subjects to a limited
degree.

3. This method is utilized with individuals who consider themselves "sick" or possessing malfunctions of their personality, or
who believe there could be significant changes and improvements
in their personalities.

4. Conclusions are reached in the following way: As the analyst registers observations and impressions during the course of
the analysis, he develops certain hypotheses. He tests these by repeated observation, by asking questions, and by making interpretations, some of which lead to changes within the personality of
the patient, and by assessing the meaning of those changes. It is
assumed that a "good" psychoanalyst, after being well trained
and having enough experience to develop his potentialities, *can*
reliably draw conclusions and arrive at valid data.

Modifications Involving the Technique of Interviewing

We now move on to the "modifications" from the "traditional" psychoanalytic research model which we utilized. We will
state the reasons for instituting these modifications and briefly
discuss the possible values and limitations of each one. Be it said

that the most important modifications involved the technique of interviewing.

In the usual psychoanalysis, psychologically significant issues are idiosyncratically developed. As the analysand "free-associates," as the analyst observes and interacts with the analysand and his material, a picture slowly develops of what the "problem" is of that analysand. Once the problem or problems are identified, it becomes possible to search for and identify the significant psychological data which are related to those problems.

Note the modifications in our interviewing technique. To some degree, we encouraged the analyst to follow a procedure similar to the one used in "usual" analytic interviewing. But, in addition, we asked each analyst to study a long list of general and specific issues in regard to which we wished him to obtain as much information as possible from each subject. We did this because we wished to gain data which would help us support or nullify preconceived hypotheses regarding the self-destructive nature of accidents. Our choice of this method of hypothesis-testing was quite deliberate.

It is our belief that research can be divided into hypothesis-generating and hypothesis-testing methods. The psychoanalytic method has been excellent for the accomplishment of hypothesis-generating with its opportunity to observe in a very broad way many of the innumerable vicissitudes of psychological occurrences. However, the usual psychoanalytic approach (what we previously called the "traditional" model of psychoanalytic research) is not as effective a tool for hypothesis-testing. Because theoretical issues are not firmly linked to predicted phenomena and because often many alternative hypotheses can be used to explain the same psychological occurrence, and because preconception, bias or distortion of the analyst may affect his interpretation of data, serious questions are raised in utilizing the usual psychoanalytic method as to the validity of conclusions.

We wished to eliminate these possible sources of error in our study. This we did by making predictions (that is, we predicted that if certain hypotheses were true, certain data would be found). If those data were indeed found, our hypotheses would

tend to be supported. If *not* found, they would not be supported. It is thus obvious that our interviewing method was different
from the usual psychoanalytic one, although it did retain a number of similarities.

FURTHER MODIFICATIONS IN
PSYCHOANALYTICAL TECHNIQUES

In addition to the changes in interviewing technique, there
were a number of additional modifications in our study. These
involved the characteristics of the subjects, the setting of the interviews and the amount of time spent in interviewing. We will
now discuss each of these additional modifications.

Modifications Involving the Subjects

Our subjects were not patients or analysands in the usual understanding of this term in psychoanalysis. None of them voluntarily came to us or requested to be interviewed. It is true that
a number of subjects in all three groups (auto accident, suicide
attempt and appendectomy) were interested in and positively
oriented toward the interviews and/or the interviewers. Questions arise concerning the motivation for this interest. In the
usual case coming for psychoanalytic treatment, the main conscious motivation is that of wanting to have anxiety relieved, to
get over an illness, or to find a better way of conducting one's
life. It is believed, however, that there are many additional motivations, some of which are unconscious. For example, many people feel that the analyst has a powerful way of improving their
conditions. They come to him to have him magically remove
their difficulties.

What motivations existed for our subjects to cooperate with
us? We cannot be sure, but we believe the following motivations
were probable: (1) They were anxious in regard to a number of
issues and welcomed the chance to talk to a "doctor" whom they
felt might relieve their anxiety. (2) They were bored and lonely
in the hospital and welcomed the opportunity to spend time with
another human being. (3) Some (particularly in the suicide
group) considered themselves emotionally ill and wanted help.

(4) Some were curious and wanted to see what would happen if they went ahead with the interview. And (5) some were acceding deferentially to the request of an "authority" figure.

These motivations are somewhat (but not entirely) different from those present in individuals who come for therapeutic analysis. Do these different motivations impair the quality of the analytic situation and therefore the validity of the material? We cannot answer this question with certainty. Many analysts feel that the need to relieve anxiety, to leave "sickness" and enter "health" is the most powerful motivation for analysis. Only such an extreme need can enable an analysand to endure the difficulties and deprivations of the long analytic process.

Other psychoanalysts[1] have worked with non-patients and have recovered what they feel to be valid data. We presume there is a good likelihood that our data were valid. In company with many other psychoanalysts, we do not feel there are overwhelming differences between those people who consider themselves neurotic and those who do not. We feel that the motivations which are identified in our subjects could produce a fruitful "research" alliance between the interviewers and the interviewees.

The advantage of dealing with non-patients was that it enabled us to gain access to relatively large groups of subjects who had undergone experiences which we wished to study. It is possible that we could have obtained equal numbers of patients in two groups (accident and suicide attempt) had we attempted to gather them from individuals voluntarily coming to psychoanalysts. However, it would have been much more difficult to obtain a large number of people in our "normal" (that is, appendectomy) group from volunteers. But going to the non-patients in the hospital enabled us to choose individuals who were matched in a number of ways. (They were all males of comparable age; they had all undergone recent traumas which required emergency hospitalization; they were all subject to the same environmental situation.) This made it possible for us to construct a much better comparative study than had we not taken such measures.

We wished to study the psychology of accidents, but we did not exclusively interview individuals who had sustained "accidents." Instead, we spent time not only with "accident" subjects but also with people who had made serious suicide attempts and with those whom we considered normal or non-self-destructive, that is, people in the appendectomy group. This procedure was followed because we wished to determine if a certain number of accidents had suicidal or self-destructive psychological phenomena involved in them. By comparing our target group (the "accidents") with a group of severely self-destructive people (the suicide attempters), on the one hand, and a group of presumably non-self-destructive people (the appendectomies), on the other, we hoped to sensitize ourselves to similarities and differences which would help us more clearly identify self-destructive psychological factors in accident.

Modifications Involving the Setting of the Interview Situation

Our subjects were seen in general surgical and medical wards of a large general hospital. The patients themselves were often in moderate degrees of organic distress and pain. Many had sustained fractures and were in traction. The wards were fairly large (each had from four to ten patients), cluttered and often noisy, as a number of other conversations plus the sound of radio, television and hallway noises added to the decibel count. Most of our analysts had not done analytic work in such settings. It was obvious that there was an adjustment necessary to both the hospital setting and the task of working with patients who were more disabled than the usual analysand.

The analysts, however, had had some preparation for this transition. Many of them had worked on previous projects in hospital wards. All of them had discussed the procedures and the milieu on several occasions before they actually entered the hospital for the first time.

Could these differences in the setting of the interview have made a difference in the quality of the material we elicited? There are certain values associated with the isolation, comfort and quiet of the "traditional" psychoanalytic setting. All three of these conditions were diminished in our endeavor.

It is thus possible that, to the degree those qualities enhance the setting up of a close and intimate relationship between analyst and interviewee, there was a significant negative input to the total interviewing situation. However, we did have skilled psychoanalysts at work and would surmise that they would be able to take advantage of whatever psychological motivations impelled our subjects to voluntarily cooperate in the study.

Modifications Involving the Time of Interviewing

The usual psychoanalysis arrives at its final conclusions after several hundred hours of work. The conclusions result from repeated observations, the utilization of transference, and the observation of the effects of carefully thought out and modified interpretations. The total time spent with our subjects was quite small in comparison with those hundreds of hours. Our analysts spent only 2 to 10 hours with each subject.

This shortness of time was the result of a number of considerations. We felt we were not offering the subjects enough to keep them coming over a long period of time. Most were content and some were even happy to work with us while they were in the hospital. However, since many did not consider themselves "sick" and in need of psychological help, they might have readily discontinued their cooperation after they left the hospital. In addition, it was an important part of our research plan to see a large number of subjects in each of the three categories. Since it was quite expensive to conduct our study, we had to limit the time spent with each subject. We quite deliberately set an upper limit of ten hours of interviewing time, feeling that we would be able to obtain meaningful material during that period of time.

Did the short period of time spent with each subject limit the value of the material from each subject? We feel that it probably did. We believe that had we spent 20, 40 or 100 hours with each subject, we would have obtained more accurate answers to our specific questions and better ideas of the characters, psychological resistances and adaptations of the interviewees.

Yet we obviously felt that the material which we did obtain would be of value. There were several reasons for this impression. First, we had skilled workers as information gatherers. Secondly, although psychoanalysts can undoubtedly obtain more firm and specific ideas of the psychological state of affairs over long periods of time, they can also gather good material and great amounts of it in relatively short periods of time. Every psychoanalyst does arrive at ideas and impressions on many psychological issues early in his contact with his analysands. Through the specific questions we asked our interviewers to answer in regard to each subject, we undoubtedly forced them to come to earlier decisions than they might have otherwise done. Yet we believed that they could obtain valuable data even though the conditions for obtaining same might not be ideal. The results of our reliability evaluations provide support for these beliefs.

ASSESSING RELIABILITY

A "reliable" method is one which can be utilized by two or more interviewers with the assurance that all would have a high degree of agreement in their interpretation of data. That is, if interviewer A believes that subject X is impulsive on the basis of his interview data, then interviewers B and C are highly likely to come to the same conclusion after evaluating the same data.

Reliability assessments are infrequently performed in psychoanalytic researches. There are a number of reasons for this. Many researches are based on the study of individual cases by individual analysts. In addition, the methods which each analyst uses to elicit and evaluate data may be different. Also, specific questions and comments of the analyst are likely to develop idiosyncratically in each analysis. It is assumed, however, that well-trained analysts are likely to come to the same conclusions even though they may arrive at these conclusions by different routes.

In our research, we had a specific series of questions which each analyst answered in regard to each case. Thus, we had a standardized data list even though the methods used to elicit data might vary from one analyst to another.

We tested for reliability by tape recording in their entirety all interviews with each subject. Then the tape recordings were evaluated by an independent group of raters who answered as many of the questions as they felt possible. In this way, we were able to ascertain to what degree our research approach was reliable, to improve its reliability in every way possible, and to evaluate the significance of any *interviewer bias* on our data (certain procedures are involved here which will be described in later sections of this book).

Interviewer Bias

A thorny issue linked to that of reliability is that of interviewer bias. By "bias" is meant the possibility that a particular "set" or preconception of the interviewer analyst may produce distortion of the data which he records. This may be done in at least two ways. First, he may tend to interpret data to fall in line with his bias. Secondly, his belief that a certain situation exists may prompt him to influence the interviewee to produce material which substantiates his preconception.

Although analysts are well acquainted with the possibility of biases in individuals (for example, they routinely find such biases in their analysands), they have rarely evaluated the significance of such biases in themselves. It is assumed that most analysts are trained to recognize and to hold in check the effects of their biases by virtue of their personal analysis and their analytic training.

There is good reason to question this assumption. In many situations which we have observed, it would seem that analysts' biases have unrealistically distorted their judgment. Furthermore, we know that individuals' psychological capabilities change from time to time. It is quite possible that biases may exert their distorting effect at certain times in an analyst's life but not at others.

Finally, it can be questioned whether a personal analysis plus much analytic training and experience can effectively deal with all the possible biases in an analyst. His personal analysis, for example, tends to focus on those areas of his personality that produce psychological pain. A successful analysis will deal with unconscious determinants of the painful situations. However, there may be many areas in his personality which are unconnected with psychological pain and yet may contain biases. These may be reflected in his evaluation of data when he is functioning as a psychoanalytic researcher (or therapist).

We wished first to evaluate the presence of bias in our interviewers. Specifically, we wished to identify possible biases in regard to the hypotheses we were investigating. Secondly, we wished to evaluate the effect of the interviewer's bias (if such was present) upon the evaluation of the material which they elicited and reported.

Evaluations of reliability and of interviewer bias are, in our opinion, valuable methodological additions to psychoanalytic research projects.

REFERENCE

1. Hendin, Herbert, Willard Gaylin, and Arthur Carr: *Psychoanalysis and Social Research*. Garden City, Doubleday and Co., 1965.

PART TWO

THE
→ RESEARCH PLAN ←

CHAPTER 3

DEVELOPMENT AND IDENTIFICATION OF THE HYPOTHESES

Summary

This chapter specifies the hypotheses which were utilized in the "Data Sheet" part of our research. It also details how these hypotheses were developed.

The central question of our research was, Do suicidal and self-destructive trends predispose certain human beings to serious automobile accidents? *Our method was to develop a series of hypotheses dealing with suicide and self-destructive trends and to note the concentration of the trends in three groups of subjects. These groups were: (1) Severely suicidal patients; (2) drivers seriously injured as a result of one-car collisions; and (3) post-appendectomy patients (postulated to be non-self-destructive).*

We would expect the hypotheses to be most positive in the suicide group. If, for any hypothesis, the accident group proved to have a higher positive rate than the appendectomy group, that hypothesis would be supported. The total number of supported hypotheses would represent a configuration of self-destructive factors in automobile accident (more specifically in drivers involved in one-car automobile accidents).

In our theorizations regarding suicide and self-destruction in accident, we did not focus exclusively or even largely on the possibilities of the death instinct. Along with many other psychoanalysts, we have strong questions about the applicability of this theory to psychological thinking. However, whether or not a death instinct exists, certain psychological patterns and certain action patterns can be conceptualized as being linked to suicidal

45

*and self-destructive potentialities. (For our own more detailed
view as to significant psychoanalytic theories of suicide, see
"Psychoanalytic Theories of Suicide."[1])*

How DID WE SELECT our hypotheses? At the Suicide Prevention
Center, we had long been interested in issues of "indirect
self-destruction." This term was used by us to designate activities
of human beings which contributed to their injury or death but
were not linked with classic suicidal configurations. The most
important difference between suicide and "indirect self-destructive modalities" is that in the suicidal situations, there is a clear
intention to do away with oneself. A plan is formulated, either
impulsively or at length, to implement this intention. The plan
is acted on, and self-injury or death results. In "indirect self-
destruction," the injury or death does not result from the sequence, "Intention-self-destructive plan-carrying out the plan."

There are presumably other connections between self-destructive intention (which may be unconscious) and action which results in self-injury or self-inflicted death.

Prominent among the presumed self-destructive modalities of
an indirect nature is accident. One of the most prevalent and
important causes of accidental death, injury and property damage is automobile accident. As a result of these considerations,
we initiated a series of research investigations in 1963. Two of
us (Drs. Norman Tabachnick and Robert E. Litman) enlisted
the support of a number of our psychoanalytic colleagues at the
Southern California Psychoanalytic Institute to assist in these investigations. From that time on, the work was a collaborative effort of the Psychoanalytic Institute and the Los Angeles Suicide
Prevention Center.

During those years of research and consideration of the results of research,[2-7] a series of hypotheses which are the ones
used in the present study were developed. What were the most
pressing and crucial psychological issues which resulted from our
research?

Depressive and Counter-Depressive Trends

First we asked, *Are certain situations of accident, in fact, con-
cealed or masked suicide attempts?* Linked hypotheses were that

although certain accidents might not have resulted from direct suicide attempts, they might have occurred in individuals who were having strong or mild suicidal preoccupations without a specific plan, or who might have had a suicidal plan but one which did not involve accident. These individuals, however, might "accidentally" have had a serious one-car automobile collision just at that point in their lives. We therefore looked for communication of suicidal ideas and self-destructive preoccupations both of direct and indirect nature.

There are some important affective states linked to suicide. Most prominent among these is depression. Considering the accident group as a whole, *would we find evidence of more depression in it than in the non-accident population?* A frequent finding among suicidal and depressed individuals is that efforts are made to combat and overcome depression. Thus, we looked for manifestations of counter-depressive trends. We felt that evidence for an increased frequency of such trends in the accident group would be supportive of a tendency toward suicide in them.

Counter-depressive psychological trends might be associated in another way with automobile accident. These trends are often characterized as impulsive, adventurous, action-oriented modalities of living. In psychoanalytic theory, they are characterized as "manic" or "hypomanic" states. Such states are often accompanied by poorly planned or poorly judged action. Thus, an individual in a counter-depressive "manic" state might tend to drive carelessly and, as a result, become involved in an accident.

Individuals deeply affected by depression and also involved in counter-depressive thinking and acting may exist on a kind of psychological teeter-totter between these polar existential modes. If they swing rapidly, lack of coordinated action can result. This might contribute to the production of accident. When one considers the need for quick actions and quick relaxations, the need for rapid alternation between states of activity and passivity which occur during driving, one can appreciate the significance of a lack of appropriate coordination. One of our hypotheses dealt with a lack of integration between depressive and counter-depressive trends.

Past research had demonstrated high rates of drinking among both suicidal people and those involved in automobile accidents. We wished to test again for the presence of high drinking patterns in our three groups to find if there were similarities or differences.

Linked to the issue of increased drinking in "accident-producing" drivers is the possibility of "drug abuse." By this we mean the self-prescription and self-medication of drugs. Most prudent individuals would probably not take drugs which can be dangerous without the advice of a physician or someone else skilled in the knowledge of the effects and dangers of the drug. Not following such a pattern is in itself a kind of "self-destructive" activity. Would such patterns be found to be high among accident subjects? We already believed that they were high among suicidal individuals.

Drinking and drug abuse, however, can lead to accident because of the physiological effects of alcohol and other drugs. These substances lead to a disintegration of those perceptual, action and coordinated faculties which are necessary for safe driving (a fact best documented in the case of alcohol). Thus, not only can the ingestion of these substances be a kind of self-destructiveness in itself, but it can be productive of another type of self-destructiveness when it is combined with driving. For these reasons, we wished to investigate in a detailed manner the drinking and drug abuse patterns of our subjects.

One group of hypotheses deals with patterns of action that can be associated with self-destructive trends. These include: not following medical advice; behavior which seems to be injury- or death-seeking; and impulsive actions which have destructive implications. (The destruction may be directed toward the self, toward others, or toward property.) The thinking here is that if a tendency toward accident is one manifestation of suicidal or self-destructive trends, then additional self-destructive manifestations might be found in individuals who possess these trends. Thus the questions about not following medical advice and about behavior which seems to be injury- or death-seeking need to be posed.

The last hypothesis in this group, "Impulsive actions with destructive implications," deals with a pattern of behavior that has been frequently noted in suicidal people, that is, impulsive activity. It is true that impulsivity is not always a continuing characteristic of suicidal people. Often it occurs only when the suicidal person is in the grip of strong emotion. Previous theorization and research had postulated that accident-prone people were often of an impulsive action-oriented type. We wished to test that concept.

A final group of hypotheses dealt with precipitating factors of self-destructive states. Previous research suggested that individuals encountering new responsibilities or dealing with recent significant life changes might enter a tense period of life during which they would be more likely to have an automobile or other type of accident. A factor frequently noted to precede successful and unsuccessful suicide attempts, and occasionally noted to precede accidents, was a loss of self-esteem. Sometimes loss of self-esteem is conceptualized as part of the tense state that precedes suicide or accident. Sometimes it is thought of as a factor which leads to those tense states.

The key questions which we asked are dealt with in the following thirteen hypotheses. Most questions in our Data Sheet were linked to these hypotheses. (The complete Data Sheet is reproduced in Appendix I.) They were also used as the focal points for the dynamic interviews and dynamic evaluations which our psychoanalysts made of each subject.

The Hypotheses of Our Study

Drivers who sustained near-fatal injury in auto collisions:

A. Have utilized these collisions as deliberate suicide attempts to a greater degree than subjects in the appendectomy group.

B. Have made suicide attempts and communications of suicidal preoccupation to a greater degree than subjects in the appendectomy group.

C. Manifest depressive symptoms to a greater degree than subjects in the appendectomy group.

D. Manifest a counter-depressive attitude to a greater degree than subjects in the appendectomy group.

E. Indulge in excessive drinking and/or drug ingestion to a greater degree than subjects in the appendectomy group.

F. Tend to self-injuriously not seek and/or not follow medical advice to a greater degree than subjects in the appendectomy group.

G. Engage in behavior which risks injury or death to themselves to a greater degree than subjects in the appendectomy group.

H. Have, in a period closely prior to the accident, had unusual difficulty in dealing with a new responsibility. This difficulty may manifest itself in (a) having doubts that the new responsibility can be handled adequately; (b) not having comfortably mastered the problems involved in the new responsibility; or (c) not having achieved a personal feeling of comfort in regard to the assumption of the new responsibility. These circumstances will occur in serious accident victims to a greater degree than subjects in the appendectomy group.

I. Have a greater tendency than others to utilize impulsive actions which have a destructive implication. Their actions will have less concern for the physical and/or emotional harm directed toward physical objects or other individuals or themselves. These circumstances will occur in serious accident victims to a greater degree than with subjects in the appendectomy group.

J. Show a lack of integration between depressive, passive and inactive styles of life, on the one hand, and counter-depressive, active, energetic styles of life, on the other hand. This will be manifested by a greater degree of fluctuation between these styles of life in the serious accident victims than in the appendectomy group.

K. Will, just prior to their accidents, have suffered a loss of self-esteem. This loss will be in respect to feeling that they have done poorly in some area (work performance, having others admire them) from which they characteristically draw a great deal of self-esteem. This circumstance will occur in serious accident victims to a greater degree than subjects in the appendectomy group.

L. Will, in a period shortly prior to their hospitalization, have undergone an important recent life change which has involved an increase or decrease in personal responsibility. This circumstance will occur in serious accident victims to a greater degree than in subjects in the appendectomy group.

M. In terms of a number of characteristics (those specified in hypotheses A through L), drivers involved in near-fatal accidents will be closer to a criterion group of serious suicidal attempters than will the group of appendectomy subjects.

REFERENCES

1. Litman, Robert E., and Norman Tabachnick: Psychoanalytic theories of suicide, *Psychoanal Q*, 36:248-259, 1967.
2. Litman, Robert E., and Norman Tabachnick: Fatal one-car accidents. In *Suicidal Behavior: Diagnosis and Management* (H. L. P. Resnick, Ed.). New York, Little, Brown and Co., 1968.
3. Osman, Marvin P.: A psychoanalytic study of auto accident victims, *Contemp Psychiatry*, 5:62-84, 1968.
4. Tabachnick, Norman: The Psychoanalyst as accident investigator, *Behavioral Research in Highway Safety*, Vol. 1, No. 1, 1970.
5. Tabachnick, Norman: The Psychology of fatal accident. In *Essays in Self-Destruction* (E. Shneidman, Ed.). New York, Science House, Inc., 1967.
6. Tabachnick, Norman, and Robert E. Litman: Character and life circumstances in fatal accident. *Psychoanal Forum*, 1:65-74, 1966.
7. Tabachnick, Norman, Robert E. Litman, Marvin Osman, Warren L. Jones, Jay Cohn, August Kasper, and John Moffat: Comparative psychiatric study of accidental and suicidal death, *Arch Gen Psychiatry*, 14:60-68, Jan. 1966.

CHAPTER 4

THE METHOD
Summary

This chapter details the various methods used in the research study. Three groups of subjects were studied: I. A critical accident group; II. a critical suicide attempt group; *and* III. a post appendectomy group. *These groups were matched for age and sex. All subjects were taken from the wards of a large general hospital.*

An attempt was made to distribute the different types of cases uniformly among the interviewers so that no interviewer had a preponderance of any one or two types of subjects.

For each case, a Data Sheet *consisting of 205 items was utilized. In addition, the analyst-investigator in each case provided a summary of its dynamic features. This focused on characterological reactions and specific resistances of the subject. The 205 items on the Data Sheet were made reliable by pre-planning evaluation pilot studies and reformulation of unreliable items. Evaluations of the presence and effect of the bias of the interviewer were conducted.*

After completing his work on the project, each analyst interviewer discussed his impressions of and reactions to the project with a member of the central research group. This was called the debriefing *procedure.*

Finally, a significant other *study was performed. In this study, certain data analagous to that elicited from the subjects was obtained from relatives or friends. This study yielded additional data on the subjects and provided an opportunity to evaluate similarities and differences in the significant others of subjects in the three groups.*

OUR RESEARCH FOCUSED on the evaluation and comparison of hypothesized self-destructive factors among three groups of subjects: (1) A critical accident group; (2) a critical suicide attempt group; and (3) a post-appendectomy group. All of our subjects came from the wards of a large general hospital in Los Angeles.

The Sample

We included new patients in our three categories by making rounds of the appropriate admitting rooms of the hospital two and three times a week. Every patient who might possibly fit into one of our three categories was identified. He was then evaluated by members of our research group. If he fitted all the criteria for inclusion in any one group, he was made a possible subject for study. We attempted to include every person so selected in our study (which subjects stayed in our study group, which ones dropped out, and for what reasons will be detailed in Part III— The Results, particularly in Chapter 5, entitled The Sample).

THE CRITERIA FOR ADMISSION

All patients were male, ages 18 to 48. We chose male patients because most of the subjects available in our critical accident group were males. (This paralleled the fact that most drivers involved in accidents are males.) We chose the age group of 18 to 48 since it is in this group that the majority of automobile accidents occur. The following is the listing of the specific criteria for each group:

I. THE CRITICAL ACCIDENT GROUP

1. The accident must have involved only one car and the patient must have been the driver. Drivers of one-car accidents were selected since it was believed that suicidal and self-destructive trends would be most likely found in this group. In addition, the subject fits into at least one of groups 2, 3, 4, 5 or 6 below.

2. Admission to an intensive care unit at any time.

3. Patients necessitating surgical intervention in the operating room. These patients might fall into one of the following groups:

   a. Patient with severe internal damage, e.g. ruptured spleen.

   b. Patients with severe soft tissue damage.

   c. Patients with single fractures with complications, e.g. compound or comminuted fractures. Patients needing surgical reduction of fracture or insertion of mechanical devices such as pins in hip fractures.

4. Patients with multiple fractures of either one or several bones.

5. Patients with fractures of the skull, spine or pelvis.

6. Patients admitted to Neurology, Neurosurgery or any other wards who have been unconscious for at least one half-hour any time prior to or during hospitalization, or who have exhibited neurological signs at any time.

II. THE CRITICAL SUICIDE ATTEMPT GROUP

1. Patients whose charts indicate an acknowledged suicide attempt and who, in addition, fit into 2, 3 or 4 below.

2. Admission to an intensive care unit at any time.

3. Patients who have been in coma at any time.

4. Patients admitted to Neurology, Neurosurgery or any other wards who have been unconscious for at least one half-hour at any time prior to or during hospitalization, or who have exhibited neurological signs at any time.

III. THE POST-APPENDECTOMY GROUP

1. Patients operated on for appendicitis, with the surgical note confirming a diseased appendix by gross inspection.

B. Clinical Interviewing

The crucial and central method of data-gathering was clinical interviewing by psychoanalysts. Seventeen psychoanalysts acted as clinical interviewers. They were all members of a research seminar at the Southern California Psychoanalytic Institute specifically involved with this project.

Approximately half of the interviewers were members and half were senior clinical associates (analysts in training) at the Southern California Psychoanalytic Institute. Two were psychologists with considerable psychoanalytic training and experience.

About two-thirds of the interviewers had participated in earlier accident research seminars. The remainder joined the group just prior to the beginning of this project or shortly after it had begun. Those analysts who had been in our group for some time were familiar with our hypotheses as well as with the methods which would be utilized in the interviewing. (Similar methods had been used in previous projects.)

All clinical interviewers had as the minimum the following training prior to their actual clinical work: at least two hours of discussion regarding the theoretical and methodological aspects of the project. The theoretical briefing was provided by two of the central research group (Norman Tabachnick or John Gussen). The methodological briefing was given by two of our technical staff (Judith Davis or Celeste Dorsey) who were knowledgeable in matters dealing with hospital procedure, utilization of tape recorders, etc.

The interviews during which the data was obtained were performed, for the most part, on the wards of the general hospital. Some patients were ambulatory so that they could move to more private sections of the ward, but the vast majority had to be interviewed at bedside. Privacy would be attempted by the placing of cloth shields around the subject's bed. Rarely, some subjects had the later part of the data-gathering performed at the analyst's office or at the subject's home.

The analysts first familiarized themselves with the hypotheses of the study. They were able, by reading the Data Sheet, to gain a specific idea of our questions. Subjects were interviewed from two to ten hours. Data was reported in two general ways, as follows:

RECORDING OF DATA

1. THE DATA SHEET: A Data Sheet was constructed around the hypotheses of the study. This sheet had 205 specific inquiries. (The Data Sheet in its entirety is included at the end of this volume as Appendix I.) The analysts answered as many of the questions on the Data Sheet as was possible in each case. It is important to note that the answers to the questions were based on the *judgment* of the analysts. In some cases, the analyst believed the most appropriate answers to the questions were different

from the overt statements of the subject. In other cases, the subjects may not have specifically commented on certain points; however, the analysts felt that they could provide answers to those questions. There was an answer available for each item called "No Information."

2. THE NARRATIVE SUMMARY: A second source of data was contained in a narrative summary of certain pertinent events detailed in each interview. This summary contained the following information:

   a. A narrative description of the patient's past and recent history, as well as genetic and dynamic formulation of the patient's character structure, conflicts and main defenses.
   b. A dynamic evaluation of circumstances surrounding the event for which the subject was hospitalized.
   c. In each accident case, the interviewer's opinion as to the presence of significant self-destructive elements.
   d. An evaluation of unconscious self-destructive trends in the subject.
   e. A dynamic evaluation of the interview transactions.

C. Reliability

How reliable was our data-gathering procedure? We thought it would be possible to make one part of it (that utilizing the Data Sheet) quite reliable. We shall here describe the procedure which we used.

Our first version of the Data Sheet included those questions which we felt would appropriately give us data on our hypotheses. The questions fell along a spectrum whose two poles were (1) very largely objective, and (2) very largely subjective. To exemplify this, some questions could be answered with almost no necessity for the interviewer to evaluate what the subject was saying. (Such a question was, "Is your driver's license in effect or suspended?") Other questions involved a relatively large degree of judging on the part of the interviewer (for example, "Subject communicates suicidal ideas.")

It was our initial intention to assess the reliability for each clinical interview by having three analysts (who had no prior connection with the study) listen to the tape recordings of all the interviews for that case and, on the basis of that experience, fill out the Data Sheet. However, it occurred to us that we had, at this point, an excellent opportunity to contrast the reliability ratings that could be achieved by analysts, on the one hand, with ratings achievable by less well-trained and experienced individuals, on the other hand. Since, in many questions, we were reducing abstract and theoretical psychoanalytic hypotheses into specific bits of data, it seemed possible that individuals other than sophisticated psychoanalysts might be able to obtain that data from the interviews.

Pursuing this possibility, we selected one group of professionals who had just achieved their degrees in clinical psychology, and a second group of intelligent laymen. (These were clinical associates trained by the Suicide Prevention Center to handle crisis calls at the Center. A detailed description of the training which these volunteers undergo has been published.[1])

With these three groups (three members in each group), we performed our first reliability study using two cases, one of near-fatal accident and one of suicide attempt. The results of this study were as follows:

	Average Percentage of Agreement
Critical Accident	
Analysts	70.0
Psychologists	69.9
Lay Raters	68.0
Suicide Attempt	
Analysts	66.9
Psychologists	67.1
Lay Raters	65.1

Following the first evaluation, we identified the questions for which there was poor reliability.* After consultations with the

---

* Almost all questions which were changed involved broader definitions of time intervals. In the original version, many questions listed the distribution of specific factors over periods of one day, one week, one month, etc. In the revision, these categories were collapsed so that five time periods were changed to two or three time periods.

interviewers and raters and after discussions on the part of the
Central Research Group, we altered those particular questions
or substituted different ones in the hope that the changes would
allow us to achieve higher reliability.

We then performed our second reliability study, this time
using four cases. The results of the second reliability study were
as follows:

	Average Percentage of Agreement
Critical Accident	
Analysts	87.0
Psychologists	87.4
Lay Raters	88.0
Intermediate Accident†	
Analysts	69.7
Psychologists	69.8
Lay Raters	70.1
Suicide Attempt	
Analysts	81.3
Psychologists	80.0
Lay Raters	84.8
Appendectomy	
Analysts	82.3
Psychologists	80.7
Lay Raters	81.8

At this point, we will comment on two issues. First, it will be
seen that a high rate of reliability was achieved. Secondly, the
degree of agreement varied only slightly between the three types
of raters. Actually, the greatest variation was only 3½ percentage
points. In most cases, the difference between the three groups
did not exceed two percentage points.

As a result of these early evaluations, we believed that we had
established a reliable instrument—the final Data Sheet. However,
in order to establish that certain intervening factors did not
make some of the cases in the study unreliable, we elected to
perform reliability studies on every case in the study. Nine raters

---

† In early phases of the project, we used a fourth category of subject called
"Intermediate Accident." We subsequently had to drop this category because we
could not obtain enough "intermediate accidents" to fulfill the statistical require-
ments of the study.

from among the non-professional clinical associate staff at the Suicide Prevention Center participated in these reliability evaluations. Provisions were made for the reliability evaluations to be carried out without communication between the raters in regard to their work.

Every case in our study demonstrated a high degree of reliability in regard to the questions on the Data Sheet. The overall reliability of the study was 77 per cent. The reliability in each category was as follows: Critical Accident — 77%; Suicide Attempt — 76%; and Appendectomy — 78%.

D. Statistical Methodology for Evaluation of Hypotheses

To facilitate the evaluation of our findings by readers not familiar with statistical methods, we shall briefly review some of the major statistical procedures which were employed to analyze the data of the study.

The Chi Square test (X^2) is a statistical procedure which is employed when one is dealing with data that can be reduced to frequencies, such as the percentage of accident, suicide attempt, and appendectomy subjects who have had suicidal thoughts. Using X^2, we can determine if there is a statistically significant difference in the percentage of subjects having suicidal thoughts from among these three groups. When we say the difference is *statistically significant,* we mean that it is unlikely that the difference is due to chance. In the present study, we accepted a difference as statistically significant if it could have occurred by chance five times out of 100 or less. This is known as the .05 level of significance.

In order to use the X^2 test, certain criteria must be met which have to do with the number of groups and the frequencies in each group. When these criteria are met, the results provide an *exact probability* of the level of significance. When these criteria cannot be completely met, the results can still provide an *approximate probability* of the level of significance.

The X^2 test was employed to analyze each of the individual items on the Data Sheet. The significant items are identified as providing either exact or approximate probabilities.

The Analysis of Variance Test (F test) is a statistical procedure which is employed when one is dealing with averages or means, such as the mean suicide potential score for the accident, suicide attempt and appendectomy groups. Using analysis of variance, we can determine if there is a statistically significant difference in the mean suicide potential score between *any* of the three groups. If we do obtain a significant F test, we know that some of the groups differ from each other, but the test does not tell us exactly which ones.

To determine the specific sources of differences, a second statistical test is employed, the Duncan Multiple Range Test. This permits us to determine exactly which groups differ from each other. The Duncan Multiple Range Test is employed after a significant F test is obtained.

All of the described methods were used to deal with various parts of the data obtained through the Data Sheet. In addition, the Analysis of Variance and Duncan Multiple Range tests were used to analyze much of the data in the Interviewer Bias Study.

E. *Interviewer Bias Study*

A major effort was made to evaluate the effect of interviewer bias in our study. We conceptualized *bias* as *attitudes, preconceptualizations or hypotheses of the interviewer* which related to the phenomena we studied.

There were three questions which we were able to evaluate in regard to issues of bias: (1) Did the psychoanalytic interviewers, as a group, demonstrate biases or preconceptions held in common? (2) If pre-existing attitudes existed in the group of interviewers, was there a correspondence between those pre-existing attitudes and the data which each interviewer reported? (3) After the clinical interviewing was completed, were there any changes in the biases or preconceptions of the interviewers?

Before we detail the specific methods of bias evaluation, it should be stated that at least two safeguards against bias probably already existed:

1. The personal psychoanalyses and psychoanalytic training of the interviewers probably provided them with some knowledge of their personal biases. It also probably provided them

with an understanding of some of their own ways of protecting against the recognition of unwelcome concepts. This, in turn, should have made it possible, to some degree, for them to recognize such unwelcome material when the presence of such material clashed with their personal preconceptions.

2. The design and development of the Data Sheet, with its emphasis on providing data from which similar conclusions could be extracted by a number of raters, would tend to eliminate the influence of *individual* biases. Of course, if the entire group of interviewers and raters shared common biases, the design and refinement of the Data Sheet would not protect against the distorting effect of such biases.

The method used to pursue the three aims of the bias study was as follows: Prior to their work with actual subjects in the study, all psychoanalytic interviewers were asked to complete a Data Sheet for a hypothetical subject from each of the experimental categories.

Instructions to interviewers for the hypothetical "Accident Person" were these: *Fill out a Data Sheet to represent a typical one-car automobile accident victim. He should be between the ages of 18 and 48, male, and have been seriously injured in the accident. There are no other restrictions on your formulations.*

Instructions for the hypothetical "Suicide Attempt Person" were as follows: *Fill out a Data Sheet to represent a typical suicide attempt victim. He should be between the ages of 18 and 48, male, and have made a near-lethal suicide attempt. There are no other restrictions on your formulations.*

Instructions for the hypothetical "Appendectomy Person" were as follows: *Fill out a Data Sheet to represent a typical appendectomy patient. He should be between the ages of 18 and 48, male, and have just undergone an operation which was a confirmed appendectomy. There are no other restrictions on your formulations.*

Following the completion of data-gathering in the study, all interviewers were asked to again fill out Data Sheets for hypothetical accident, suicide attempt and appendectomy persons. This was accomplished before the results of the clinical data were processed. Thus, no one knew what the actual results of the study were at that time.

By examining the pre-data-gathering hypothetical sheets of the group of psychoanalyst interviewers, we would be able to determine if there were any shared preconceptions or biases in that group. If there were systematic biases demonstrated by the first evaluation, we could make inferences as to whether those preconceptions had influenced the data-gathering from the actual subjects by comparing the systematic preconceptions or biases with material reported from the actual subjects. By comparing the data from the hypothetical cases which were described after the data-gathering with the hypothetical cases described *prior* to the data-gathering, we could form an opinion as to whether the participation in the project had brought about any changes in bias.

In addition, members of the Central Research Group had been in contact with the psychoanalytic interviewers during the course of the data-gathering and were able to gather a number of impressions dealing with issues of bias. At the end of the clinical interviewing, each interviewer had a formal "debriefing" session with a member of the Central Research Group. Some of the material obtained during the debriefing dealt with issues of bias.

F. Debriefings

Following the completion of clinical data-gathering, each clinical investigator was "debriefed." This meant that he had a one to two hour discussion with a member of the Central Research Group. Here we had a number of purposes:

1. We wanted the analyst's subjective impressions of his participation in this research project. We wished to know how he felt about the specific topic of the research (self-destruction in automobile accident) and how he felt about his role as a researcher.

2. We wanted to know how these psychoanalyst clinicians felt about the methodology of the study.

3. Along the same line, we wondered whether the participa-

tion in the project had stimulated ideas concerning the psycho-analytic implications of the project and ideas regarding research design.

4. We wished to understand how the thinking about these various issues had progressed during the course of their partici-pation.

5. We wondered if the interviewers had developed any new theories not comprised in the hypotheses.

6. We were interested in their thoughts about possible biases with which they might have approached the project and/or the different subject groups.

7. Would they have liked to have seen the project designed differently?

8. What ideas derived from this experience did they have for future research?

This material was considered to be more impressionistic than "hard" research data. Yet we felt that it would have several val-ues: (1) It might contribute to an understanding of the role of bias in psychoanalytic and other interviewing; and (2) it would give us some impression of the way in which psychoanalyst clini-cians at this time in history react to the type of research method-ology which we were using. Do they accept it readily or do they feel uncomfortable with it? Based on the data derived from the debriefing, could we draw conclusions as to the problems in-volved in psychoanalysts doing research along lines similar to ours? And how might such problems be dealt with?

G. The Significant Other Study

A study of eighteen "significant others" of the subjects was conducted. The main evaluations made in this study were:

1. To what degree does the subject answer similar questions in the same way as his designated significant other? Are there any differences among the three experimental groups in this regard?

2. How does the significant other evaluate changes in his life and in the life of the subject prior to the hospitalization? Again, are there any differences among the three groups?

3. How did the significant others explain the event that brought the experimental subject into the hospital?

4. How did the significant others judge the experimental subjects in terms of a number of human qualities?

THE SAMPLE

The subjects in this "significant other" study represented a sample of eighteen obtained from the major study. The subjects in the major study were asked to designate a significant other who might be contacted and interviewed. There were very few refusals of this request. After he designated the person in his life whom he considered most significant, each subject was asked to give a second and third choice. If the first choice was not available, the second or third significant other designated was asked to participate.

No criteria to screen significant others were made, although in some cases it was learned that some other *significant others* who had *not* been designated, might have provided more information. The significant others were related to the subjects in the following ways: there were five wives, three mothers, two fathers, two girl friends, three male friends, one guardian and one sister. This variability in the nature of significant others was an uncontrolled source of differences in the results. We felt that this method was preferable to designating in advance who the particular "significant other" might be (that is, saying it would always have to be the wife or mother or a sibling).

INTERVIEWERS: Interviewers were four second-year students in a graduate school's M.S.W. (Master of Social Work) program. They participated in the project in order to gather data for their own master's theses. The four interviewers were randomly assigned to interview cases.

THE INTERVIEW SCHEDULE: The schedule was designed to ascertain what, if any, change occurred in the relationship between the two persons in the six weeks prior to the ensuing event. The schedule was similar in some ways to the schedule used for the major study, but had a number of differences as well (it can be found in Appendix III at the back of this book).

Areas covered in the Significant Other Schedule were: Suicidal Acts; Actual History of Depression; Emotional Problems;

Alcohol and Drug Usage; Medical History; Adjustment to Change; Violence; and others. The average interview required about 45 minutes and was usually done in the informant's home.

Data Analysis

Because of the small sample involved, in many cases, the application of statistical techniques was inappropriate here. In cases where such techniques were used, percent of agreement was obtained to ascertain reliability. Chi square tests were run to evaluate differences between the accident, suicide attempt and appendectomy groups.

REFERENCE

1. Heilig, Sam M., Norman L. Farberow, Robert Litman, and Edwin Shneidman: The role of the non-professional volunteers in a Suicide Prevention Center, *Community Ment Health J*, Vol. 4, 1968.

PART THREE

→ THE RESULTS ←

CHAPTER 5

THE SAMPLE
Summary

In this chapter, we describe the methods by which our sample of subjects was selected. We also characterize the sample from a number of standpoints. Finally, we consider the representativeness of our sample of one-car accident drivers in regard to the total group of such drivers in Los Angeles County.

How were the subjects for our inquiry regarding suicide, self-destructive trends in accident and factors affecting appendectomy patients finally selected? As we mentioned earlier in these pages (see Chapter 4), the subjects were all patients on the wards of a large general hospital in the eastern part of metropolitan Los Angeles. All were males between the ages of 18 and 48. Three groups of subjects were utilized: (1) Drivers injured in one-car accidents; (2) suicide attempts of a serious nature; and (3) post-appendectomy patients. (When we began the study, we attempted to include two groups of accidents, critical and intermediate. However, too few intermediate accidents came into the hospital to compose a statistically significant group.)

SELECTING SUBJECTS FOR THE RESEARCH SAMPLE

A list was made of all wards in the hospital where patients in the three groups were treated. Two or three times a week, members of our Central Research Group visited these wards and checked new admissions. When subjects were found which might fit the diagnostic categories, they received brief interviews from members of the Central Research Group. The purpose of these interviews was to definitely include or exclude the prospective subjects from our research study. In each instance, if the subject was found to fit the criteria for inclusion into any of our three groups, he was immediately so listed and assigned to a clinical interviewer. Thus, all cases in the three diagnostic groups which fit our criteria were considered as possible subjects for clinical interviewing.

The first four cases were selected during August 1969. They were utilized as the subjects in our second reliability evaluation. Since the reliability achieved in those cases was high, we decided to make no further changes in our Data Sheet and therefore these cases were utilized as the first ones of our study. We resumed selecting cases on October 9, 1969, and the last case was selected on November 5, 1970. Thus, almost all cases were selected in a 13-month period.

All in all, one hundred and thirty cases were listed for possible interviewing. We completed 96 of these cases. There were 25 completed critical accident cases, 29 completed suicide attempt cases, and 31 completed appendectomy cases. In addition, there were 11 completed intermediate accident cases. This means that 34 of the 130 cases were aborted for some reason.

What were the reasons that certain assigned cases did not go to completion? We here list the various ones in this study:

1. An analyst could not be found to interview the patient before he was ready to leave the ward.

2. The analyst started a series of interviews but the patient left before they could be finished, and no subsequent arrangements could be made.

3. The recording equipment was not used or, if used, the quality of reproduction was poor. (These cases had to be rejected because of our intention to complete a reliability study on each case.)

4. On more intensive interviewing, the case was found not to fit criteria for inclusion.

5. The subject first agreed to participate in the research study but subsequently withdrew his approval.

6. One patient died.

7. The subject's command of the English language was so poor that it was decided not to include him.

8. The subject demonstrated such severe organic brain confusion that the interviewer believed the data would be inadequate.

We note that a relatively high percentage of the cases were completed (about three-fourths of all the ones which fit our criteria). We believe that these were all or most of the cases that were brought to the hospital during the data-gathering period. During the complete data-gathering period, we never became aware of any case which should have been included in our study which we missed. Since we were frequent visitors to the hospital, we were well acquainted with hospital personnel. They volunteered much information to us and almost surely would have let us know if there was a patient suitable for our study who was on some other ward. It is, of course, possible that such cases could have existed but not have been known to any of our communicants, or that the latter, even if they did know, did not relay the information to us.

CHARACTERISTICS OF THE SAMPLE

1. *Sex:* All subjects were male.
2. *Age:* The mean ages for the three groups were as follows:
   a. Critical Accidents — 27.92 years
   b. Suicide Attempts — 29.89 years
   c. Appendectomies — 27.06 years

Social Class

Identification of social class is based on the work of Hollingshead and Redlich.[1] They divide social class into five categories. These range from Class I, which describes the highest social class in terms of education, occupation and place of residence, through Class V, which describes the lowest social class according to the same three criteria. It was found that one of these criteria, occupation, correlated .88 with the overall predicted variables, and since information on occupation was readily available, this was used as our single indicator of social class.

The following diagram shows the social class breakdown for the three groups in our study. The accident group includes both the critical and intermediate accident cases.

	Percentage in Accident Group	Percentage in Suicide Attempt Group	Percentage in Appendectomy Group
Class I	0	7	3
Class II ...	2½	7	0
Class III ...	12½	24	18
Class IV ...	75	49	58
Class V	10	7	18
Unknown ..		6	3

REPRESENTATIVENESS OF THE SAMPLE*

Our study concentrated on a comparison of psychological factors between an accident group and two other groups of patients in a general hospital. How representative of one-car accident drivers is the data arising from our particular subjects? To answer this question, we made a number of calculations.

Our first question was, What percentage of the total one-car critical and intermediate accident picture was represented by the subjects in our study? We contacted the Los Angeles Police Department, and with their cooperation were given access to all accident records in Los Angeles municipal areas. (The geographical areas dealt with comprised approximately 65 per cent of the total Los Angeles County area.) During a two-week period, there were 73 reported cases of intermediate and critical accidents involving one-car drivers. For a 13-month period, there should thus

---

* Although the data of this study comes from critically injured drivers in one-car accidents, in the following discussion there are references to both critical and intermediate accidents. This is based on a vicissitude of the sampling evaluation. We would have preferred to have a Total Los Angeles sample of only critical accidents. However, that sample, as actually gathered by the police, included both critical and intermediate accidents. (The criterion to be included in the Total Los Angeles sample at all was "necessity for medical treatment.") There was no way to differentiate in the Total Los Angeles sample between the critical and intermediate accidents. Therefore, to accurately compare the representativeness of our study's sample with the Total Los Angeles sample, we decided to include the intermediate accidents we gathered at the hospital together with the critical accidents. Fortunately we were able to do this since we had identified all intermediate as well as all critical accidents which came into the hospital during our data-gathering period.

be 1,973 such cases. During a 13-month period, we gathered 38 cases of critical and intermediate accident. This means that our sample covered approximately 2 per cent of the total number of such cases recorded in the Los Angeles municipal area. If the accident rate is assumed to be approximately equal in proportion in the 35 per cent of the county not covered by the Total Los Angeles survey, our sample was approximately 1.3 per cent of all critical and intermediate one-car driver injury cases in Los Angeles County.

What were the similarities or differences in social class between the research sample and the Total Los Angeles sample? This diagram demonstrates social class differences by percentage in the two groups:

	Percentage in Research Sample	*Percentage in Total Los Angeles Sample*
Class I	0	0
Class II	2½	25
Class III	12½	27
Class IV	75	23
Class V	10	22
Unknown		3

It is evident that in the research sample, there was a high concentration of subjects in a relatively low social class, Class IV, with small percentages in Classes II, III and V. The Total Los Angeles sample showed a more uniform distribution with approximately one-fourth of the cases being distributed in each of the social classes from II to V. Our explanation for this difference is that the location of the general hospital was in an area of the city where lower social classes predominated. An additional factor may have been that people in higher social classes, even if taken to the general hospital for emergency treatment, may have quickly been transferred to private hospitals. Lower class people would not arrange such transfers.

Finally, we compared the distribution of accident subjects according to ethnic origins. Below is a diagram which compares the ethnic distribution of subjects in the two groups.

	Percentage in Research Sample	*Percentage in Total Los Angeles Sample*
Black	27	15
Chicano	22	5
White	51	79

First, it is noted that there is a significantly smaller proportion of white people in the research sample, with significantly larger groups of blacks and Chicanos. This is probably accounted for by the location of the hospital in a lower socioeconomic section of the city. Here one would expect to find a higher representation of ethnic groups which tend to be clustered in lower socioeconomic classes.

Of additional interest is the discrepancy between the percentage of Chicanos in the research sample as contrasted with the Total Los Angeles survey. There were over four times as many Chicanos in the research sample. The probable reason for this difference is that there is a large Chicano population which lives close to the general hospital. However, the areas in which the Chicanos live, because they are separate incorporated cities, are not included in the Total Los Angeles survey. Thus the social class and ethnic differences between the two samples can well be accounted for by geographical factors.

In summary, the accident subjects in the study constituted a little over 1 per cent of the total accident group (drivers in one-car accidents) in the Los Angeles area. The differences which exist between the study group and a group more representative of the total Los Angeles area can be explained in terms of the location of the hospital where we conducted our study.

REFERENCE

1. Hollingshead, A. B., and F. C. Redlich: *Social Class and Mental Illness: A Community Study.* New York, John Wiley and Sons, 1958.

CHAPTER 6

EVALUATION OF DATA SHEET RESPONSES

Summary

The major hypothesis of this study was that important suicidal and self-destructive features would be found in drivers who seriously injured themselves in one-car automobile accidents.

Based on previous literature and research, twelve suicidal and self-destructive modes of thinking, acting and experiencing were identified. The frequency of these modes was noted in three groups of experimental subjects: (1) Critically injured drivers involved in one-car accidents; (2) critical suicide attempts; and (3) post-appendectomy patients. The prediction was that the suicidal and self-destructive modes would be most prevalent in the suicide attempt group, next most prevalent in the accident group and least prevalent in the appendectomy group. If this prediction was substantiated, it would support our major hypothesis.

Date was obtained by interviewing subjects and answering 205 items linked to the twelve self-destructive modes for each subject.

The first result of this evaluation was that none of the twelve self-destructive modes were distributed in the predicted distribution and that, therefore, our major hypothesis was not supported. A number of evaluations revealed additional interesting data.

Drinking Behavior

Both the suicide attempt group and the accident group manifested a significant increase in drinking within two days prior to the suicide attempt or accident. Approximately 75 per cent of the accident group drink every day, while only about 25 per cent of the suicide attempt and appendectomy groups drink daily. The effects of the drinking (in regard to loss of consciousness or unusual social behavior) are not different among the three groups.

Unsupported Predictions

Our prediction was that all postulated self-destructive modes would be most frequent in the suicide attempts. This prediction was not supported in regard to several modes:

1. Contrary to prediction, suicide attempters followed medical advice to a greater degree than subjects in the other two groups.

2. There was no difference among the three groups in regard to injury or death-risking behavior.

3. There was no difference among the three groups in regard to difficulties in dealing with new responsibilities.

4. There was no difference among the three groups in regard to impulsive activity with destructive implications.

5. There was no difference among the three groups in regard to lack of integration between depressive and counter-depressive life styles.

DETAILED REPORT OF DATA SHEET RESPONSES

A MAJOR EFFORT was directed toward obtaining data on 205 specific questions for each of our subjects. These questions were designed to elucidate various aspects of thirteen major hypotheses which dealt with the presence of suicidal and self-destructive trends in persons who were both drivers and victims in one-car accidents. (The hypotheses are identified in Chapter 3, the methods utilized to obtain data in Chapter 4, while the Data Sheet in its entirety is reproduced as Appendix I.) The present chapter presents *the results* of the evaluation of the Data Sheet. It is focused entirely on evaluations of data dealing with our hypotheses. (The next chapter will deal with additional interesting findings from evaluations of the Data Sheet, which are not directly linked to our hypotheses.)

Methods of Obtaining and Evaluating Data

A few words about our methods are in order. As one might expect, we were unable to obtain data on every question on the Data Sheet for every subject. We were, for purposes of computation, however, able to answer all questions since one of the categories available for each question was "No Information." Because the groups of subjects were large, there were few questions which could not be utilized in our study.

Our method does entail a disadvantage. The results which come from such an evaluation do not reflect the specific and individual peculiarities of each subject. We believe that we do have a good picture of the general presence or absence of certain psychological qualities in our subjects, but putting these together into a meaningful dynamic picture does not come from this part of the study alone. That dynamic picture must flow from an interpretation of this material plus the dynamic evaluations of our subjects as individuals plus a correlation of those data with other research material.

We utilized two groupings of questions for the evaluation of most of the hypotheses. We called these the direct and the indirect tests (results are shown in Appendix II). The direct test consisted of an evaluation of those items on the Data Sheet which had been constructed specifically to elucidate a particular hypothesis. However, we also noted that questions which had been specifically designed to test one hypothesis might also be used to evaluate one or more additional hypotheses. We grouped such additional questions into the indirect tests for each hypothesis. We do not report those indirect tests in this chapter. However, we may report that in every situation where indirect tests were performed, they paralleled the direct test for that hypothesis. Thus, if our direct test indicated that there was no greater incidence of suicidal threats and communications in the accident group than in the appendectomy group, the indirect test supported the same conclusion.

Some readers will be interested in learning which specific items on the Data Sheet related to each hypothesis. Appendix II at the end of the book contains this information. In Appendix II, a group of questions is linked to the topics of each hypothesis. In addition to the group score which yielded the evaluation of each hypothesis, many analyses of the data of individual items supported that hypothesis.

Now we present the results of the Data Sheet evaluation, considering each hypothesis separately.

Hypothesis A

In our first hypothesis, we predicted that hospitalization among subjects in the accident group would result from a deliberate suicide attempt in greater frequency than among subjects in the appendectomy group, yet in a lesser frequency than among subjects in the suicide attempt group. Table I presents the statistical evaluation of this hypothesis.

Table I shows that all hospitalizations which resulted from a deliberate suicide attempt were to be found *only* among the suicide attempters (93% of that group). The suicide attempt group was different in a statistically significant way from both the accident and the appendectomy group, but *the accident and the appendectomy group were not different from one another.*

TABLE I

HOSPITALIZATION RESULTED FROM DELIBERATE
SUICIDE ATTEMPT

	Accid (n = 25)	*S/A* (n = 29)	*Appy* (n = 31)
Chi Square	%	%	%
Yes	0	93	0
No	100	7	100

$X^2 = 76.40$, p $<$ .001 (exact probabilities).

Component Chi Square Analysis

	Accid	*S/A*	*Appy*
Accident		46.55*	.02
S/A			52.47*
Appy			

* p $<$ .001 (exact probabilities).

TABLE II

SUICIDE ATTEMPTS AND COMMUNICATION

Analysis of Variance

Source	DF	MS	F
Between	2	300.38	202.95*
Within	82	1.48	

Duncan Multiple Range Test

	Mean Accid (.12)	Mean Appy (.19)	Mean S/A (1.46)
Accident		.07	1.34*
Appy			1.27*

* Significant, p < .01.

Hypothesis B

This hypothesis predicted that the accident group would show a greater history of suicide attempts and suicidal communications than the appendectomy group but not as great a frequency of such attempts and communications as the suicide attempt group. The statistical evaluation of this hypothesis is presented in Table II.

Table II indicates that the results of hypothesis two parallel the results of hypothesis one. Suicide attempt subjects showed a greater history of suicide attempts and communications than accident and appendectomy subjects. The accident and appendectomy subjects were just about the same, and the slight difference between them was not statistically significant. It is interesting that the slight difference between accident and appendectomy subjects reflected a greater frequency of suicidal attempts and preoccupations in the appendectomy group.

Suicide Risk

At the Los Angeles Suicide Prevention Center, extensive work has been done on correlating various psychological features with suicidal risk.[1-7] As might be expected, many of the questions in our Data Sheet had received such prior correlation. We therefore decided to construct a test of suicidal risk which consisted

TABLE III

SUICIDE RISK

Analysis of Variance			
Source	*DF*	*MS*	*F*
Between	2	1368.48	32.22*
Within	82	42.46	
Duncan Multiple Range Test			
	Mean Appy (5.16)	*Mean Accid* (5.96)	*Mean S/A* (17.60)
Appy		.80	12.44*
Accident			11.64*

* Significant, p < .01.

of the evaluation of about 70 such items. The evaluation of suicidal risk in the three groups is statistically shown in Table III.

Table III shows that the suicide attempt group had a statistically significant greater suicide risk than either the accident or the appendectomy group. The suicide risk of the appendectomy and accident groups was not significantly different; in fact, the scores on these two groups were almost the same. The average score for the accident group was 5.96; the average score for the appendectomy group was 5.16; and the average score for the suicide attempt group was 17.60.

Thus, the analysis of suicide risk continues to support the trend that suicidal manifestations are high in the suicide attempt group but that accident and appendectomy groups are not differentiated by suicidal manifestations.

Hypothesis C

This hypothesis dealt with depressive symptoms. The prediction was that depressive symptoms would be found most frequently in the suicide attempt group, next most frequently in the accident group, and least frequently in the appendectomy group. In order to test this hypothesis, we developed two indices. The first evaluated recent depression, that is, depressive symptoms present during the week prior to hospitalization. The index of past depression dealt with depressive signs or symptoms which occurred earlier in the life of the subject than the week prior to hospitalization. Table IV summarizes the analysis of the index of recent depression.

Table IV shows that the suicide attempt group experienced recent symptoms of depression to a statistically significant greater degree than either the appendectomy or accident group. The differences between the appendectomy and accident groups were not statistically significantly different.

The statistical evaluation of the index of past depressive symptoms is presented in Table V.

Table V demonstrates that past depression also characterized the suicide attempt group. This affect was demonstrated in a higher frequency in that group than in the other two groups. The accident and appendectomy groups did not differ from each other.

TABLE IV

RECENT DEPRESSIVE SYMPTOMS

Analysis of Variance

Source	DF	MS	F
Between	2	73.16	30.61*
Within	82	2.39	

Duncan Multiple Range Test

	Mean Appy (.48)	Mean Accid (.80)	Mean S/A (3.37)
Appy		.32	2.89*
Accident			2.57*

* Significant, p < .01.

TABLE V

PAST DEPRESSIVE SYMPTOMS

Analysis of Variance

Source	DF	MS	F
Between	2	221.99	13.71*
Within	82	16.19	

Duncan Multiple Range Test

	Mean Accid (2.08)	Mean Appy (2.19)	Mean S/A (6.65)
Accident		.11	4.57*
Appy			4.46*

* Significant, p < .01.

Hypothesis D

Hypothesis D dealt with counterdepressive attitudes among the groups. The statistical evaluation of this hypothesis is presented in Table VI.

Table VI shows that suicide attempt subjects manifested counterdepressive attitudes to a statistically significant greater degree than accident subjects. Differences among any other comparisons of the three groups were not statistically significant. (The mean score for the accident group was .32, for the appendectomy group .54, and for the suicide attempt group 1.00.) Again, interestingly, although this is not statistically significant, the trend is for the accident subjects to less frequently demonstrate a counterdepressive attitude than either the appendectomy or the suicide attempt group. It is clear that the accident subjects did not show a greater frequency of counterdepressive trends than appendectomy subjects.

Hypothesis E

Here our prediction dealt with the frequency of drinking and drug ingestion among the three groups. The general prediction was that we would find more drinking and drug ingestion in the accident group than in the appendectomy group. Since we postulated the drinking and drug ingestion to be symptoms of the self-destructive trend, we felt that there would be most drinking and drug ingestion among the suicide attempt subjects.

TABLE VI

COUNTER-DEPRESSIVE ATTITUDE

Analysis of Variance			
Source	*DF*	*MS*	*F*
Between	2	3.28	3.41*
Within	82	.96	

Duncan Multiple Range Test			
	Mean Accid (.32)	*Mean Appy* (.54)	*Mean S/A* (1.00)
Accident		.22	.68*
Appy			.46

* Significant, p < .05.

TABLE VII

INCREASE IN DRINKING WITHIN TWO DAYS PRIOR
TO EVENT LEADING TO HOSPITALIZATION

	Accid (n = 20)	S/A (n = 23)	Appy (n = 26)
Chi Square	%	%	%
Yes	20	35	0
No	80	65	100

$X^2 = 10.41$, $p < .01$ (approximate probabilities).

Component X^2 Analysis

	Accid	S/A	Appy
Accident		1.16	5.69*
S/A			10.80†

* $p < .05$ (approximate probabilities).
† $p < .01$ (approximate probabilities).

First, the issue of drinking. We will describe two different tests of the drinking hypothesis. The first deals with increasing drinking within the two days prior to the event which led to hospitalization. The second is a measure of the intensity of the drinking pattern for the subject. Intensity is measured both by how frequently the subject drinks and how excessive the drinking is in terms of its effects on states of consciousness, and extreme changes in social behavior.

What was the situation in regard to increase in drinking within two days prior to the event leading to hospitalization? The results of this evaluation are shown in Table VII.

Table VII demonstrates that drinking increased significantly during the two days prior to hospitalization among subjects in both the accident and suicide attempt groups as compared to the subjects in the appendectomy group. The subjects in the accident group are not statistically different from the subjects in the suicide attempt group. Note the figures in Table VII: 20 per cent in the accident group, 35 per cent in the suicide attempt group, and 0 per cent in the appendectomy group.

For the first time, one of the "self-destructive" hypotheses is supported. (However, the *exact* prediction is not supported. That prediction is that the drinking should be highest in suicides, next highest in accidents and lowest in appendectomies.)

TABLE VIII

CUSTOMARILY THE SUBJECT DRINKS DAILY

	Accid (n = 17)	S/A (n = 20)	Appy (n = 21)
Chi Square	%	%	%
Yes	76	30	24
No	24	70	76

$X^2 = 12.36$, $p < .01$ (exact probabilities).

Component X^2 Analysis

	Accid	S/A	Appy
Accid		7.94*	10.45*
S/A			.19

* $p < .01$ (exact probabilities).

The next issue dealt with the intensity of drinking behavior. This was first evaluated by comparing the customary daily drinking pattern among the three groups. The results of this evaluation are presented in Table VIII.

Table VIII indicates that accident subjects in high proportion (over three-quarters of them) customarily drink every day. The other two groups, the suicide attempt and appendectomy groups, are approximately equal in terms of their daily drinking and are both much lower than the accident group.

The second evaluation of intensity of drinking behavior focused on how frequently subjects drank to the point of severe impairment of consciousness or extreme changes in social behavior. The results of this evaluation are present in Table IX.

Table IX indicates that a third or more of each group did apparently demonstrate such extreme drinking. However, more im-

TABLE IX

SUBJECT DRINKS TO POINT OF SEVERE IMPAIRMENT OF
CONSCIOUSNESS OR EXTREME CHANGE IN SOCIAL BEHAVIOR

	Accid (n = 20)	S/A (n = 22)	Appy (n = 22)
Chi Square	%	%	%
Yes	35	45	32
No	65	55	64

$X^2 = .94$ (not statistically significant).

TABLE X

RECENT DRUG USE—MODERATE OR HEAVY
(Within 7 Days Prior to Event
Which Led to Hospitalization)

	Accid (n = 23)	S/A (n = 24)	Appy (n = 22)
Chi Square	%	%	%
Yes	9	67	9
No	91	33	91

X^2 = 25.38, p < .001 (exact probabilities).

Component X^2 Analysis

	Accid	S/A	Appy
Accident		16.70*	.01
S/A			15.97*

* p < .001 (exact probabilities).

portantly from the standpoint of our interest, there was *not* a significant difference between any of the three groups. We emphasize—extremes of drinking did not differentiate the three groups.

Continuing with hypothesis E, we come to the evaluation of drug abuse. First we tested recent moderate and heavy drug usage, that is, within the seven days prior to the event which led to hospitalization. The statistical evaluation of recent drug abuse is presented in Table X.

TABLE XI

PAST DRUG USE—MODERATE OR HEAVY
(Prior to 7 Days Before Event
Which Led to Hospitalization)

Analysis of Variance

Source	DF	MS	F
Between	2	9.00	11.25*
Within	82	.80	

Duncan Multiple Range Test

	Mean Accid (.16)	Mean Appy (.16)	Mean S/A (1.14)
Accident		.00	.98*
Appy			.98*

* Significant, p < .01 (exact probabilities).

Table X indicates that the subjects in the suicide attempt group were greatly involved in moderate or heavy drug usage. The accident and appendectomy groups, on the other hand, were both much lower and were not statistically different from each other.

Next we evaluated drug use in a somewhat more chronic period, that is, in the entire period of life prior to seven days before the event leading to hospitalization. The results of this analysis are shown in Table XI.

Again, Table XI shows the same trend as noted in the previous evaluation of drug usage. The suicide attempt group demonstrated heavy usage of drugs to a much larger degree than the accident and appendectomy groups. The latter two again did not significantly differ from each other.

Thus, the prediction that heavy drug usage would be found to a high degree in the accident group was not supported by our study.

Hypothesis F

This hypothesis predicted that accident subjects would have a tendency to seek or follow medical advice to a lesser degree than appendectomy patients but to a greater degree than suicide

TABLE XII

SEEKING MEDICAL ADVICE
(Within 7 Days Prior to Event
Which Led to Hospitalization)

	Accid (n = 10)	S/A (n = 7)	Appy (n = 13)
Chi Square	%	%	%
Yes	20	86	38
No	80	14	62

$X^2 = 7.46$, p $<$ .05 (approximate probabilities).

Component Chi Square Analysis

	Accid	S/A	Appy
Accident		7.13†	.90
S/A			4.10*

* p $<$ .05 (approximate probabilities).
† p $<$ .01 (approximate probabilities).

TABLE XIII

NOT FOLLOWING MEDICAL ADVICE
(Prior to 7 Days Before Event
Which Led to Hospitalization)

Analysis of Variance

Source	DF	MS	F
Between	2	1.66	1.23
Within	82	1.35	

Not significant.

Group Means

Accident	1.08
S/A	.64
Appy	.64

attempters. The statistical evaluation of this hypothesis is presented in Table XII and Table XIII.

Table XII deals with seeking medical advice within seven days prior to the event leading to the hospitalization. The results indicate that suicide attempters sought medical advice to a significantly greater degree than either the accident or appendectomy groups. While there was no statistically significant differentiation between the accident and appendectomy groups, only a small percentage of accident victims sought medical advice, while a much larger percentage of appendectomy subjects sought medical advice.

Habitual patterns of not following medical advice are evaluated in Table XIII.

The results indicate that the accident group was slightly high-

TABLE XIV

RECENT EXCESSIVE RISK TAKING

Chi Square

	Accid (n = 24) %	S/A (n = 24) %	Appy (n = 31) %
Yes	8	17	10
No	92	83	90

$X^2 = .97$ (not statistically significant).

er than the other two groups in not following medical advice, but this difference was not statistically significant.

Hypothesis G

This hypothesis predicted that excessive risk-taking would be found to a higher degree in the accident group than in the appendectomy group. We first evaluated risk-taking behavior within the seven days prior to the event leading to hospitalization. The results of this evaluation are shown in Table XIV.

Table XIV indicates that there are no statistically significant differences among the three groups in terms of excessive risk-taking.

Excessive risk-taking behavior prior to seven days before the event leading to hospitalization is statistically evaluated in Table XV.

Table XV indicates that the mean differences between the three groups of subjects in terms of excessive risk-taking prior to seven days before the event are not statistically significant.

In summary, excessive risk-taking behavior is not shown to occur to a higher degree in accident victims than in appendectomy patients. The hypothesis is not supported.

Hypothesis H

This hypothesis predicted that there would be recent difficulties in dealing with new responsibilities. The period evaluated

TABLE XV

EXCESSIVE RISK TAKING BEHAVIOR
(Prior to 7 Days Before Event
Which Led to Hospitalization)

Analysis of Variance			
Source	*DF*	*MS*	*F*
Between	2	.03	.12
Within	82	.26	

Not significant.

Group Means

Accident	.20
S/A	.17
Appy	.12

TABLE XVI

NEW RESPONSIBILITY—LAST SIX MONTHS

Analysis of Variance

Source	DF	MS	F
Between	2	.05	.71
Within	82	.07	

Not significant.

Group Means

Accident	.12
S/A	.03
Appy	.09

was the six months prior to the event which led to hospitalization. It was predicted that the accident group would show this trend to a higher degree than the appendectomy group, but to a lower degree than the group of suicide attempt subjects. Table XVI shows the statistical evaluation of the three groups.

The differences among the three groups are not statistically significant. The conclusion is that there are no differences demonstrated by this evaluation which differentiate among the three groups of subjects in regard to difficulties over new responsibilities.

Hypothesis I

Hypothesis I predicted that accident subjects would tend to use impulsive actions with destructive implications to a greater degree than appendectomy patients but to a lesser degree than

TABLE XVII

IMPULSIVE ACTIONS

Analysis of Variance

Source	DF	MS	F
Between	2	.20	1.54
Within	82	.13	

Not significant.

Group Means

Accident	.04
S/A	.21
Appy	.12

TABLE XVIII

LACK OF INTEGRATION BETWEEN DEPRESSIVE
AND COUNTER-DEPRESSIVE STYLES

	Accid (n = 15)	*S/A* (n = 20)	*Appy* (n = 19)
Chi Square	%	%	%
Yes	20	25	21
No	80	75	79
X^2 = .14 (not statistically significant).			

suicide attempters. The statistical evaluation of this hypothesis is set forth in Table XVII.

The evaluation indicates no statistically significant difference between the three groups of subjects.

Hypothesis J

Hypothesis J predicted that subjects in the accident group would demonstrate a lack of integration between depressive and counterdepressive life styles to a greater degree than subjects in the appendectomy group but to a lesser degree than subjects in the suicide attempt group. The statistical evaluation of this hypothesis is presented in Table XVIII.

This evaluation shows that there are no statistically significant differences among the three groups on this dimension.

Hypothesis K

Hypothesis K predicted that accident victims would demonstrate a recent loss of self-esteem which would be greater than that found in the group of appendectomy patients and less than the amount found in the group of suicide attempters. The statistical evaluation of hypothesis K is presented in Table XIX.

In this table, we see that a significantly higher percentage of suicide attempt subjects demonstrate a loss of self-esteem than do the accident and appendectomy subjects. The accident group shows less recent loss of self-esteem than the appendectomy group, but this difference was not statistically significant. Thus,

TABLE XIX

RECENT LOSS OF SELF-ESTEEM
(Within 7 Days Prior to Event
Which Led to Hospitalization)

	Accid (n = 24) %	S/A (n = 29) %	Appy (n = 21) %
Chi Square			
Yes	25	93	38
No	75	7	62

$X^2 = 28.20$, p $<$ .001 (exact probabilities).

Component Chi Square Analysis

	Accid	S/A	Appy
Accident		25.92*	.89
S/A			17.55*

* Significant, p $<$ .001 (exact probabilities).

hypothesis K was not supported by the results of this evaluation.

Hypothesis L

Hypothesis L dealt with recent life changes. Included were such issues as significant losses or increases in responsibility. The prediction was that accident victims would show a higher incidence of such life changes than appendectomy patients but less changes than suicide attempters. The statistical evaluation of this hypothesis is presented in Table XX.

Table XX demonstrates that the average scores of the three

TABLE XX

RECENT LIFE CHANGE

Analysis of Variance			
Source	DF	MS	F
Between	2	.13	.28
Within	82	.47	

Not significant.

Group Means	
Accident	.48
S/A	.46
Appy	.35

groups are not significantly different from each other. The conclusion is that recent life changes were the same among subjects in each of the three groups and that the hypothesis is not supported.

Hypothesis M

Hypothesis M was not tested by a particular item on the Data Sheet. It was a general hypothesis dealing with the overall position of the accident group vis-à-vis the other two groups. The prediction was that on some or all of the first twelve hypotheses, the accident group would lie somewhere in between the group of appendectomy subjects who would be low in the hypothesized trends and the group of suicide attempt subjects who would be high in the hypothesized trends.

Since none of the first twelve hypotheses were supported, hypothesis M is not supported.

REFERENCES

1. Brown, Timothy R.: The judgment of suicide lethality: A comparison of judgmental models obtained under contrived versus natural conditions. Unpublished Ph.D. dissertation, University of Oregon, 1970.
2. Farberow, Norman L., and Alcon Devries: An item differentiation analysis of MMPI's of suicidal neuro-psychiatric hospital patients. *Psychological Reports, 20*:607-617, 1967.
3. Litman, Robert E.: Suicide Prevention Center patients: A follow-up study, *Bull Suicidology,* Spring 1970.
4. Litman, Robert E., and Norman L. Farberow: Emergency evaluation of self-destructive potentiality. In *The Cry for Help* (Farberow and Shneidman, eds.), New York, McGraw-Hill Book Company, 1961.
5. Litman, Robert E., Norman L. Farberow, Carl I. Wold, and Timothy R. Brown: Prediction models of suicidal behaviors. In *Measurement of Suicidal Behaviors,* New York, Charles Press (in press).
6. Wold, Carl I.: Characteristics of 26,000 Suicide Prevention Center patients, *Bull Suicidology,* Spring 1970.
7. Wold, Carl I.: Sub-groupings of suicidal people, *Omega,* 2:19-29, 1971.

CHAPTER 7

EVALUATION OF DATA SHEET RESPONSES

SUGGESTIONS AND IMPRESSIONS

Summary

This chapter continues a report of the Data Sheet findings. A scrutiny of certain individual items and groups of items gives rise to some interesting suggestions and impressions. Of particular interest are a series of observations relating to activity and impulsivity in accident victims and suicide attempters.

THE PREVIOUS CHAPTER evaluated the main hypotheses of our study. The method utilized was the evaluation of groups of items from our Data Sheet which had been specifically designed for particular hypotheses.

A POTPOURRI

As we went through the individual items and groups of items on the Data Sheet, a number of additional interesting suggestions and impressions emerged. The actual data which we will be reporting in this chapter is a potpourri. A number of individual items yielded statistically significant chi squares. Some groups of questions revealed interesting trends when looked at together. In the previous chapter, we only utilized questions for which statistical significance had been achieved. However, in this chapter, we sometimes cite non-statistically significant trends. These trends, particularly when seen in a group of related items, suggest certain possibilities in the elucidation of factors related to self-destructiveness.

Since the data we cite and discuss in this chapter come from varied and diffuse parts of our Data Sheet, it did not seem possible to organize it into a meaningful classification. We will therefore present issues as we discovered them—that is, by going over the individual items related to each hypothesis.

A statistical note: In some of these evaluations, a glance at the percentage figures might suggest that the groups have differed significantly. In these cases, many of the subjects had "N.I." (No Information) listed for that question. Since we could not know what the reckoning would have been had those subjects been able to give information on these questions, we can only say that we have come across *possible* trends.

Communication of Suicidal Ideas

Question 13 dealt with the communication of suicidal ideas during the entire lifetime of the subject prior to one year before hospitalization. An attempt may be made here to establish some trend: although the difference between groups was not statistically significant, there were more positives in the accident and appendectomy groups than in the suicide attempt group. This suggests that *people who make suicide attempts are less prone to think about suicide or to communicate suicidal ideas than other groups of subjects.* Alternatively, they may attempt to deny suicidal preoccupation to a greater degree than other people.

Early Morning Waking

Early morning waking was utilized as an indicator of depression. In the period of seven days prior to hospitalization, five people in the suicide attempt group, three people in the accident group and one in the appendectomy group were judged positively on this item. Although this is a non-statistically significant comparison, there is a suggestion that the accident group might have been close to the suicide attempt group in this dimension.

Despondency Prior to Hospitalization

Here two items were of interest. In the period of seven days prior to hospitalization, 90 per cent of the suicide attempt group demonstrated despondency. This was anticipated. What was unanticipated was that approximately one-third of the accident and one-third of the appendectomy groups were also despondent.

In the period of seven days to six months prior to hospitalization, 82 per cent of the suicide attempt group demonstrated despondency. Unanticipated but of interest was that 40 per cent of the other two groups also manifested despondency.

What might be the meaning of these findings? That there is more despondency than one would anticipate in the entire population? That there is a high level of despondency in these socio-economic groups? Perhaps there is a high level of despondency which is found in people in our hospital for any of the reasons which brought our subjects into the hospital. This mood may be retroactively projected onto the patients' views of their lives in the time periods noted.

Subject's Thoughts About His Own Death

How many people thought about their own deaths every day? Of those subjects that gave data for this item, five appendectomies answered *yes;* one suicide attempt subject answered *yes;* and none of the accidents answered *yes.*

How many subjects thought about their own deaths at least once a week? Appendectomies—6; Suicide Attempts—6; Accidents—1.

These data were non-statistically significant, but it is of interest that the appendectomies were high in both cases, and that as a group appendectomies were closer to the suicide attempt group than to the accident group, in which this manifestation was almost entirely absent. There is a suggestion that *accident victims have a tendency to repress thoughts about death or not to report them if they do have them.*

Frequent Bursts of Activity

Here are the findings on four items dealing with frequent bursts of activity.

Frequent bursts of activity seven days prior to hospitalization:

Accident — 27%
Suicide Attempt — 13%
Appendectomy — 26%

Frequent bursts of activity seven days to six months prior to hospitalization:

> Accident — 21%
> Suicide Attempt — 33%
> Appendectomy — 15%

Frequent bursts of activity six months to one year prior to hospitalization:

> Accident — 25%
> Suicide Attempt — 20%
> Appendectomy — 15%

Frequent bursts of activity one year or more prior to hospitalization:

> Accident — 27%
> Suicide Attempt — 11%
> Appendectomy — 17%

All four of these evaluations are statistically non-significant, but there is a definite trend among the four questions for accident victims to demonstrate a higher degree of activity. Add to this another item:

Frequent bursts of activity when exposed to disappointment or being "put-down":

> Accident — 33%
> Suicide Attempt — 25%
> Appendectomy — 22%

Again this is non-statistically significant, but again the accident group figure is higher. These items which we used as tests of counter-depressive attitudes suggest that *people who have accidents tend to have more frequent bursts of activity than other groups.*

Restless Irritability With Other People

Let us now present four items dealing with the issue, "Restless Irritability With Others."

Seven days prior to hospitalization:

> Accident — 23%
> Suicide Attempt — 71%
> Appendectomy — 35%

Seven days to six months prior to hospitalization:
>Accident — 32%
>Suicide Attempt — 63%
>Appendectomy — 26%

Six months to one year prior to hospitalization:
>Accident — 30%
>Suicide Attempt — 52%
>Appendectomy — 22%

One year or longer prior to hospitalization:
>Accident — 18%
>Suicide Attempt — 57%
>Appendectomy — 30%

The first two items listed were statistically significant and demonstrated that the suicide attempt group had a higher degree of restless irritability than the other two. The last two items were not statistically significant but showed trends in the same direction. The suggestion is thus quite strong that *restless irritability prior to hospitalization is highly linked to suicide* in all time periods but *most strongly in the periods closest to the suicide attempt group.*

Excessive Driving

Following are four items dealing with excessive driving in various time periods prior to hospitalization.

Seven days prior to hospitalization:
>Accident — 28%
>Suicide Attempt — 18%
>Appendectomy — 17%

Seven days to six months prior to hospitalization:
>Accident — 37%
>Suicide Attempt — 26%
>Appendectomy — 14%

Six months to one year prior to hospitalization:
>Accident — 6%
>Suicide Attempt — 22%
>Appendectomy — 15%

One year and longer prior to hospitalization:
>   Accident — 18%
>   Suicide Attempt — 21%
>   Appendectomy — 7%

These items were all non-significant statistically. However, the first two demonstrated *a trend toward increased driving among the accidents.* This trend, however, is only demonstrated in the period up to six months before hospitalization. After that, the trend is no longer noticeable. Thus, the finding reported by early researchers that individuals who have automobile accidents tend to drive excessively is somewhat supported by our study. This finding is particularly significant when linked to the finding about frequent bursts of activity which, it will be recalled, also occurred to a greater extent in the accident group than in the others.

The Effects of Disappointment, Loss or Being "Put Down"

Next we will present three items dealing with disappointment, loss or being "put down."

When exposed to disappointment, loss or being put down, there was restless irritability with others:
>   Accident — 18%
>   Suicide Attempt — 67%
>   Appendectomy — 43%

This item did achieve statistical significance.

When exposed to disappointment, loss or being put down, there were episodes of excessive time spent driving:
>   Accident — 6%
>   Suicide Attempt — 33%
>   Appendectomy — 4%

This item did achieve statistical significance.

When exposed to disappointment, loss or being put down, there were episodes of using driving to "work off steam":
>   Accident — 7%
>   Suicide Attempt — 24%
>   Appendectomy — 7%

This item is non-statistically significant, but there is a trend to suicide attempt being highest.

These items, taken together, indicate that *there is a tendency toward various types of activity, including driving activity, in individuals who make suicide attempts.* The hypothesis that such activity is highly linked to individuals who have accidents is not supported by these items.

Drinking to the Point of Severe Impairment of Consciousness

A complex evaluation was made of "drinking to the point of severe impairment of consciousness" in the three groups. This covered many time periods from every day to less than once a year. Although the answer was not statistically significant, it was judged to be close to significant. The finding was that there was a trend for the suicide attempts to be highest, and that the appendectomies and accidents were close to each other.

A similar evaluation was made for "drinking to the point of moderate impairment of consciousness." This finding was similar to the previous one.

Chronic Drug Abuse

The following data come from several items relating to drug abuse.

DRUG ABUSE AND PHYSICIAN CONTACT

First, let us present findings in a series of hypotheses relating to drug taking. In the seven day to six month period prior to hospitalization, was the subject taking drugs?

> Accident — 23%
> Suicide Attempt — 73%
> Appendectomy — 45%

This is significant for *suicide attempt*.

In the six month to one year period prior to hospitalization, was subject taking drugs?

> Accident — 30%
> Suicide Attempt — 71%
> Appendectomy — 40%

This is significant for *suicide attempt*.

In the period of one year or longer prior to hospitalization, was subject taking drugs?

Accident — 29%

Suicide Attempt — 76%

Appendectomy — 47%

Again, this is statistically significant for *suicide attempt*.

There are two points we would now make. First, people who make serious suicide attempts take drugs to a statistically significant higher degree than accidents. Second, although it is not statistically significant, postappendectomy patients also take drugs to a higher degree than do accident victims.

When considering whether the drugs in the different groups come from legal or extra-legal sources, the finding is that suicide attempters get their drugs from legal sources (mainly physicians), while accident victims tend to get their drugs from extralegal sources.

Next we present a finding in regard to contact with physicians:

Suicide attempters, in the seven-day to six-month period prior to hospitalization, *have contact with physicians to a statistically significant higher degree than the other two groups.*

These findings suggest to us that suicidal people take drugs and have contact with physicians so that they identify themselves as "sick" people, whereas accident victims do not do these things.

New Responsibilities

In regard to this issue, there were two questions. The first asked whether there was a change of job at all within many years. The answers were:

Accident — 77%

Suicide Attempt — 63%

Appendectomy — 48%

These findings were non-significant statistically.

Another question dealt with various time periods in which change of job may have occurred. Here we report one finding:

change of job within seven days to one month prior to hospitalization. Here are the statistics in this regard:

Accident — 60%
Suicide Attempt — 14%
Appendectomy — 0%

This was a non-statistically significant difference. However, there is a suggestion that accident victims tend to change their jobs to a significantly greater degree within one month prior to hospitalization than the other two groups.

Impulsive Activity

Here are the data from three questions relating to impulsive activity.

The subject never acts impulsively so as to destroy physical objects. Response:

Accident — 67%
Suicide Attempt — 37%
Appendectomy — 59%

The non-statistically significant trend is for suicide attempt subjects to act more impulsively.

The subject never acts impulsively so that injury occurs to himself. Response:

Accident — 76%
Suicide Attempt — 64%
Appendectomy — 85%

The non-statistically significant trend is for suicide attempt subjects to act more impulsively.

The subject never acts impulsively so that physical damage is done to others. Response:

Accident — 74%
Suicide Attempt — 48%
Appendectomy — 68%

The non-statistically significant trend is for suicide attempt subjects to act more impulsively.

A frequent concept related to individuals who are involved in accidents, particularly driving accidents, is that they tend to be impulsive and action-oriented. Since suicide is often an impulsive act, we would also expect suicide attempters to show a high degree of impulsivity. The trend in this series of questions is for suicide attempters to show the highest degree of impulsivity.

There is *no* support for even a trend for accident victims to manifest increased impulsivity.

CHAPTER 8

NARRATIVE SUMMARIES
Summary

The interviewers' dictation on dynamic aspects of the cases was reviewed by three psychoanalyst members of the central research group. This material was gathered and evaluated in a more subjective way than that obtained through use of the Data Sheet.

This review yielded a number of suggestive differences among the three groups of subjects—the accident group, the suicide attempt group, and the appendectomy group. We evaluated these dynamic summaries from four standpoints:

I. What can be said about the accident, suicide or appendicitis process, that is, what psychological experiences seem significant as the subject lived through the episode that led to his hospitalization?

The Accident Group

There were two important sub-groups:
a. *A "Depressed" group. There were people who had recently suffered some important loss and had many clinical manifestations of depression.*
b. *A "Counter-Depressive" or "Action-Oriented" group. These were people who were dealing with some new responsibility. It might entail moving to a higher responsibility such as job promotion or advanced schooling, or it might mean coping with a readjustment such as a separation from one's family. They reacted with denial, activity and manifestations of psychodynamic "manic" behavior.*
There was a monotonous repetition of regressive experiences. Almost all of the accident victims had been at a party or had been drinking with friends or at a bar prior to the accident. This accompanied the high incidence of drinking and probable

drunkenness which had been established through use of the Data Sheet.

The accidents themselves occurred, for the most part, in one of two ways: (1) Many subjects fell asleep at the wheel. (2) Some subjects lost control of the car. They often did this as they were attempting to avoid what they felt was an impending collision. However, the result of their hopefully protective driving was to involve themselves in another collision.

The Suicide Attempt Group

These people were all undergoing a sense of loss. They were depressed. They drank, which probably increased their feeling of hopelessness. Under these conditions, they made a suicide attempt.

The Appendectomy Group

It was not possible to delineate one or two "appendicitis" processes. Rather, a variety of circumstances occurred preceding and during the development of the appendicitis.

II. Is unconscious self-destructiveness present? If so, what are its manifestations?

The Accident Group

Unconscious self-destructiveness manifested itself in excess drinking and drug-taking. Another manifestation was extreme denial, a denial which did not allow necessary dependent gratifications to take place.

The Suicide Attempt Group

Unconscious self-destructiveness seemed quite high in this group. Manifestations included depression, fantasies and acts of rage directed both at the self and the outside world, and much discussion of automobile accidents. There were many dreams of anger, isolation, loneliness, depression, suicide and death. In addition, there was a high rate of utilization of drugs and alcohol. Finally, there was a higher incidence of psychotic-like manifestations in the suicide attempt group.

The Appendectomy Group

Although some evidence for self-destructive characteristics in certain subjects were noted, this seemed to be at a much lower incidence than in the other two groups.

III. What life changes preceded the incident?

The Accident Group

As already indicated, some of the accident victims had suffered recent loss. Others were trying to deal with new responsibilities without a sense of loss.

The Suicide Attempt Group

Almost all suicide attempt subjects had suffered recent loss. Many of them had, in addition, feelings of chronic loss.

The Appendectomy Group

No characteristic life changes could be designated for the appendectomy group.

IV. The transactional encounter between the subject and the interviewer.

The Accident Group

The accident subjects as a group were cool and evasive toward the interviewers. The interviewers had a hard time with them and were glad to end the interviewing.

The Suicide Attempt Group

The suicide attempt subjects were needy and dependent. They interested and engaged the interviewers. The interviewers responded sympathetically and tried to help but finally were glad to get away from them.

The Appendectomy Group

These subjects seemed to be normal, interested in and respectful toward the interviews and the interviewers. The interviewers responded positively. Both parties to the interview seemed to enjoy it and parted with a feeling of accomplishment.

T HE PREVIOUS TWO CHAPTERS present data obtained by utilizing a Data Sheet as a guide and a relatively objective methodology. The specific judgments which constitute this data were made by psychoanalyst interviewers. As we stated earlier, we felt that psychoanalysts make good interviewers because of their ability to move interviews in the direction of psychologically meaningful material. They have an additional value in being sophisticated judges of the disguises, subterfuges and obscurations which human beings use when they talk.

But making judgments on pre-formulated issues is not the only or, indeed, the chief method of psychoanalyst function. They usually obtain large masses of material (both historical and immediately interpersonal, that is, based upon the transactional dynamics of their communication with their subject). Then they skillfully evaluate those data. They look at the patterns, the contradictions and the regularities behind different modes of presenting data, and from these and other observable attributes of their subjects, they formulate hypotheses concerning the motivations of the subjects and the conflicting forces within their personalities. In addition, they identify those elements of the external world which are crucial in setting off conflicts and mobilizing defenses against uncomfortable motivations, affects and thoughts.

SIGNIFICANCE OF THE SUMMARY

An important division of this research was the narrative summary. Each analyst was asked to utilize his intuitive and hypothesizing abilities to obtain material and form impressions about the patient's psychological mode of life. In addition to those judgments made in response to the Data Sheet, he was asked to formulate a dynamic impression of the subject's life history, crucial conflicts, precipitating stresses connected to the hospitalization event and the transactional aspects of the interview.

From these summaries, we hoped to obtain data which would add to our research in a number of ways. First, we might discover additional important material not considered in our hypotheses. Secondly, we might find material which would support the evaluations of the hypotheses made through the utilization of the Data Sheet answers. Finally, we might find material which would contradict those evaluations.

Immediately upon completion of each series of interviews, the psychoanalyst interviewer dictated a dynamic summary of the case. In the summary, he commented on a number of points (these are outlined in Chapter 4 on the Method). The analyst himself, however, made the final decision as to which points he would emphasize. There was no restriction as to time spent on his description.

These narratives were then typed and made available to members of the Central Research Group. The three psychoanalyst members of that group then read and evaluated the dynamic summaries.

There was great variation among these summaries. The length of the reports ranged from 2 to 15 pages. There were differences in what was reported. Some cases would have much concerning the early history of the subject, while others contained little. Some would detail the events which preceded the hospitalization; others would make almost no mention of them. In addition, there was variation in regard to the sophistication of the dynamic formulations. Some cases had relatively brief and simple dynamic descriptions, while others were quite sophisticated. There was variation among interviewers and further variation according to the specific case. Thus, the same interviewer would be terse and guarded in one case and more elaborate in the next.

Because of these differences in a number of dimensions, there were problems in evaluating these data. We could not exclusively utilize the comfortable method of counting responses across groups of subjects. Rather we had to immerse ourselves in the material, attempt to empathize with the feelings and impressions of the interviewers, try to feel ourselves into their position, vis-à-vis the subjects, and finally come to some understanding of the similarities and differences between the three groups.

There are, no doubt, reasons to question or criticize such a method of obtaining data. We will only point out that it is (a) the one that we used, and (b) one that is suited by tradition to the discipline (psychoanalysis) which was utilized in obtaining data in this study.

As we read and tried to understand the significance of this data, we felt that it could be most meaningfully summarized and presented under four main headings. They are:

I. A description of the psychological experiences of each subject as he went through the episode connected with his hospitalization.

II. Evidence for conscious or unconscious self-destructiveness in the personality of the subject. This might take many forms. It could appear in behavior, dreams, fantasies or unusual defenses.

III. The life changes or other stresses which occurred to the subject in the period prior to the incident. The changes could be in the direction of greater success, greater achievement, greater responsibility or greater satisfaction. There might also be negative stresses entailing loss or failure. In some cases, we might find no changes in life direction or no stresses.

IV. A report of the psychoanalytic encounter between the subject and the psychoanalyst. We looked at the interviews as a micropsychoanalysis with resistance, interpretations or other maneuvers to deal with the resistance. We looked also for evidence of transferences and counter-transferences.

We will now detail our findings and impressions regarding these points.

I. DESCRIPTION OF THE ACCIDENT, SUICIDE AND APPENDECTOMY PROCESSES

These evaluations deal with the actual processes which led to hospitalization. They include descriptions of the events which immediately preceded and led up to the physical trauma. We call them the accident, suicide and appendectomy processes.

The Accident Process

1. *There was no report of the accident process in about one-quarter of the cases.* It is interesting to speculate on this finding. The interviewers were specifically told that this was an area of interest, although we did not insist that there be a report on it.

As we will presently see, there was amnesia for many cases but we do not include the amnesia cases in this 25 per cent. In many of the amnesia cases, the victims had learned a good deal about the details of the accident from others. They related this information to the interviewer who reported it.

To repeat, there was simply no mention of the details of the accident itself in 25 per cent of the cases. Did the interviewers feel that the accident had nothing to do with psychological issues? Were they so involved with other aspects of their report (such as their descriptions of the dynamics) that they overlooked the accident itself? Perhaps the subject volunteered no details of the accident.

2. *Amnesia was reported in about one-third of the cases.* As we previously indicated, this did not preclude our getting details of the accident event from our subjects.

What was the meaning of the amnesia? Was it a result of temporary brain dysfunction (caused by the trauma of the accident)? In some cases, this may well have been so, but we believe that unconscious denial and conscious distortion was responsible for much of the "amnesia." We noted that many of the accident victims tended to deny sensitivities and hurts and to present a wall which effectively kept the interviewers from close emotional contact. Denial of painful or humiliating events, such as as an automobile accident, may fit in with this characterological picture. It should be noted that the ability to drive a car safely and to avoid ending up in a hospital "all cracked up" is probably an important source of pride to drivers.

There are several reasons why our subjects may have lied about remembering the accident. Many of them admitted drinking. A few admitted taking drugs. It is our impression that the total number who were drinking or on drugs was larger than reported. These habits in individuals who are responsible for accidents could certainly arouse the fear of legal difficulty. (This fear was well justified in many cases since a great deal of damage resulted from the accidents. In some cases, injury or death of others was a result of the accident also.) In addition, fabrication might have been utilized in an effort to construct a more favorable history to be used in negotiating with insurance companies.

3. Most victims had been drinking within a few hours of their accident. *Many had been drinking quite heavily.*

Two or three victims reported that they had been on drugs. Some reported marijuana smoking; others reported the use of stimulants. It seemed possible that many more were taking drugs. In several accidents in which neither drinking nor drug-taking was reported, there were impressions or suggestions that they had in fact been used. In one case, some young people stole a car and were being pushed by another car in order to get moving. The car which they were in finally started. They went around a corner and lost control. This resulted in the accident. The entire episode is reported in terms of a frivolous, fun-seeking group of young people out to enjoy themselves. What is almost essential to this picture is alcoholic or other drug intake.

4. With monotonous regularity, there was *a history of drinking with friends, drinking at a party,* or having a few drinks and then being on the way to a meeting with friends or a party where more drinking would occur.

Examples of Drinking Behavior

A. A 30-year-old man who had done a lot of drinking and who has a history of having abused drugs was at a party with friends. He was doing a fair amount of drinking. He left the party suddenly after midnight and drove off at high speed alone in his car. Within a few blocks, he drove into a power pole.

B. Another man was out with some friends. They did a lot of drinking. At one point in the evening when they were all fairly high, they got into the car and were driving off to the next drinking place. Suddenly someone thought that he saw a police car pulling up alongside. The driver jerked the car out of control and ran into the freeway center divider.

C. One man spent Saturday evening with his mother and sister and her family and a few old friends. They were drinking continuously throughout the evening and listening to music. He finally decided to go home at about 2 or 3 o'clock in the morning. He got into his car. Then he doesn't remember what happened. He must have fallen asleep and a collision occurred.

In addition to the intoxicating effects of alcohol and/or drugs, an additional important feature is suggested. These people seem to be trying to relax, to regress, to be together with others who will gratify them and take care of them. Can this state of regression have something to do with the accident-prone state?

5. What driving characteristics might have contributed to the accident? Most reports of driving characteristics fall into one of two categories. Either there is *a lack of sufficient reactivity* on the part of the driver or there is an *impulsive, poorly planned and probably poorly coordinated over-reactivity.*

Earlier we mentioned the group of young people who were unable to retain control of their car as it went around a corner. Many of the victims state that they were getting drowsy and probably fell asleep. Others who have amnesia for the event believe that that is what must have happened.

However, certain drivers react in an impulsive way so that they get into an accident by doing more than they planned to. For example, they will swerve to avoid what they believe to be a car coming close to them or coming at them and thus set themselves on a collision course.

One driver unexpectedly traveled onto a gravel road. When he felt the different texture under his wheels, he gripped the wheel firmly and tried to gain control of the car. In so doing, he lost control and hit a tree.

(Incidentally, the lack of sufficient reaction and its opposite, the compulsive over-reaction, do not correlate completely with the depressed and counter-depressed ego characteristics which we will later be describing.)

Two subjects gave evidence for unique driving patterns different from those just described. One person was a compulsive, non-flexible individual whose mind could not easily shift from one focus to another. His accelerator got stuck and he tried to stop the car by jamming on the brakes. In retrospect, he and his interviewer speculated that had he remembered that he could turn the motor off with the ignition switch, the accident might have been averted.

Another individual seemed to be ambiguous and hazy about all his activities. (In fact, he seemed to be schizoid, according to the dynamic and symptomatic description.) We speculated that he was intensively fantasizing and did not have sufficient energy left to focus on his driving task.

Three individuals had a strong need to do something to avoid a collision, but their fear of collision seemed greatly exaggerated. We have already noted the case in which the driver felt a police car was at his side. Another individual felt that he was being overtaken by a large truck; while a third driver felt that he was so close to the vehicle ahead of him that a collision was imminent. All three of these drivers impulsively swerved out of what they thought was the collision course, only to find themselves involved in *another* collision course. One of them who later went over the details of the accident with his interviewer realized that he had misjudged his supposed danger.

The Suicide Process

First, we note that our findings in regard to the actual suicide attempts reveal no data or speculations which have not been previously reported.

Depression, at least moderate, in most cases severe, was a constant feature in the suicide attempters. In general, our subjects were confronted with losses which seemed important, indeed overwhelming, to them. Although about one-third reacted to a specific recent loss, the others seemed to have been on a downhill trend for from several months to several years. Many made their suicide attempts in response to an event which seemed to be "the last straw." That is, they had suffered previous frustrations, deprivations and losses and felt that they could not deal with the latest one.

A. An example of the "last straw": Mr. A's difficulties had been increasing for at least six months. The initiating external event was an automobile accident. This resulted in an injury which prevented him from working. He lost his job. He attempted many types of work over the next six months but each one resulted in failure. At that time, he began to think of himself as a failure. He consulted a psychiatrist. This man could not treat him and referred him to other psychiatric facilities. By that time, he was feeling so bad that he didn't follow through. Two weeks prior to the suicide attempt, some money which he had expected did not materialize. He began withdrawing from people and started to think seriously about suicide. He finally attempted it.

Three of our subjects denied making suicide attempts. One said that he took a great amount of medication in an attempt to get high, while two others talked about varying degrees of panic and confusion. In two of these cases, the interviewer's opinion was that there was a conscious suicide attempt. The third interviewer did not comment on this issue, and it is unclear as to whether he believed that a conscious suicide attempt had taken place.

The types of losses suffered by our subjects were most importantly losses of people who were important to them. However, occasionally financial loss, loss of good health and other losses were sustained.

Here are some examples which detail types of losses as well as other factors:

B. Four months ago, he slipped off a truck and suffered a head concussion. He did not feel his usual self. He was unable to secure psychiatric treatment at first but finally got some. He was becoming despondent about his medical condition and about not earning enough money. There was increasing dissention between his wife and himself. Three or four weeks before the suicide attempt, she left and went to live with a sister who is seeking a divorce herself. On the day of the attempt, he called various people. His idea was to try to get together with them. No one was home. He got more depressed. Then he thought of suicide consciously and took some sleeping pills. After a while, he got frightened and called friends.

C. He decided to separate from his wife several days ago. Following an argument with her, he went to a friend's house and drank. Then he went back to his own house. He had been thinking about taking his own life, thinking that rather than face being apart from his wife, he would prefer to be dead. He also thought that if he took his life, she would see that he really meant it and feel sorry or get together with him. Then he came home and took some pills.

D. He had mounting financial difficulties. He was trying to create his own business but was having psychological and practical difficulty in doing that. Then he thought of several ventures to generate immediate cash. He made appointments with two possible lenders but these were postponed. At that time he began drinking heavily and decided, "What the hell." He then took a number of sleeping pills. He does not recall it, but apparently he called his best friend on the telephone and told him what he had done just before he became unconscious.

The last two cases demonstrate an important feature of the suicide cases—that is, how alcohol is importantly intertwined with the movement toward actual suicide. Perhaps with continuing feelings of loss and failure, regressive movements take place. We do not know how many people in such a situation drink, feel better and move away from suicide. However, in many of our suicidal cases, it is clear that the regressive pull is either not decreased by the drinking or may actually be enhanced by it. The interesting point is that this movement toward regression corresponds with what we have already seen in the accident cases. There also, drinking and regression go hand in hand as the subject moves toward his trauma.

Most frequently, our interviewers comment on the sense of loss in the suicidal individuals. Occasionally they note a need or desire to rejoin a warm, maternal figure at the time of the attempt. We will discuss the possible implications of these regressive movements in suicide attempt and accident at later points in the book.

The Appendicitis Process

It is somewhat difficult to formulate an "appendicitis process." A "suicide process" describes those events leading to a situation in which an individual tries to end his life. It seems clearly to be an intentioned act with a good deal of structure. Although an "accident process" is not as clear-cut, there has been enough past research and thinking about accident, and there is a strong enough feeling that an accident victim does some things to contribute to his accident, so that there are guidelines. In the case of appendectomies, we are not on such sure ground. Very few people have considered appendectomies to be psychologically motivated. Appendicitis is something that *happens* to one. From this standpoint, we are on entirely new ground as we try to delineate possible components of a psychological "appendicitis process."

First, it is of interest that only a minority of the appendectomy cases seemed to be totally disconnected from immediate precipitating factors. In a little less than one-quarter of the cases, the interviewers indicated that they could discern no psychological precipitating factors. In the remaining cases, there were precipitating factors or at least possible precipitating factors noted. These were in the nature of stresses which the individual was undergoing immediately prior to the onset of the attack.

The stresses took a number of forms. No predominant trends can be identified. A number of the individuals were under stress which can be characterized as loss. They were undergoing marital disputes, job or school difficulties, or having financial reverses.

A. Several individuals were involved in intensely conflictual and somewhat complex situations. An example of this was a young man who was getting "serious" with his girl friend. He then decided to try to get into the service. He was not accepted and returned to his girl friend. An engagement was announced. At precisely this time, he became ill.

B. Another subject had been tense for about a year since his return from the Vietnam War. He decided to re-enlist even though the war had held a number of traumatic situations for him. Re-enlisting, however, meant that he had to live with his in-laws whom he did not like. It was at this time that the first symptoms of the appendicitis began.

C. A notable trend in some of the subjects was a strong regressive pull. One man who was falling behind in school was watching television and had the feeling, "Oh, what the hell! I ought to give in." Shortly after this, he began to have his first symptoms.

D. Another patient had just finished a vacation in which he had been doing much more drinking than usual and started to have his symptoms.

E. Yet another man was being treated for drug withdrawal in a residential setting. He had improved and was scheduled for discharge. He learned, about twelve days prior to the appendicitis attack, that his sister had run away. He was very worried about her. She was found after nine days, but three days following her return his pain began. In this situation, it is possible that his fear of leaving the residential setting was enhanced by his concern for his sister. When we add to this that he was probably the kind of person who has an "oral" character and is made extremely anxious by the loss of security, it might seem that there were strong motivations for regression. A similar postulation could be made for the other subjects.

F. Other examples. Several of the appendectomy subjects demonstrated a stoic or masochistic trend. Two had their symptoms for over a week, and it was only at the insistence of friends or relatives that they came to medical attention. Another one did seek medical attention shortly after his first symptoms but was told that nothing definite could be diagnosed. He then went home and proceeded to develop a severe case of appendicitis. It was only when he was practically unconscious that he was taken to the hospital. Finally, one young man experienced the appendicitis attack as if he had been struck down.

One professional person had been overwhelmed by everyone in his family being ill and his having to take care of them. In addition, he found his professional work boring and seemed to welcome his hospitalization after it occurred.

II. CONSCIOUS AND UNCONSCIOUS SELF-DESTRUCTIVE TRENDS

In suicide, there are conscious thoughts of self-destruction and movement toward implementing them. As far as is presently known, such conscious trends exist in neither accident nor appendicitis. One purpose of this evaluation was to ascertain if such conscious and willful self-destructive trends are present in accident and appendicitis subjects.

In addition to conscious self-destructive trends, we can postulate unconscious ones. There are a number of ways in which such trends might manifest themselves. The presence of certain affective states, like depression, are associated with self-punitive attitudes and feelings of hopelessness which downgrade the value of life. Such feelings probably are precursors to many suicidal life segments.

There are a great number of psychological defenses which may become maladaptive. The specific maladaptation may take the form of an increased risk to the continuance of life. Some of these defenses are an uncontrolled use of alcohol and drugs, impulsive life-threatening activities (for example, impulsive speeding, feeling that one needn't bother to use seatbelts), and a general tendency toward risk-taking (for example, enjoying the thrill of speeding on rain-slicked highways or flying in "bad" weather).

Finally, we mention the presence of dreams or fantasies which clearly speak of death or injury to the subject. Less extreme punishments, such as humiliations, disappointments or deprivations, may also be indications of self-destructive trends.

Let us now proceed to evaluate the dynamic summaries of the subjects in our three groups for clues to self-destructive trends.

The Accident Group

Evidence of conscious self-destruction was meager among the accident cases. No subjects admitted that their accidents were suicidal or self-destructive. We asked our analysts to evaluate each of the 25 accidents in terms of its self-destructive component. In only four of the cases was there a positive reaction. Three of these were strongly positive: (1) "There is a self-destructive element in his accident." (2) "His accident to me is a suicide." (3) "My hypothesis is that there was a strong self-destructive element involved in this accident." (4) The fourth opinion was expressed in a tentative manner: "As far as the question of whether there were significant self-destructive elements involved in the accident, if I am forced to have a simple *yes* or *no*, I would say that in my opinion I think *yes*."

In regard to unconscious self-destructive trends, there was evidence of depression in a number of our cases, but going along with our more objective evaluations, the rate of depression in the accident group did not seem higher than in the appendectomy group. There were also a number of modes of living or defenses which could be associated with self-destructive trends. There was a high rate of drinking (alcohol) among the accident subjects. There was also a fairly high incidence of drug-taking, but it was not clear that this was increased over the appendectomy group nor that it had more serious sequelae. (It should be kept in mind that the taking of certain drugs is a serious criminal offense and that therefore the presence and intensity of drug-taking may be one of the most carefully guarded secrets of individuals who do utilize drugs.)

There was evidence of impulsive activity in some areas which could be dangerous, such as driving. There was a lesser degree of other risk-taking. However, in neither of these areas were there significant differences in rate or in self-destructive implications between the accident group and the appendectomy group.

Dreams and fantasies of self-destruction were not a prominent feature of this group. One person characterized as depressed had some dreams of death. Another subject had a dream in which an authoritarian man was approaching him to beat him because of forbidden sexual activity with a woman. The analyst felt that this dream not only was revelatory of the man's personality but, more specifically, represented his understanding of the accident as a warning against Oedipal temptations. These dreams are noted not because they are felt to be typical of accident cases, but rather because they are rare examples of possible self-punishing or self-destructive dreams in this group.

It will be seen that up to this point, our evaluation of conscious and unconscious self-destructive trends in the accident subjects does not give too many positive clues. Indeed, apart from the heavy drinking, there seem to be none. However, when we look at the character defenses or coping trends of the accident subjects from the standpoint of self-destruction, some rather striking impressions are obtained.

Of the 25 cases, there are five that are clearly so individualistic that they do not fall into either of the two groups we are about to portray. Of the remaining 20 cases, five can be characterized as a "depressive" group and the remaining 15 constitute an "action-oriented" group.

The depressed group is responding to some recent loss or stress with a feeling of depression and a diminishing of their self-esteem. They have many of the usual clinical signs of depression: affect changes, slowing in behavior, a cognitive self-depreciating attitude, and a feeling that life does not hold much that is good for them. The depression is moderate in degree.

What could the mechanism of accident production (at least that contribution to it which is made by the individual) be in these individuals? Their self-destructive trends are, for the most part, unconscious. They speak of disappointment, frustration, a feeling of failure. The analysts postulate anger or hatred turned upon the self. We believe that there are at least three important concepts which link these depressed people to the accidents which they encountered.

1. Their state of depression carries with it an inability to focus attention on what is transpiring around them. Rather than the more usual state of alertness which makes a driver aware of potential dangers, they are preoccupied with themselves and unaware of the outside world. However, it is not (at least in the cases we saw) that they drive straight into another car or into some solid object. Rather they, too late, notice an actual danger and made a speedy and over-compensatory action, such as twisting the wheel too far or jamming on the brakes. This results in an accident.

2. A possible additional factor is a tendency to overemphasize the danger of nearby objects. These are usually cars which they feel are coming too quickly toward them or that they are too quickly approaching. From a psychoanalytic viewpoint, we postu-

late that these objects are seen as dangerous because of a projection of negative and hostile feelings from within the driver to the nearby vehicle. Then he is frightened and must excessively protect himself from that projected danger.

3. A third important characteristic of the depressed state is the need to take in valued, gratifying substances. These are often alcoholic beverages and drugs. The tragic consequences of the ingestion of these substances is that they deaden the sensorium or make it less reliable and therefore increase the possibility of collisions.

Now for a few examples of the depressed group:

A. This subject drove off at high speed from a party alone in his car. It was after midnight and he soon hit a power pole. He is a 30-year-old man who has a history of drug abuse and has spent six years in jail on charges of armed robbery, burglary and felonies. At the time that he had this accident (he was probably drunk), he was about to go to court to face a charge of drunk driving from the previous night. Under these conditions, it is probable that he would have drawn a prolonged jail sentence.

The history reveals a continuing series of events which are compounding his misfortune. He is involved in crime, he takes drugs, and has had extreme penalties imposed for these activities. As a result, he is depressed. In order to counter the depression, he takes more drugs and the cycle goes on and on. To add to his misery, he had a falling out with his mistress three weeks before. He had been living with her, but after a violent disagreement between them, the parole officer made him move from her house. She has subsequently been seeing other men. His depression has been increasing. This, incidentally, was the case that the analyst strongly considered was a consciously attempted suicide. However, the subject denied it.

B. A second man had a history of early childhood deprivation. In his youth, he lived alone on the desert in primitive surroundings. He is married. He has had several marriages, but none of them worked out. During the last few years, he has been struggling with feelings of hopelessness and defeat. He has, for the moment, given up on women, but he feels particularly bad about his difficulties in the work area. The analyst felt this crucial trauma was tearing at his self-esteem. He doesn't feel strong enough to do his work, yet he had to push himself relentlessly in order to keep a job. He has had self-destructive ideas and dreams of death. He wants again to withdraw as he did when he was a child, and there are hints that he wishes to withdraw from life.

When he described his accident, he first said that a car had swerved directly in front of him and he, in attempting to avoid a collision, hit the curb. Later on, a more detailed description was obtained. This indicated that the other car turned into his lane several hundred feet ahead of him but he overreacted. He turned the steering wheel excessively and violently. The car went out of control, hit the curb, and flew through the air. He had not fastened his seatbelt. The car rolled over on him. He was lucky to be alive. Of course, he had been drinking prior to the accident.

Now let us survey the "action-oriented" group. These people tend to be independent and self-assertive. They do not care to get too involved with the interviewer. They seem to shy away from any relationships or activities which might seem dependent. These traits, however, are related to a conflict about dependence. These people are usually conscientious and hard-working. Indeed, that is their trouble. They work so hard at getting things done, at discharging responsibilities, and at denying their own gratification that they have large unmet dependency needs.

How do they cope with these needs? For one thing, they do a lot of drinking. It is as if that way of obtaining gratification is unconnected with the shame of taking from another person. Sometimes they drink in a solitary way so that no one knows about it. Sometimes they drink in the company of other "men" where drinking is a "manly" thing. But the drinking and the other modes which they utilize to satisfy their dependent needs do not completely gratify them. When they are by themselves and no one can closely scrutinize them, when they can relax their own vigilance as to what they are doing, they let go. They decrease the compulsive nature of their driving, and through that letting go they gain some relief.

However, as this "letting go" occurs, they move into the accident-prone state because the letting go, which does so much for their dependency needs, is, unfortunately, poorly adapted to the necessities of safe driving. These are the people who fall asleep at the wheel or who do not adequately judge distances and perhaps neglect other of the minutiae of safe driving.

Let us cite examples:

A. Here is a young man who during the interview was friendly but had a manner of studied ease. He was cool and casual. The interviewer felt that he had to pull information from him and noted at the time that the subject was trying to control the situation and limit the amount of self-expression: He denies strong affects, aggressiveness, violence, feeling hurt or disappointed. He does admit to being a fast driver. He has had his license suspended and many tickets. The interviewer feels that he is dependent upon his wife, mother and family, but the subject denies it.

About two months ago, the subject moved for the first time in his life. He left an apartment near his parents and moved to an outlying city. He did this so as to be near work. On the Saturday evening of the accident, he had spent the evening with his mother, sister and her family, and a few old friends. He was listening to music and drinking. He stayed with them until 2:00 or 3:00 a.m. It was as if he wanted to stay away from his new home, the new responsible situation. He had agreed to take on the new responsibility, but he was not quite willing to do it. He came home for a big feed of gratifying dependent experiences. Then, as he drove back to the new responsibility, the conflict intensified. This, plus the effect of the alcohol, may have contributed importantly to the accident.

B. This subject was an intensely conscientious person who had always worked hard. However, for about two weeks prior to the accident, he was working even harder. He was holding down two jobs plus being involved in a teaching project. The day before the accident, he was setting up a party. The accident occurred on a Sunday morning. He had not had any sleep since Friday night. After he had helped set up the party, he enjoyed himself at it. He stayed to clean up after the party. Then while driving home, with intense and excessive conflicts around the dependence-independence area, he had his accident.

His whole life history centers around the dependence-independence theme. His ambition is to succeed, to work hard. He identifies with hard-striving people like Jews and once even kiddingly changed his name to a Jewish one. But as he does all this hard work, he denies his passive dependent needs. He is apparently fairly successful at doing this, but it is our postulation that at certain points there is a breakthrough of the passivity. It is as if the compulsive, hard-working efforts wear out because they are spread too thin!

The Suicide Attempt Group

Much has been written about self-destructiveness in suicide.[1,2,3] Since our present series of suicidal subjects did not reveal much that was strikingly new in this regard, we will not give a detailed survey of our findings. What follows, then, is an outline of the aspects of self-destructiveness noted in our suicide attempt group.

Conscious suicidal trends were, of course, overwhelmingly evident. All of the subjects except three acknowledged that their hospitalizations were due to current suicide attempts. The three who demurred had previously acknowledged making suicide attempts.

In addition to their most recent suicidal preoccupations, fully two-thirds of our subjects had thought about suicide earlier, and a good many of them had made prior attempts. In many cases, there was *a combination of both chronic and recent suicidal preoccupation.* That is, individuals had thought about taking their lives on a number of occasions in a period of from two weeks to several years prior to the actual attempt. They may not have carried their intentions to the point of action previously (although, in some cases, they did). However, all had new stress which made them move into the present suicide attempt.

On a less conscious level, there were many indications of self-destructiveness. A majority of our subjects were depressed. Many were chronically depressed. Others had episodes of depression alternating with depression-free periods.

There was a great deal of rage in their discussion of current situations and past events. In about one-third of the cases, there was acting-out of this rage on the outside world. To a greater extent, the rage was turned upon the self, and there were varying kinds of self-mutilation, self-castigation and actual previous suicide attempts.

Fantasies of rage and anger were present *in almost every subject*. These feelings were directed both toward outside people and toward themselves, but there seemed to be a preponderance of self-direction. Fantasies of being persecuted were present in a smaller sub-group.

Accidents, and automobile accidents specifically, were frequently mentioned. Probably about 40 per cent talked of past and recent automobile accidents. It is perhaps not so striking that such an incidence of accidents occurred. Most people driving in this automobile-saturated land will have had one or more accidents. What may be of more significance is the degree to which this group of people talked about their accidents. However, we must add that the suicide attempt group did not seem significantly different from the appendectomy group in terms of number of accidents.

There were many dreams of anger, isolation, loneliness, depression, death and suicide in this group. There was no question that they occurred much more frequently in the suicide attempt group than in either of the other two.

There was a high utilization of alcohol and drugs. As we surveyed the dynamic summaries, that incidence seemed as high in the suicide attempt group as in the accident group.

There was a higher incidence of psychotic-like manifestations and actual psychotic diagnoses in the suicide attempt group than in either of the other two. Psychosis may be an indication of self-destructiveness because of its association with poor "reality testing." Because of poor "reality testing," psychotic people may have less concern for life-preservative actions than non-psychotic people. In addition, psychosis often carries with it a higher rate of impulsive actions. Putting these two characteristics together may yield a higher self-destructive potentiality.

Finally, let us give two brief examples of suicidal situations:

A. Six months ago, the subject was in Vietnam in the Army. He received news that his grandmother died. This brought on a depressive reaction which was perhaps intensified by his having to leave Vietnam. He got into behavioral difficulties with the Army and his commanding officers. He acted rebelliously and got into fights. Then a few days before the suicide attempt, he came to Los Angeles. He saw his mother who was anxious. This added to his depression. Also adding to it was his seeing his former girl friend who had married another man and recently had had a child. His drinking increased to a very high level. Then he took an overdose of sleeping pills.

The interviewer felt there was tremendous underlying rage because of a feeling of deprivation. The subject felt he had been deprived in childhood, and each frustration seemed an additional deprivation to him. We quote the interviewer: "He constantly fights impulses to lash out, to attack and to kill."

There are many daytime fantasies of hurting those who frustrate him. There are also self-mutilative and self-destructive fantasies which he has acted out on a number of occasions. For example, at the age of nine, he attempted to hang himself "to see how it feels to be dead."

B. The second suicidal patient was depressed at the time of the interview. He stated that he had a self-destructive pattern. "I get in my way or screw myself up." This man spoke about desertions, about being beaten up by his father and stepfather. He had pleasure when his stepfather died, but this was short-lived as the stepfather was replaced by another brutal one. He has always gotten in trouble with the law. There was much talk of death and funerals and fantasies of killing his father. He had had an automobile accident. He was facing a court action in which he would be charged with driving under the influence of alcohol and possession of dangerous drugs. This accident occurred while he was on probation for a previous conviction in which he had been found guilty of using marijuana while being involved in an accident. He has beaten up his wife when he was "blind with rage."

The Appendectomy Group

The appendectomy group was less self-destructive than the other two. This does not mean that indications of self-destructiveness were absent in this group. Almost every category which we evaluated—suicide attempts, accidents, depression, fantasies of rage and anger, alcohol and drug taking—was represented in the appendectomy group. But fewer subjects demonstrated the self-destructive characteristics, and the intensity of the characteristics was less. There were many people who took drugs but they tended to take marijuana rather than "the harder stuff." Many drank but not to as great a degree as those in the other groups, nor did one get the impression that they drank as frequently. There were fewer suicide attempts and less talk about accidents.

There were not many people in this group who would fit the average psychoanalyst's concept of a healthy, happy, creative individual or his concept of someone who is relatively conflict-free. Of course, psychoanalysts often wonder in which group of people in the whole world they would find a high incidence of those "happy" or "normal" individuals.

Although these people have conflicts and hardships, they are not in as much distress as the suicidal people and they get more pleasure in relating to others than the accident people.

Let us note the self-destructiveness in two representative subjects:

A. This is a man who is somewhat anxious. He has a constant dread that he will not "make it" or that something terrible will happen to him. He thinks of death frequently. He keeps himself busy at work and uses "positive thinking" to minimize difficulty. He drives his car around. Sometimes that makes him feel better. He smokes pot occasionally, more rarely will use another drug. When disappointments occur, he may get irritable and touchy. Then he will start working harder and this will make him feel better.

B. This young man willingly agreed to participate in the interview. He identified with the psychiatrist, telling him that he (the patient) was planning to do similar work. He was arrested once for possession of marijuana, but it could not be proved and he was not convicted. He is a light drinker. He was divorced about three years ago, and he lives with his mother and stepfather who take care of his children. The interviewer felt that he regarded his own children as siblings. He seemed to be quite contented with what he was doing and was looking forward, but without specific plans, to making changes which would improve the quality of his life.

III. LIFE CHANGES PRECEDING HOSPITALIZATION INCIDENT

First a few words concerning the validity of our impressions about precipitating incidents. In two groups, accident and appendectomy, there are important questions as to the importance of psychological factors in "producing" the event. In the case of appendectomy, there is almost no past research to suggest that psychological features are important in causing appendicitis. In accidents, although there have been numerous suggestions as to the importance of psychological features, their actual significance can be questioned in at least three ways:

1. The data supporting the presence of such factors is uncertain. Many postulated psychologically related "causes" have been shown to lack support. (The accident-prone hypothesis is one example.)

2. There are so many factors related to the occurrence of an "accident" that it is important to consider to what degree and in what way "psychological" factors make their contribution.

3. When psychoanalysts who are educated and experienced in looking for "psychological" factors focus their diagnostic skill on any group, it is possible that their own bias may lead them to note "psychological" issues in an invalid way. We do not know to what degree we may have done this in this part of the research. However, there are suggestions (from our bias and debriefing studies) that biases did operate in us and may have distorted our interpretation of the data.

Here are our impressions as to the validity of the data in this section. In the suicide attempt group, we felt convinced that the feeling of loss and the various losses which the subjects enumerated were importantly linked to the state of increasing despondency and hopelessness which preceded the suicide attempt. In the accident and appendectomy groups, we were less sure of such an important linkage. This unsureness probably reflected our own subjective attitude as well as the impressions of our subjects. They probably questioned that there were important connections between the events they were relating and the hospitalization incident.

Notwithstanding these reservations, we did form impressions of psychological events preceding the incident which may have been significantly linked to it.

The Accident Group

As a group, these subjects were not displaying anywhere near the degree of distress or conveying as much of a feeling of breakdown of defenses as was true in the suicide attempt group. (Appendectomy subjects did not seem distressed or in stages of defensive breakdown.) Although about five of the cases did not fall clearly into the two main categories we are about to describe, almost all of the other twenty cases fell into one or both of these categories.

The "Responsible" Person

About three-fifths of the subjects fell into this group. In essence, it consisted of people who had, in a period of the last few days to the last several years, been assuming new responsibilities. It was the impression of the interviewers that they were in conflict about these responsibilities. On the one hand, they *wanted* to assume them, and on the other hand, there was anxiety and unsureness about being able to stand up to the new responsibilities. A seeming variation of this was a person in whom important new responsibilities were not present but who had an extremely "responsible" attitude toward the commitments which already existed. Thus he would always seem to be striving hard and to be concerned about how well he was doing. He seemed to put out great effort and concentration as he dealt with his duties and responsibilities.

A. Here is an example of someone who took on a new responsibility. This subject had been having difficulties with his wife for some years. For a while, they had been separated. Divorce was the next event. However, about two months ago, she rejoined him. This meant that once again he would have to deal with a responsibility which had given him great anxiety. In addition, the new situation entailed a number of other life changes. He would have to make more money, keep a steadier job, and give up some other associations which had been gratifying to him.

B. Next, an example of a compulsive hard worker. This man was mentioned earlier. He is the person who was doing a great deal of work. He was holding down two jobs and at the same time he was involved in a teaching project. He is the type of person who gives of himself unstintingly, often exhausting himself in the process. Actually the accident followed such an extreme giving of himself. In addition to his other responsibilities, he took on the job of setting up a party. Then, after participating in it for a number of hours, he spent several hours in cleaning up. His accident occurred as he was driving home after all this work.

C. On occasion, it is seen that the new responsibility is connected with important long-standing conflicts in the subject. One man had his accident in the context of an increasingly intimate relationship with a girl friend. He had been in love with her, and three days before the accident he declared that he wanted to marry her. He was very happy that he had made the decision and had made some accompanying resolves to work harder and become more serious about life. As a matter of fact, a few days following the accident, he had planned to start school and he was also making plans to buy a new car.

He had chronic fears of authority and superego punishments for unacceptable desires, such as love desires. These fears reflect an incorporation of experiences he had with a father who, to him, seemed strict and punitive.

Later we will describe a second category of preceding events which focuses on loss. A number of our subjects who were in the "new responsibility" or "overly-responsible" group were also experiencing simultaneous feelings of loss. What follows is an example of combined "new responsibility" and "loss" preceding the accident.

D. This man is a hard-driving person. He works at several jobs. He is also a very serious kind of person who is deeply concerned about the status of the country and various social and racial problems. However, he recently separated from his family and even more recently has been separated from his wife. The interviewer felt that he was masochistic and depressed. He was trying to deal with his depression by overactivity. It should be stressed that his overactivity is not only a recent coping mechanism but a lifelong one.

In regard to precipitating life stresses, the interviewer felt that this subject was still dealing with feelings of loss of his family and of his wife. He was also recovering from an ulcer attack.

The Person Responding to "Loss"

The larger group of preceding life situations in the accident group focused on individuals who were intent on dealing with and mastering *responsibility*. Now we describe our second and smaller group. Their preceding life situations were centered around *losses*. We have already described one such person. Here are two additional examples:

A. This man was somewhat irritable and made some complaints about being mistreated and neglected. He is chronically depressed. The depression started three years ago when he finished high school. Several months ago, he had met a young woman who had many desirable features and he had become quite close to her. He had given up drinking alcohol, taking drugs, and other companions in order to devote his energy exclusively to this girl and to become "a better man" for her. However, three weeks ago, his girl friend began dating someone else who our subject felt, far surpassed him. In fact, she fell in love with the other man and indicated that she wished to break off the relationship with the subject. At that time, he became increasingly depressed.

B. The subject was a person who had been delinquent, who had actually been convicted of a criminal charge. Now he is on parole. He started to work as a truck driver two or three days before the accident. This was something of a problem because he did not have a driver's license or insurance. He was married three months ago. On the day of the accident, he had returned from his first run on the new job to discover that his wife was in the hospital because of a miscarriage. He became tearful in the interview. He mentioned that his wife and mother had not visited him that day and again became tearful.

The Suicide Attempt Group

In an earlier section of this chapter, we previewed the main precursors of suicide attempts. The subjects in this group were typically concerned about some recent loss and had feelings that they were unable to continue life in the face of that loss. The losses were of various kinds. The most common one was the loss of an important significant person. This loss was most usually through divorce or separation of a mate. Less frequently there were interruptions of a love relationship or a close friendship. In other situations, the loss of good health, the loss of finances, or the loss of opportunity to succeed was present. Rarely the most important feature was a loss of nerve, a loss of confidence in oneself even though the external disappointment seemed, in itself, not overwhelming. The subject had the feeling that he would be unable to do anything to make himself feel better.

We previously noted that in many situations, the recent loss was "the last straw." There had been a series of preceding losses which the subject had managed to endure without coming to a decision for suicide. However, on the occasion of the most recent loss, a suicidal decision and action occurred.

The Appendectomy Group

A few general comments about this group. It is interesting that in about half of the appendectomy group, interviewers became aware of important stresses in the lives of the individuals.

What does this mean? Do individuals in lower socio-economic classes have more stresses than other people? This is possible, but we doubt it. We were dealing with a group of relatively young people (under 30). These are people who were facing many real external problems. In addition, longitudinal studies indicate that this is a stressful developmental period. We believe that the number of stresses in our appendectomy group are not greater than the number of stresses in most men of this age.

We observed a broad diversity of conflictual and threatening situations. In the suicide attempt group, there seemed to be a fairly uniform type of precipitating event and character reaction. In the accident group, although matters were not as clear, there seemed to be two fairly well defined reaction types. In the appendectomy group, we have no such feeling of uniformity. Rather, we seemed to be looking at a decidedly heterogeneous group of people.

One last general point. Of the three groups, the appendectomies seemed most "normal." Their problems did not seem large to them, and they had the easiest and most comfortable relationship with the interviewers (as we shall presently detail).

Now some examples of preceding life situations:

A. One man became engaged a week prior to his appendectomy. There is indication of conflict about marriage. Just prior to the engagement, he tried to enlist in the service but was turned down. Deeper questioning revealed that he partially wished to avoid marriage.

B. Another young man had recently moved away from his family. He had been having interpersonal problems, particularly with his mother. He had fought with her many times and also struck out at his 19-year-old sister who is pregnant. He had had suicidal ideation (although no plans to commit suicide). He had thoughts of getting a job and going to school but had encountered difficulty in both areas. He was also unsuccessful in making friends. As a result of being ill with appendicitis, he turned to his grandparents and established a closer relationship with them.

Could his appendectomy have been a somatic expression of weakness? Perhaps illness was more acceptable to him than his openly stating that he wanted to be closer to parental figures.

C. Another man had been discharged from his job two months before the appendicitis attack. He was quite discouraged. He was the type of man who feels very good when he is taking care of other people. Thus, being out of work was doubly distressing to him.

Others were, as might be expected, anticipating major changes in their lives. We have already mentioned some who were dealing with situations of getting into or out of marriage. A number of the men planned to go to school.

Let us now suggest a formulation. Many people in this group were undergoing stressful situations of various kinds. To some degree, they may have felt "over their heads" with responsibility, yet they made no conscious decision to give in. At that point, they had an appendicitis attack. That may have been the symbolic way of expressing their distress. In some cases it (that is, the hospitalization for appendicitis) provided a pathway for moving to new and hopefully more gratifying dependent relationships. Does this mean that the appendicitis was unconsciously intentional, that it was a "somatic" compliance to an unconscious but unacceptable type of living (that type of living which would mean regressing to a less responsible position)? We do not feel that sufficient evidence to support this hypothesis was present in our data.

IV. THE ENCOUNTER BETWEEN THE SUBJECT AND THE ANALYST

Since analysts did our interviewing and since analysts evaluated the interviews, it is meaningful to look at each of the three groups of interviews from the following standpoints: (1) What attitudes, feelings, defenses and resistances were manifest in the subjects? (2) What attitudes, feelings, defenses and resistances were manifest in the interviewers? (3) What were the transactional aspects of the interview?

As might be expected, there were a number of factors which probably affected our evaluation of the above stated issues. First, individual interviewers had personal orientations. One or two interviewers seemed intensely interested and involved with every subject no matter what group he was in or what his individual personality was like. Others tended to maintain a "cool" attitude toward all subjects. No doubt the specific events in the lives of each interviewer and each subject which were operating at the time of the interview affected the quality of the interview. One could go on at length as to the number of variables which might have affected *specific interviewing situations.*

Yet, in spite of these individual factors, it was possible to discern distinct differences between the three groups. As was true with the other evaluations, it should be kept in mind that we are speaking about general group characteristics. We do not imply that every interview in a given group displayed all of these characteristics.

The Accident Group

We have already identified two sub-groups within the accident group. The smaller one was the "depressed" group. Those subjects expressed a need for the analyst to which he responded positively. A relatively close bond was established between the two. There was mutual "good" feeling.

In the other group, the "action-oriented" or "counter-depressive" group, there was much withdrawal and denial on the part of the subjects. The denial was prominently manifested in an attitude of coolness and distance from the interviewers. Many times the interviewers had to question repeatedly in order to get data. The interviewers finished their work with an irritated feeling.

The great number of individuals in the "action-oriented" group was most responsible for the identification of denial and withdrawal as a characteristic of the accident group as a whole. But even in the "depressive" sub-group, there were greater manifestations of withdrawal and denial and less of a tendency to manifest dependence in a comfortable way. Thus, this "depressive" sub-group differentiated itself from the "suicide attempt" group who were likewise depressed. The suicide attempt group did not manifest as much denial and left the interviewers with a much less irritated feeling.

Here are examples of the two sub-groups in the accident group. First, an example of the "depressed" sub-group:

A. This man tried to maintain a light and airy attitude during the interviews. However, he often brought up depressed feelings and spoke of deprivation. Although he tried to seem friendly, he was actually quite angry. He was taken to the prison ward during his series of interviews. At that time, his anger and depression increased. At first he was seen as suspicious and even manipulative. The analyst developed a little respect and positive feeling for the subject as the interviews progressed, but he was far from liking him. The analyst thought that the "accident" had been a suicide attempt.

B. Next an example of the "counter-depressive" type. Early in his report, the interviewer mentions denial in the subject. He states that the subject was friendly but had a manner of studied ease and was cool and casual. Later he notes that he had to pull or drag information from him. The interviewer felt that the subject was trying to control the situation and limit the amount of self-expression. There were many statements like "I don't remember." There was also denial of information which had previously been volunteered.

The interviewer felt that he had to do a lot of work and a lot of putting together of data. (We thought he meant that he had to consider that many of the explicit answers which the subject gave were false.) The interviewer stated that he felt if he pushed the patient, he might get into difficulty so he did not do this. He ended the interview with the dissatisfied feeling that he had not gotten as close to or as much into the subject as he would have wished.

The Suicide Attempt Group

This group was the most homogeneous of the three in terms of interview evaluation. There was less of the irritating denial characteristic of the accident group. Most of the subjects expressed a desire and need for help. Most interviewers reacted with sympathy and interest.

There were frequent comments by the interviewer that the subject was "cooperative," "relatively non-defensive," "volunteering a good deal of information," etc. The interviewers found the subjects interesting, responded to them, and on many occasions tried to initiate or further the attempts which the subjects were making to obtain psychiatric help. However, it is interesting that rarely did the interviewers offer themselves as psychotherapists. We concluded that the interviewers had worthwhile and interesting interviews with the subjects. However, they were glad to be done with them.

Here is a typical example of an interview with a suicide attempt subject:

A. In the early part of the interview when listing some of the subject's defenses, the interviewer says that the subject has conflicts around expressing his sadness and affectionate feelings but is able to do so. He also says that the subject is compliant to authority. Later in the interview, it is noted that the patient speaks frequently about his suicide attempt and his shame. He tells of looking for psychiatric care, at first being unable to secure it but continuing his search. When he discusses his actions on the day of the suicide attempt, he notes that he repeatedly tried to call people. (It seemed to us that all of these were indications of active movement toward the interviewer.) The interviewer comments on the self-esteem being low, also that the man has difficulty in reaching out for help. The interviewer did not make attempts to secure psychiatric help for the subject, but it seemed that the thought was in his mind. (This subject was already in psychotherapy and therefore did not need further help in securing it.)

The Appendectomy Group

This was the most heterogeneous of the groups in regard to interview interaction. There did not seem to be distinct subgroups as was true for the accident subjects. However, there were characteristics which seem to differentiate this group from the other two.

These interviews as a group tended to be shorter than those in the other two groups. (Those two could not be distinguished from each other in terms of length of interview.) One reason for the shortness of the interviews is that the appendectomy patients had much shorter hospital stays. They were often due to be discharged shortly after they were first seen. Under such pressure, the interviewers probably wished to complete the entire evaluation at one sitting. Perhaps they felt that a lower class group of patients would be relatively untrustworthy in regard to making and/or keeping future appointments. These latter interviews would have had to be conducted either at the subject's home or at the analyst's office.

Before we reviewed the reports, we thought that the appendectomy subjects might have been less interesting to the analysts in terms of their individual psychodynamics. This was definitely not true. They were a fascinating group for dynamic speculation. The analysts were caught up in the intriguing problem of trying to find dynamic accompaniments to the appendicitis attack. They seemed surprised by and interested in the frequent presence of psychopathology in this supposedly "normal" group.

Following are excerpts from one of the appendectomy interviews:

A. The interviewer designates the subject by his first name. He states early in his report that the subject willingly agreed to participate. Indeed, the subject identified with the psychiatrist, telling him that he himself was planning to do similar work. He is anxious to please and is respectful. He was described as a little boy. Later on, the analyst mentioned that there are no recent traumatic situations. He has had some difficulties in the past but seems to be coping quite well at the present time.

We felt that the interviewer had a positive feeling about the subject and that he appreciated the cooperation and admiration which the subject had for him. It was evident that he was not going to have any explicit or implicit demands put upon him. At the end, he might have wished to continue a relationship with the subject, but neither of them could think of any reason for doing so.

The degree of interview intimacy and positive feeling in the appendectomy group was somewhere between the degrees of closeness noted in the accident and suicide attempt groups. In the suicide attempt group, there was a close, dependent relationship. In the accident group, there was a cool, warding-off relationship. This coolness emanated from the subjects and was responded to in kind by the analysts.

In the accident group, our feeling was that the analysts conducted their interviews, responded to the "coolness" of the subjects, and were rather relieved to bid adieu to them.

In the suicide attempt group, the analysts were, during the series of interviews, drawn quite close to, in fact, *into* the lives of the subjects. This was accompanied by feelings of being engulfed by the subjects and their problems. The analysts wished them well, tried to get help for them, and wanted to escape their clutches.

The appendectomies constituted an interesting group of subjects who related well. The analysts enjoyed their contacts with them. Since neither the subjects nor the analysts felt that there was any great need for further psychiatric help, they were able to say goodbye with a mutual feeling of satisfaction and no regrets.

REFERENCES

1. Litman, Robert E. and Norman Tabachnick: Psychoanalytic theories of suicide. In *Suicidal Behaviors: Diagnosis and Management* (H. L. P. Resnik, Ed.). Boston, Little, Brown and Co., 1968.
2. Menninger, K. A.: *Man Against Himself.* New York, Harcourt, Brace and Co., 1938.
3. Tabachnick, Norman and Norman L. Farberow: Emergency evaluation of self-destructive potentiality. In *The Cry for Help* (Farberow and Shneidman, Eds.). New York, McGraw-Hill Book Co., 1961.

CHAPTER 9

THE BIAS STUDY
Summary

The bias study focused on three questions: (1) Did the psycho-analytic interviewers as a group demonstrate biases or beliefs held in common? (2) If pre-existing attitudes existed in the group of interviewers, was there a correspondence between these pre-existing attitudes and the data which each reviewer reported? And (3) after the clinical interviewing was completed, were there any changes in the biases or beliefs of the interviewers?

The answers to these questions were (1): The psychoanalytic interviewers as a group did demonstrate biases or beliefs. (2) There was not a correspondence between these pre-existing attitudes and the data which each interviewer reported. That is, data contrary to the biases of the interviewers were elicited in this study. (3) After the clinical interviewing was completed, there were no significant changes in the biases or beliefs of the interviewers. Even though they had elicited and reported data which contradicted their biases, they maintained their original beliefs.

W_HAT DO WE MEAN_ by "interviewer bias," and how were we concerned with it in this research? The issue arises when we consider the task of the interviewer. He explored the hypotheses of our study during psychoanalytic interviews with the subjects. From this experience, he was asked to gather data and make judgments about the subjects which he reported on a structured data sheet. In this study, the interviewer was aware of the event which precipitated hospitalization for each subject. As a result, bias might easily influence the data he elicited and reported. We define *bias* as attitudes or preconceptualizations or hypotheses of the interviewer which relate to the phenomena under study.

These biases, if present, may or may not influence the findings of the study.

THE PROBLEM OF BIAS

There have been a number of previous reviews and researches dealing with interviewer bias. Matarazzo[1] reviewed studies of interviewer bias in the area of social science research. Hollingworth[2] and others demonstrated interviewer bias operating in employment situations. More to the specific point of our study, Rice[3] reported interviewer bias among twelve trained social workers as they evaluated applicants for social welfare. It was found that the interviewers' feelings about the ill effects of drinking and their feelings about the social system influenced their response to a group of drinkers. Hyman et al.[4] reported age and sex of the interviewers as a source of bias.

More relevant to our accident research are the findings of Raines and Rohrer.[5, 6] They studied the role of interviewer bias in psychiatric interviews. In their first study, using nine experienced Navy psychiatrists, they reached two conclusions: (1) Two psychiatrists, each interviewing the same man, observed different personality traits in this man and also reported different dominant defense mechanisms used by him in his everyday behavior. And (2) any given psychiatrist had a preferred personality type classification which he utilized more frequently than on a chance basis, with different psychiatrists preferring different personality type categories. When five of the psychiatrists re-interviewed the subjects five weeks later (no psychiatrist interviewing the man he had previously seen), the same biases persisted.

The authors concluded that a clinical interviewer's subject served as a projective device for the interviewer and reflected significant aspects of the psychiatrist's own personality. They felt that each psychiatrist's own life experiences made him more sensitive to certain facets of the patient's dynamics and led him to perceptually distort other facets of the patient's psychology.

In their second study, Raines and Rohrer asked psychiatrists to make independent assessment of interviewers. This study demonstrated a correlation between independently judged facets of the personality of the interviewer and the interviewer's reports of his subjects.

In our study, bias might play a role during the psychoanalytic interviewing of the subjects. Bias might be influential not only during the *data-gathering* but in the way *the data was reported* as well. Primarily a structured data sheet was used by the interviewer to make public the findings of the interview. Bias was controlled for and measured during this study, as reported below.

Controlling Interviewer Bias

It is likely that the psychoanalytic training of the interviewers provided one control of bias in this study. A fundamental tenet of the psychoanalytic method is that the analyst's awareness of his own conscious and unconscious biases allow him to make patient-centered observations. In spite of this control, however, the interviewer's bias might significantly influence the findings of this study.

Further control over bias was provided by the design and development of the data sheet. Most of the items required structured, objective answers in an attempt to minimize or eliminate ambiguous responses and highly interpretive data. Research with projective techniques[7, 8] has amply illustrated that individual bias is more evident in responses to unstructured stimuli.

The inter-rater reliability of the items in the data sheet provides another control of bias. All research interviews were voice-recorded, and each interviewer's data sheet answers were compared with independent ratings of the recorded interviews. On this basis, as the research plan was developed, items were changed or eliminated with the goal of using only the highly reliable items.

For each of the 205 items on the data sheet, the percent agreement between the answer given by the interviewer and those of independent raters was calculated. Table XXI shows the average (mean) percent agreement between interviewers and independent raters, over all items, at the conclusion of the data-gathering.

TABLE XXI

AVERAGE (MEAN) PERCENT) AGREEMENT

Actual accident cases (n = 25)	77%
Actual suicide cases (n = 29)	76%
Actual appendectomy cases (n = 31)	78%
Overall cases (n = 85)	77%

Analysis of variance of the interviewer-rater percent agreement showed that any differences were not statistically significant. What this means is that the answers given by interviewers filling out the data sheet were very much in agreement with answers of the raters who listened to the interviews on tape and completed the data sheet independently.

Since the raters and the interviewers were different in a number of ways—for example, educational achievement, specific training and experience, degree of involvement with the study, etc.—the following inference is plausible. The high degree of agreement between raters and interviewers indicates that interviewer bias did not influence the findings of the study. However, the possibility must be considered that despite the differences between the interviewers and the raters, they shared a common bias in regard to the hypotheses of the study. This common bias might have accounted for the high degree of agreement.

Measuring Interviewer Bias

There were three questions which we evaluated in regard to issues of bias: (1) Did the psychoanalytic interviewers as a group demonstrate biases or preconceptions held in common? (2) If pre-existing attitudes existed in the group of interviewers, was there a correspondence between those attitudes and the data which the interviewers reported? And (3) after the clinical interviewing was completed, were there any changes in the biases or preconceptions of the interviewers?

The method which obtained data to answer these questions is detailed in Section E (Interviewer Bias Study) of the Method chapter (Chapter 4). In essence, this method consisted of having each psychoanalytic interviewer complete a data sheet for a hypothetical subject from each of the experimental categories before the clinical interviewing began. This procedure was repeated after all the clinical data was gathered but before the results of its evaluation were known. These hypothetical evaluations were compared with the data resulting from interviews with the experimental subjects to arrive at conclusions regarding bias.

To what extent did the interviewers begin the study with a shared conceptual bias about the subjects whom they were to interview? Table XXII shows the average (mean) percent agreement among all psychoanalytic interviewers for their initial description of hypothetical accident, suicide and appendectomy subjects.

There was a good deal of agreement among the interviewers' descriptions of hypothetical subjects. In large measure, interviewers began the project with shared conceptual biases about a prototypic accident subject, suicide subject and appendectomy subject.

Was there a correspondence between the interviewers' preconceptualizations and what they actually found during the research interviews? Table XXIII shows rank order correlations (Rhos) between the percent agreement among interviewers on hypothetical cases with their agreement on the actual cases.

These correlations were all statistically non-significant, indicat-

TABLE XXII

AVERAGE (MEAN) PERCENT AGREEMENT
(Before Interviewing Actual Subjects)

Hypothetical accident cases (n = 16) 60%
Hypothetical suicide cases (n = 16) 62%
Hypothetical appendectomy cases (n = 16) 75%

TABLE XXIII

RANK ORDER CORRELATION (Rho)

Hypothetical vs. actual accident cases .... .08 (not significant)
Hypothetical vs. actual suicide cases .... .13 (not significant)
Hypothetical vs. actual appendectomy cases ..... .11 (not significant)

ing that there was very little agreement between the interviewers' initial bias and the descriptions of actual subjects. Apparently the initial bias had not been imposed upon the actual data.

In order to assess in more detail the correspondence between the interviewers' answers about hypothetical subjects and the data from actual subjects, comparisons were made item by item for the entire data sheet. Table XXIV shows the number of items which interviewers judged to discriminate between accident, suicide and appendectomy subjects, the number of items which *actually* discriminated between the subjects, and the number of items which discriminated both the hypothetical and actual subjects.

It can be seen that the interviewers judged a large number of items differentially among hypothetical accident, suicide and appendectomy subjects. In fact, among actual subjects during the research, only 40 items differentiated among the three experimental groups. Only 27 items, which were judged significant among hypothetical subjects, turned out to be significant among the actual subjects. This finding further substantiates the discrepancy between the interviewers' initial bias and the empirical findings with actual subjects. An inspection of the items themselves reveal that hypothetical accident subjects were described by the interviewers as similar to hypothetical suicide subjects and quite different from hypothetical appendectomy subjects. This is in contradistinction to the main findings of the research. Ratings of the actual subjects showed similarity between the accident and appendectomy subjects; both groups were different from the suicide group.

Had the interviewers' initial bias been influenced by the actual interviewing experience? As noted above, interviewers completed

TABLE XXIV

NUMBER OF ITEMS JUDGED TO DISCRIMINATE BETWEEN
ACCIDENT, SUICIDE AND APPENDECTOMY SUBJECTS

Hypothetical subjects (before interviewing actual subjects)	126
Actual subjects	40
Characteristic of both hypothetical and actual subjects	27

data sheets for hypothetical subjects once again upon completion of their interviews with actual subjects. When these data sheets were compared with the original hypothetical ratings completed before the actual interviewing was initiated, no statistically significant changes had occurred (using an Analysis of Variance test). In spite of their experience with actual subjects which produced findings to challenge their initial biases, interviewers maintained their initial biases substantially unchanged.

DISCUSSION

It was not surprising that the psychoanalytic interviewers entered the experimental situation with shared conceptual biases about subjects whom they were to interview. In addition to rather homogeneous professional background and training, all of the psychoanalytic interviewers were members of the same Training Institute, and many participated in a research seminar studying automobile accident in the context of developing a more general psychoanalytic theory of action. Initial agreement about hypothetical appendectomy cases was even closer than the agreement among hypothetical accident and hypothetical suicide attempt cases. Examining the individual items, it seemed that the reason for the consistency among interviewers (their initial bias) toward appendectomy cases was the fact that most of the items on the data sheet were in a pathologic direction, and most of the interviewers gave "No" answers for hypothetical appendectomy cases. This meant that the interviewers came to the study with the belief that appendectomy subjects would show little psychopathology, which resulted in consistent answers among interviewers on the data sheet.

Interviewers had the initial bias that accident subjects would be more similar to suicide attempt subjects than to appendectomy subjects. They believed that strong self-destructive personality factors characterized accident victims, were important in the etiology of the accident, and were analogues of components of the suicidal state. There had been prior research evidence to support these opinions.[9, 10, 11] In fact, during actual research interviewing, the interviewers were confronted with subjects who gave little evidence to support the initial biases. This was reported by the interviewers on the data sheet, although contrary to their biases.

How did the interviewers conceptualize the discrepancy between the empirical data of this study and their initial biases? When bias was measured once again upon completion of the research, it had changed little from the initial position. This finding was supported during debriefing meetings with the interviewers. Most interviewers felt that self-destructive components are to be found among accident subjects in spite of the negative indications of this in the research. They felt that the data sheet itself had inhibited the finding of self-destructive trends among accident subjects by failing to capture and make public the deeper and more important dimensions of their psychoanalytic interviews.

What are the implications of these findings?

1. First, they indicate that analysts do enter research studies of this type with certain preconceptualizations or sets of "biases."

2. Even though they develop and report data which contradicts those biases, they have a tendency to *retain* them. Both of these points are important. The finding that our analysts were actually able to develop data that countered their preconceptualization speaks well for their personal objectivity as well as the psychoanalytic method of training and the psychoanalytic method of evaluating data.

Interesting and possibly of more concern, however, is our finding that the preconceptualizations or biases did not change although contrary data was elicited. This suggests that in the interval between observing and reporting data and assimilating its meaning, there is an opportunity for distortion of the meaning of data.

3. Bearing on the above point, however, is the actual experience of this research study. By utilizing fairly rigorous and empirical methods, we may have been able to affect a more meaningful interpretation of the data than if such methods had not been utilized.

4. What we observed in this bias study may be equally true of other social scientists and their interviewing. Indeed, these same phenomena may occur in all human beings as they elicit and interpret data.

REFERENCES

1. Matarazzo, Joseph B.: The interview. In *The Handbook of Clinical Psychology* (Benjamin B. Wolman, Ed.). New York, McGraw-Hill, 1965.
2. Hollingworth, H. L.: *Judging Human Character*. New York, Appleton and Croft, 1922.
3. Rice, S.: Contagious bias in the interview: A methodological note, *Amer J Sociol, 35:*420-423, 1929.
4. Hyman, H. H.: *Interviewing in Social Research*. Chicago, University of Chicago Press, 1954.
5. Raines, J. N. and J. H. Rohrer: The operational matrix of psychiatric practice: Consistency and variability in interview impressions in different psychiatrists. *Am J Psychiatry, 111:*721-733, 1955.
6. Raines, J. N. and J. H. Rohrer: The operational matrix of psychiatric practice: Variability in psychiatric impressions and the projection hypothesis, *Am J Psychiatry, 117:*133-139, 1960.
7. Bell, J. E.: *Projective Techniques*. New York, Longmans, Green and Company, 1948.
8. Ainsworth, M. A.: Problems of validation in developments in the Rorschach technique. In *Technique and Theory*, Vol. 1 (B. Klopfer et al, Eds.). New York, World Book Company, 1954.
9. Tabachnick, Norman: The psychology of fatal accident. In *Essays in Self-Destruction* (E. Shneidman, Ed.). New York, Science House, Inc., 1967.
10. Litman, Robert E. and Norman Tabachnick: Fatal one-car accidents, *Psychoanal Q, 36:*248-259, 1967.
11. Tabachnick, Norman, et al: Comparative psychiatric study of accidental and suicidal death, *Arch Gen Psychiatry, 14:*60-68, Jan. 1966.

CHAPTER 10

DEBRIEFING THE PSYCHOANALYSTS

Summary

At the conclusion of their interviewing, the psychoanalysts who obtained data for us were "debriefed." A member of the Central Research Group discussed with them their experiences and reactions to the research.

The material was dealt with in terms of the interviewers' responses to eight general questions. These questions dealt with their personal reactions to the study, their thoughts as to its value and shortcomings, and their suggestions for future research stemming from this study.

In addition to these data, there was an opportunity to obtain supplementary material in regard to some of the other formal sections of the research (more specifically, the bias study).

SIXTEEN PSYCHOANALYTIC CLINICIANS participated in this research study. The experience was a relatively novel one for most of them. What reactions did the analysts have to their participation in the research?

We had questions both about the practicalities of utilizing our method and the analysts' theoretical impressions and reactions. During the course of the data-gathering, we formalized our inquiries into eight broad questions. At the conclusion of the data-gathering phase of the study, we had a "debriefing" session with each of the clinicians during which their responses to the questions were obtained. This material not only has intrinsic interest but also provides data which may illuminate other parts of our research (for example, the bias study).

148

QUESTIONS AND ANSWERS

Because of the way in which the data was obtained, it seemed most appropriate to deal with it in an impressionistic manner. What is now presented are our eight questions, each followed by a summary of the analysts' responses.

I. *Did you enjoy working in this project? What do you feel about the value of the project as a type of psychoanalytic research and in regard to its elucidating self-destructive factors in automobile accident?*

All of the clinical investigators enjoyed their participation in the project. However, the reasons for their enjoyment varied. A number felt that the project dealt with an important theoretical issue and was thus worthy of their effort. Some of them also felt that the individual case work stimulated new thoughts about self-destructiveness or opened up new techniques of interviewing. For example, several mentioned that dealing with subjects who did not consider themselves psychiatric patients in the usual sense brought about considerations of how they (the analysts) could establish a data-gathering relationship with non-patients.

Others became interested in problems of research method. For example, a number focused on the Data Sheet. Some felt it was a valuable adjunct in obtaining data. Others felt that it interfered with their utilization of the free-floating interview. What we stress is the analysts' gratification at the opportunity of testing and then discussing the value of this interviewing tool.

The group was almost equally divided in regard to the project's value as psychoanalytic research. About half were highly positive. The other half, although expressing the opinion that it was a valuable piece of *psychiatric* research, indicated that they felt it had shortcomings as *psychoanalytic* research.

Those who were positive made the following points:

1. The study was comprehensive and rigorous. It attempted to get detailed data on a number of hypotheses and was successful in doing this.

2. The use of psychoanalysts as interviewers was laudable.

They could pick up nuances in the material and make evaluations of it which were important. For example, they could evaluate distortions due to defense mechanisms or note the effects of repressed emotions.

3. One analyst commented that the use of both specific questioning and free-floating interviewing was excellent for gathering data from a large group of subjects. Some of these might be more talkative and some less cooperative.

The following reservations were raised about the psychoanalytic methodology:

1. There was an insufficient opportunity to deal with the traditional data of the psychoanalytic interview. With the emphasis on the Data Sheet, the development of transference and the noting of resistances and defenses received short shrift.

2. The project involved too many variables. One or two interviewers felt that they were lost in the immensity of the project. Others felt that they saw so few total subjects that they had insufficient data to draw their own conclusions regarding the hypotheses of the study.

3. Questions were raised about the extrapolation of the results to the general issue of self-destructiveness in accidents. For example, one interviewer pointed out that we studied just one end of the social class spectrum. "Could we," he asked, "generalize from this group to the entire population? Might it not be that what we are finding is characteristic only of the social classes which we studied?"

II. *What were your feelings about the methodology of the project?*

A minority of the interviewers felt quite comfortable with the method. All of those who did feel comfortable mentioned that they had previous experience with similar types of interviewing. For example, they had worked in a crisis unit at a hospital, had utilized a similar technique in the Army, or routinely asked many questions in their first interview with office patients.

Many of the interviewers indicated that they had difficulties in adjusting to the different physical conditions of the hospital interview. The noise and lack of privacy were two important problems. Another less important problem was adjusting to the recording machinery. (We utilized a small tape recorder with necklace microphones for interviewer and subject.) It was also a petty annoyance that the tape recorder needed occasional attention for verifying that it was in working order and for changing tapes.

A number of additional difficulties and problems were mentioned: One interviewer said that the patients were difficult to deal with because of their socioeconomic class. "They felt strange and different." One interviewer stated that he felt guilty and uncomfortable about the interviewing. He felt that he was exploiting the subjects. Because of this, he found it difficult to maintain an analytic stance. He had a strong feeling of having to give the patients something for his "exploitation" of them.

Another interviewer raised questions about the freedom which the interviewers had to spend as much time as they wished with each subject. He felt that this made for biased obtaining or interpreting of material. He dealt with the problem by trying to keep the number of hours for each subject standard.

Two interviewers mentioned that they were somewhat uncomfortable with the method because there were two parts to it: the interpretation of the data and the answering of the questions on the Data Sheet. Both added that they did not feel the task to be insuperable.

III. *What are your thoughts about the research design?*

A number of clinicians felt that the project was innovative in its design. One said that he thought it was a pioneering effort of serious and systematic psychoanalytic investigation. Another felt that it was important that we worked with non-patients. This was a relatively new group for psychoanalytic study.

However, others felt that the project demanded less from them than they could potentially give. These interviewers felt that they were able to construct detailed psychoanalytic formulations by listening to and interviewing patients in the traditional psychoanalytic way. They felt that less well-trained interviewers, questioners, in fact, could have done as well as they did.

There were some suggestions for additional data-gathering

methods. One interviewer suggested the use of projective tests. Another mentioned the Data Sheet was strongly slanted toward the hypotheses of the study and therefore questioned whether the results would be valid. He suggested a larger data sheet with more hypotheses.

IV. *How did your thinking change during the course of your work?*

A minority of the interviewers said their thinking did not change during the study. However, most of the interviewers did note changes in their thinking. These changes can be conveniently taken up under two headings, those dealing with the method and those dealing with theory.

There were several types of initial discomfort with the *method:* the discomfort of having to go into a general hospital, of having to work in an open ward, of having to be closely tied to the patient during the course of the interview. The most important discomfort had to do with the utilization of the Data Sheet. A number of analysts had initial difficulty in reconciling that more specific and questioning approach with their preferred way of obtaining data.

During the course of the study, all of these discomforts except one were mastered by the analysts. The one exception was one analyst's feelings that the Data Sheet increasingly interfered with his obtaining "good" data.

Some *theories* held by the analyst interviewers changed during the course of the research. One clinician stated that the theories that he had about accident were reinforced. He had originally had the notion that accidents were heavily loaded with suicidal intent. He also believed that both suicides and accidents came about as a result of changes in life style and that appendectomies were not significantly related to psychological issues. All of these feelings were reinforced during the study.

One worker started the study with the impression that at least some accidents were unconnected with psychological predisposing or precipitating factors. As the study progressed, he began to feel more strongly that accidents represent the acting-out part of the conflict between dependence and independence or hostility and love-dependence and that the accident helped resolve the conflict.

V. *Did you develop any original theories which were not dealt with in the hypotheses of the study?*

Several interviewers did develop new theories. Some of these have already been mentioned. In addition, the following were presented in answer to this question. It was suggested that in addition to acting on suicidal or self-destructive feelings, accidents may represent an acting-out of homicidal impulses or defenses against them. Another new hypothesis: The accident individual is someone very close to his family who has increasing feelings of depression as he tries to make an independent way in the world. These depressive feelings are warded off by aimless behavior and, as a result, accidents occur.

One analyst suggested that certain individuals in the grip of strong suicidal feelings have a strong need to act and that this action is an attempt to block out feelings of restriction.

VI. *Do you think that there were any biases with which you approached the project and any biases that you had about the different subject groups?*

Only two of the interviewers felt that they had no biases. The others mentioned a variety of biases in regard to the project as a whole and in regard to the different subject groups.

First, what were their biases about the project as a whole? Several felt the research was importantly limited by its exclusive use of county hospital patients. These patients, in general, were not psychologically oriented or introspective. Another limitation of a number of the county hospital patients was their poor grasp of English. It was felt that using populations in addition to the county hospital one would help provide a picture of the entities which we studied across the whole socioeconomic sphere and that this would add to the study.

In regard to the subject groups, the following biases were noted:

1. Many of the interviewers felt that the appendectomy group

would not have any characteristic dynamics or that they would be normal. They believed that they would therefore make less of an effort to look for psychological factors in those cases.

2. There was a fairly general agreement that the suicide cases would be individuals who were depressed and who dynamically would be noted to have hostility or aggression turned inward.

3. The accidents were felt to be individuals who would have high degrees of outwardly directed hostility, impulsiveness, alcohol and drug use.

4. One interviewer felt that accidents were just accidents.

5. One interviewer felt that accidents and suicides were equivalent.

Although we did not specifically ask for it, a number of interviewers (3) volunteered the opinion that although they were aware of biases in their feelings about the various groups, they did not feel that such biases affected their eliciting of information.

VII. *Would you like to have seen the project designed differently?*

There were a great number of suggestions as to different methods which might be used in such a project. It seemed that working on this research helped stimulate creativity in regard to designing research.

There were two suggestions which were made frequently:

1. Several clinicians stated that the project was too "cold." They were referring to the use of the Data Sheet. A number of the accompanying suggestions had to do with allowing more opportunity for free-floating interviews, Data Sheets that were less structured, Data Sheets that focused more on what the specific dynamics in each group were.

2. Several interviewers asked for a middle class population. One wanted this because he felt such a group would be more psychologically oriented. Another stated that he felt there would be a greater difference between accident and suicide groups in middle socioeconomic groups than in the ones which we actually utilized during this study.

Other suggestions included:

1. Formulating questions to gain a knowledge of other areas of ego functioning and object relationships.

2. The number of hours the patients were seen might have been standardized.

3. The questionnaire should have been more structured.

4. There should have been a more formal outline to be followed in dictating the dynamics.

5. There should be a follow-up study of the subjects five years later to see if there had been significant differences in their life styles.

6. The tape interviews should be evaluated after the references to the specific subject type are eliminated to see if listeners can accurately identify the subject type.

7. Investigators other than psychoanalysts could do the interviewing.

VIII. *What future research do you think could follow from this experience?*

The majority of the interviewers had no answer to this question. We believe that this reflects their reluctance to think of themselves as researchers. Note the many suggestions for extension of this research into contiguous areas or new ways of doing this research which were detailed in earlier parts of this chapter. However, two hypotheses for future investigation were volunteered specifically in answer to this question:

1. Certain people make a conscious and action-oriented adaptation to a "life script" and follow it even to the extent of killing themselves.

2. Suicidal victims tend to be very conscious of the problems in their life situations, whereas accident victims are quite unconscious of the problems in their life situations. As accident victims attempt to contemplate their problems, they tend to have accidents. The accidents help resolve these problems.

CONCLUSIONS

A few general conclusions can be drawn from the data in this chapter:

1. The analysts in this study found our methods to be somewhat strange and some were disconcerted by them.

2. Most managed to reach a working agreement with the methods.

3. Most found their work on the project worthwhile and stimulating.

4. Many questions were raised about the method, and many suggestions which might have added to the value of this study were made.

5. Ideas for new research came from the work on this project.

CHAPTER 11

THE SIGNIFICANT OTHER STUDY

Summary

As an added dimension of our study, a small number of significant others of subjects in each of the three experimental groups —the critical accident group, the suicide attempt group, and the post-appendectomy group—were interviewed. The main evaluations made in this study were in answer to the following questions:

1. To what degree does the subject answer similar questions in the same way as his designated significant other? Are there any differences among the three experimental groups in this regard?

2. How does the significant other evaluate changes in his life and in the life of the subject prior to the hospitalization? Again, are there any differences among the three groups in this regard?

3. How did the significant others explain the event that brought the experimental subject into the hospital?

4. How did the significant others judge the experimental subjects in terms of a number of human qualities?

5. Were there characteristics that differentiated the significant others of the three subject groups?

The most important findings in this study were these:

1. The general percent of agreement on similar questions between subjects and significant others was moderately high in all three groups. Suicide attempt subjects and their significant others, however, demonstrated a lesser degree of agreement than subjects and significant others in the other two groups.

2. There was a slight tendency for significant others of suicide attempt subjects to judge that those subjects had more recent changes in their lives to a greater degree than significant others in the other two groups.

3. There was a slight tendency for significant others of suicide attempt subjects to note more recent changes in the relationship between the two than was true of similar evaluations in the other two groups.

4. The significant others of the accident victims perceived more recent change in their own lives than the significant others in the other two groups.

5. In regard to the kind of force which produced the event that led to hospitalization:

   a. In the appendectomy group, all significant others judged that unexplained forces produced the event.
   b. In the accident group, most significant others attributed the event to forces within the subject.
   c. In the suicide attempt group, most significant others attributed the event to forces outside of the subject.

6. In regard to three characteristics, the researchers judged the significant others of the suicide attempt subjects to be different than the significant others of the other two groups. These characteristics were as follows:

   a. They showed more neurotic traits.
   b. They had a poorer relationship to the subjects.
   c. They were more "friendly" to the subjects.
Some interpretation of these data are provided.

MOST OF OUR RESEARCH utilized data derived from interviewing subjects who were the victims of accident injuries, suicide attempts or appendectomies. However, these people live in interrelationship with others. We therefore hoped to add another dimension to our study by interviewing "significant others" of our subjects.

The "significant others" were people who were designated by the individuals in the three subject groups. They included five wives, three mothers, two fathers, two girl friends, three male friends, one guardian and one sister. The relationships of the significant others to the subjects varied among the three groups so that a specific kind of significant other—i.e., wife—was more present in one group than in others. The details of how the significant others were selected, as well as other aspects of the method used in this study, are reported in Chapter 4 under the heading: The Significant Other Study.

Since the total number of subjects interviewed was small, the data that was obtained must be considered, for the most part, not amenable to statistical comparison. In the majority of evaluations, only trends can be noted. In a few situations, we have findings which are statistically significant.

RESULTS OF STUDY

1. To what degree did the experimental subject answer questions *in the same way* as the "significant other"? There were a total of 19 items administered to each of the 18 significant others, which had also been evaluated in regard to the experimental subjects. A percent of agreement was run to determine similarity of response on each question between the subject and the significant other.

The three groups—accident, suicide attempt and appendectomy—differed in terms of the percent agreement. The results of this evaluation were as follows:

PERCENT OF AGREEMENT

Accident Group	65.8%
Suicide Attempt Group	52.6%
Appendectomy Group	66.6%

When this data is subjected to the Chi Square evaluation, a Chi Square of 5.96 emerges. This makes the above data significant at the .05 level. What this means is that there is a lower response agreement for similar items among suicide attempt subjects and their significant others, than for the other two experimental groups and their significant others.

The highest percent agreement items were on issues of suicide and accident, and this was true for all three groups. The questions on suicide and accident yielded .72 and .83 agreement respectively.

Those items that had the lowest percent agreement were the ones dealing with the subject having seen a physician recently and having trouble with the law. These yielded .44 and .50 respectively.

2. What changes occurred in the life of the subject and the significant other *prior* to the hospitalization event?

    a. There was a slight tendency for the significant others of the suicide attempt victims to feel that those victims had more recent changes in their lives than was the case in the evaluations of the significant others of the accident and appendectomy subjects. This was not statistically significant.

    b. Were there recent changes in the relationship between the subject and his significant other? Again, there was a tendency for the suicide attempt victim's significant other to perceive more recent changes in the relationship of the two than was true in the interaction between the accident and appendectomy subjects and their significant others. There was no statistical significance.

    c. Did the significant others perceive recent changes in their own lives? The accident victims' significant others perceived more recent changes in their lives than was true with the other two groups. This data, when evaluated by analysis of variance, reached the .10 level of confidence ($F = 2.70$ with two degrees of freedom). This does not quite reach the level of statistical significance.

3. How did the significant others *explain* the event that befell the subject? The informants were asked to explain what they believed caused the event that brought the subject into the hospital. The explanations were then coded into three categories:

    a. The subject himself produced the event.

    b. Unexplained forces produced the event.

    c. Stresses coming from outside of the subject produced the event.

In the appendectomy group, all significant others felt that unexplained forces produced the hospitalization event. An example of an "unexplained force" is as follows: The significant other of an appendectomy patient stated, "It was strange. One minute he was fine and then the pain started, just sort of happened."

In the accident group, four persons felt that the subject himself caused the event which led to hospitalization, while two significant others saw it as an outside stress.

An example of the subject himself causing the event: A significant other of an accident subject stated, "What does he expect to happen if he drinks and takes 'reds' and then tries to drive? He's lucky he's not dead."

An example of stresses outside of the subject: A significant other of an accident subject stated, "Well, he couldn't very well help it. This kid ran into the street and he had to swerve his car."

In the suicide attempt group, one significant other saw the event as being caused by the subject himself. One significant other felt that an unexplained force produced the hospitalization event, and four significant others judged the hospitalization event to have been produced by outside forces.

An example of stresses outside the subject: The significant other of a suicide attempt subject stated, "First his girl friend walked out on him, then he lost his job. It's no wonder he tried to kill himself."

4. How did the interviewers in the significant other study *evaluate* the significant others in terms of a number of functions? The interviewers were asked to judge the informants in regard to a number of characteristics. There were three of these characteristics which demonstrated that suicide attempt subjects' significant others were different than the significant others of the other two groups:

    a. The suicide attempt subjects' significant others were judged as having more neurotic traits than the significant others in the other two groups.

    b. In the suicide attempt group, the relationship of the significant others to the subjects was judged poorer than was true of the relationships between significant others and subjects in the other two groups. "Poorer" meant that there were less designations of the subjects as being good, acceptable individuals, and people capable of doing things which produced pleasant and approving responses in the significant others.

c. The significant others of the suicide attempt group were judged as being more friendly than the significant others in the other two groups.

DISCUSSION OF FINDINGS

What interpretations can be made of these findings? First, let us note that there is a moderate degree of agreement between subjects and significant others over *all* three groups in regard to the way they respond to the same question. That is, if we were to call a low percent of agreement under 30 per cent, and a high percent of agreement over 60 per cent, then the overall percent of agreement of all three groups is at the borderline between *moderate* and *high*.

However, there is a statistically significant difference which differentiates the suicide attempt group from the other two groups. That difference is that suicide attempt subjects agree less on the same items with their significant others than is true of accident and appendectomy subjects.

It is possible that such a difference might be due to suicide attempt subjects' significant others not being as close to the suicide attempt victims as would be true of the relationship between significant others and subjects in the other two groups. However, our interviewing form was constructed so that a significant other who was *not* close to a subject and thus did not know much about him, could say so. As a result, such an informant's answers would *not* affect the percent agreement results. Our impression is that not knowing the subject well was not a significant factor in producing this result. Rather we believe that there was, in fact, a greater difference in perceiving or understanding the same event in the suicide attempt group as compared to the other two groups.

Characteristic Reactions of "Significant Others"

Now let us review and evaluate some of the other results of this study. In general, these results support the notion that significant others of suicide attempt subjects respond differently and are evaluated as being different (by our interviewers) on a number of issues than is true of the significant others of the other two groups.

Let us focus on the relationship between significant others and subjects. Recall that the significant others of the suicide attempt subjects reported more recent changes in the relationship between themselves and the subjects. They also reported a greater number of recent changes in the subject's life than the significant others of the other two groups. However, when significant others are asked about changes in their own lives, the suicide attempt group's significant others do not report a greater number of changes than occur in the appendectomy group (according to the appendectomy significant others). Interestingly, in response to this question, it is the accident group's significant others who report a greater number of changes than the other two groups.

One explanation that incorporates all of these findings is the following: The significant other of the suicide attempt subject is saying, "Something was happening recently with *him* that caused something to change within *our relationship,* but that was unrelated to anything going on with me."

This concept is supported by some of the observational comments that appear on the schedule protocols. Here are two examples:

A wife commented, "Just before the suicide attempt, we were hardly talking to each other, but it had been building up for a long time. He got really into himself and cranky. I just couldn't talk with him."

Similarly a father commented about the suicide attempt of his son, "We used to get along fine, but when he went away to college, he really changed. I don't know if it was his friends or drugs or what, but we just couldn't be together five minutes without fighting."

Interviewers' Interpretations of the "Significant Others"

Now some interpretations regarding the judgments which the interviewers made of the significant others. Let us recall that although the significant others of the suicide attempt subjects were seen as being friendlier to those subjects, the interviewers also judged them as having a poorer relationship with the subject and as having more neurotic traits than was true of the significant others in the accident and appendectomy groups. This suggests that suicide occurs in interpersonal contexts where people are close but have a tense and strained relationship and, as a result, neurotic manifestations are evident.

This has been known for a long time. What is interesting in our study is that we did not find similar situations occurring in the accident group. Thus, again, we could not support the hypothesis that accidents are like suicides.

Why don't the significant others of the suicide attempt group believe that the suicide attempt was caused by something within the suicide attempt subjects? (It will be recalled that the accident group's significant others attributed the cause of the accident to the victims, but the suicide attempt group's significant others attributed the cause of the suicide attempt to outside forces.)

Perhaps the suicide attempt group's significant others, although they believe that there are definitely changes which are occurring to the suicide attempt victims and to the relationship between those victims and themselves, cannot bring themselves to point the finger of blame at the suicide attempt victims. This may be because the significant others are more friendly, because the suicide attempt victims present a more helpless and forlorn attitude, or to some combination of these two factors. Another explanation may be this: The significant others of the suicide attempt victims feel guilty and responsible for what has happened. They want to deny that something was happening *within* the suicide attempt victims themselves that led to the suicide attempt. If they allowed themselves to believe that internal unresolved conflicts existed within the victims, they might also have to acknowledge that they (the significant others) might have participated in events which led to the suicide attempt.

PART FOUR

THE
→ IMPLICATIONS ←

Chapter 12

VALIDITY IN PSYCHOANALYTIC RESEARCH

Summary

The methods of the research are examined from the standpoint of contributing to validity.

Three kinds of validity are evaluated:

1. Face validity.

2. Construct validity.

3. Validity by independent criteria.

Those features of our method which bear on validity are reviewed. They include:

1. The issue of reliability.

2. The issue of bias.

3. The utilization of psychoanalysts as objective interviewers.

4. The utilization of laymen in our research.

By way of review of the various methodological aspects of this study, an outline for one type of future psychoanalytic research is proposed at the end of this chapter.

F ROM THE BEGINNING our research has been firmly grounded in psychoanalysis. This was true of the theoretical concepts which formed our early thinking about accident and suicide. It was also true of our methodological approaches. However, we felt that psychoanalytic theory and method constituted but one approach. Psychoanalysis is only one member of a broader family of approaches to knowledge called behavioral sciences, and the behavioral sciences constitute only *one* group of approaches to man's knowledge. For this reason we wished to expand the possibilities of traditional psychoanalytic approaches. To accomplish such an expansion we developed modifications of past psychoanalytic research methods.

Each reader will have to judge for himself whether these amendments and additions produced more valuable data, but he should bear in mind that to produce more valuable and relevant data was the central aim of our methodological thinking and planning. In a word, we were attempting to reach a high degree of *validity*.

Validity is what this chapter is about. We shall comment on the problems of validity and then indicate how some of our methods may have helped achieve it. (That, of course, is too ambitious a statement: it would be more accurate to state that we attempted to achieve *a higher degree* of validity than would have been possible without those methods.)

TYPES OF VALIDITY

What *is* validity? We take it to mean that the questions one is asking about a certain phenomenon have some significant relationship to that phenomenon, that is, these questions are related in an important way and focus on important qualities of *the target phenomenon*. For example, if we are trying to understand self-destruction in accident, will we be able to say at the end of a research study that suicide *is* related in some important way to accidents in general or to certain groups of accidents? We would hope not only to be able to move towards an answer to that question but even to go beyond it and to tell *how* suicide is related to accident.

Research methodologists conceptualize different kinds of validity.

First of all there is *face* validity. This means that the relationship between the answer to a question regarding a phenomenon and the phenomenon itself are so close that the answer is "self-evident."

Two examples. If we pick up a small, hard object from the ground, someone may ask us, "What is that?" We say, "It is a stone." Our friend may ask, "How do you know it's a stone?" We might reply, "Don't be stupid. It has the shape, size, texture and density of a stone. What else could it be?" Our friend looks at the object and says, "Of course, it's a stone."

Now, for the second example. Suppose we want to find out whether a certain person was trying to kill himself. We will ask him, "Were you trying to kill yourself?" or "Were you trying to commit suicide?" We will assume that he, of course, knows what "suicide" and "killing yourself" mean and that he will answer us truthfully. If he says, "I *was* attempting suicide," we will conclude that he was doing just that.

Now it can immediately be seen that this concept of face validity is not as perfect as we might like it to be. It is implied that there are certain kinds of knowledge which are so direct and self-evident that everyone could know them. It assumes common sense—i.e., "Everybody knows that." This means that there is a general agreement on the interpretation of certain data. Also, face validity takes for granted that if a question is asked of someone, he will want to answer directly and honestly. Those assumptions can be questioned for a wide variety of reasons. However, face validity is a concept that is often utilized both in day-to-day evaluation of "what is going on" and in more formal, scientific studies which, however, are directed to the same question—"What in the world is going on?"

There are more complicated ways of arriving at validity. One method is called *construct* validity. Construct validity means that one attempts to get data on an issue by asking a series of questions about it and making predictions about the answers. As the independent questions fall into certain patterns (for example, most answers are either *yes* or *no*), a larger pattern or design is discerned. For example, in our study we were interested in the general issue of self-destruction in accident. First, we had to decide how we would define self-destruction. We ended up by defining it in terms of a number of hypotheses. Each of these hypotheses was more exactly detailed by specific questions. As it turned out, most of the hypotheses were not supported for the general group of accidents. This means that we said that if self-destruction was present in accident, then accident victims would do such and such or feel such and such. However, when we asked whether accident victims were doing those things or feeling those ways, it turned out that they were *not*. Therefore, evidence that accident victims as a group are self-destructive was not found.

A third kind of validity is *validity by independent criteria.* This means that one asks the same questions utilizing different approaches. For example, a psychiatrist may interview a patient and, through the presence of clinical signs and symptoms, establish a *diagnosis.* Then a psychologist may use the specific evaluations of the Rorschach and Thematic Apperception Test and move toward a diagnosis in *that* way. Should both workers come to *a similar conclusion,* validity by independent criteria would be established.

Various procedures of our total method attempted to support and reinforce the validity of our conclusions.

THE ISSUE OF RELIABILITY

If a number of people observe the same data and agree on their meaning, we have in our hands a *reliable* method. Here we touch on a kind of consensual agreement that is an important ingredient of validity. However, it is clear that consensual agreements do not always indicate that what is being agreed on is valid. It is possible that people may agree on something, yet they all may be wrong. We are told, for example, that at one time most people agreed that the sun and stars revolved around the earth. If our present information regarding the heavenly bodies is accurate, all those agreeable people were wrong.

Nonetheless, we did try to achieve a method with high reliability, and, in the Data Sheet part of our study (Chapter 4), we were able to do this. Thus we advanced part way toward an establishment of better validity for our results.

THE ISSUE OF BIAS

In the previous section we mentioned that a number of observors could reliably agree on something and yet it might not be so. They all could, for some reason, come to the same incorrect conclusion. One of the reasons that such a thing could happen would be that all the observers shared a certain preconception or bias—which bias, in fact, was so strong that it allowed them to disregard or misinterpret certain data which would have led to conclusions against the bias. We know that we all have values and biases which prejudice us in certain directions. We are not sure to what degree a particular bias may distort our evaluation of some phenomenon. It, therefore, would seem valuable to perform evaluations of bias in many research studies. It is to the credit of psychoanalysts and other social scientists that they have become aware of the possible influence of biases on their research studies. We must now act on that knowledge and learn how to apply it specifically to each pertinent research.

THE UTILIZATION OF LAYMEN IN PSYCHOANALYTIC STUDIES

In our reliability study, laymen were able to answer and evaluate data obtained from our subjects with the same degree of agreement among themselves as were groups of psychoanalysts and graduate psychologists. At first we were somewhat surprised by this finding (although, of course, we must have secretly believed it possible or we would not even have attempted the comparison). In reviewing the details of our method, a reasonable explanation presents itself. Although some of our concepts and our hypotheses were of a sophisticated nature, the specific questions which were utilized in the Data Sheet evaluation were not highly inferential. They tended to be concrete and specific. (Of course, there was a range from very concrete questions to more inferential ones.) Another aspect of our method was that the questions on the Data Sheet were not phrased in technical psychoanalytic language. Rather, they utilized that language which seems to be the property of most educated people.

An interesting question is raised by our finding, however: Is psychoanalysis a highly specialized way of thinking, or is it, at this point in history, merely a specialized way of talking about and conceptualizing certain generally agreed upon beliefs? Seventy years ago when psychoanalysis was in its early stages, it dealt with concepts that were new and foreign to most people. Perhaps through the years the interest in and attraction to psychoanalytic hypotheses have changed all that so that today most intelligent people (at least in this culture) really understand and believe a good deal of psychoanalytic theory.

At any rate, there is strong evidence from our study that these lay people can evaluate questions and data (at least under certain conditions) with the same degree of agreement as more highly trained psychoanalysts can. Now if that is so, a further question arises: With appropriate attention paid to the kinds of questions that would be asked and with some training in interviewing (or perhaps training in interviewing would not be necessary), could intelligent laymen obtain data with as much skill and effectiveness as trained psychoanalysts can? We believe that this is possible and we are currently designing researches which could tell us whether that belief is accurate.

In doing this, we are moving with a general societal trend in which "paraprofessionals" are developing skills which allow them to do work previously reserved for highly trained and educated specialists.

THE UTILIZATION OF PSYCHOANALYSTS AS "OBJECTIVE" INTERVIEWERS

Although, in one part of this research, psychoanalysts functioned in their traditional role as elicitors and interpreters of interviewees' verbalizations, they also performed what might have seemed a less specialized task—they acted as interviewers whose task it was to answer as many as they could of a long series of questions. We felt that such a procedure had unusual value for our study. Because of their ability to evaluate and judge defenses and resistances and because of their further ability to help diminish some of these resistances so that different affective and cognitive states could be entered upon by the interviewees, we felt that our psychoanalysts were *very special* types of interviewers indeed.

It was not only their ability in evaluating and helping overcome resistances that made them important. These professionals were able to observe, understand and communicate what those resistances were. This result, in turn, told us something about the characters of the different groups of subjects. It added, we believe, to the validity of our study to have knowledgeable, insightful participant-observers as data-gatherers.

A PROPOSAL FOR ONE TYPE OF
PSYCHOANALYTIC RESEARCH

Psychoanalytic research has moved, and will continue to move, in many directions. This is as it should be. Science should not run according to prescription or else it will lose what is, perhaps, its most important value. That value is the opportunity to be innovative, free and creative. However, science can also continue to use (sometimes with modifications) certain traditional methods which seem to have demonstrated value.

Our study was a long, complicated and expensive one. Yet, in looking back at it, it seems worthwhile to have done most of the things we did. They helped add to the validity of our findings.

For the future, then, we would say that a method something like the following would be useful in certain behavioral researches: Psychoanalysts who wish to test hypotheses should work not only with colleagues in the behavioral sciences, but also with other stimulating people, to develop those hypotheses. This is crucial because being a psychoanalyst (or being any other kind of special scientist) means restricting oneself from other types of knowledge, theory and technique. One is faced with a dilemma. It is important to make a limitation to one field of knowledge in order to learn it well. Yet, at the same time, one has separated oneself from other important fields of knowledge, and knowledge is really what it is all about—not psychoanalytic knowledge, not statistical knowledge, not sociological knowledge, but knowledge which has relevance for the human being and the human condition. So when the researches are planned, designed and executed, first of all, teams of specialists who can add to one another's abilities to look for and ferret out significant data should be utilized.

The actual investigative work can then proceed in a second direction. As a contrast to the use of trained scientists referred to above, it may be possible that individuals of relatively unsophisticated backgrounds can be utilized in certain parts of the research. We made such a utilization in the present research study, and we believe that even more utilizations of this type can be made as further concentration on this issue occurs. If research strategy is well designed and takes into account what particular groups of investigators can and cannot do, such methods can be quite fruitful.

A third ingredient of future research should be an increased utilization of the implications of interviewers' biases and pre-conceptions, with attempts made to evaluate the impact of such biases on the subject matter of the study.

A fourth ingredient of future research should be an attempt to validate findings by independent criteria. In our study, we did that kind of validating by utilizing answers to specific hypothesis-linked questions as one approach, and then utilizing the interpretations, dynamic constructions and observations on character and interpersonal relationships of psychoanalysts functioning in their traditional interpretative and evaluative mode. We added yet a third way of focusing on the same issue. That was by obtaining data from the "significant others" of the individuals in each of our subject groups.

As we followed these pathways in our research, we found that certain relatively independent criteria tended to suggest similar conclusions. At other times, however, our independent methods produced data at variance one with another. These non-concordant findings raise questions as to the "real" situation and become an important source of questioning for further research.

Chapter 13

ACCIDENT AND MENTAL ILLNESS

Summary

This chapter evaluates the findings of our own and other research which bear on the relationship of accident and mental illness.

Many previous studies have suggested that suicide and self-destructiveness are present in many accidents. Some studies have suggested that they are responsible for large numbers of accidents. Our research pointed in general in the opposite direction. However, there was a suggestion that about 20 per cent of the accident group might have certain depressive or self-destructive potentialities.

Much previous research has suggested that automobile accident is linked to character disorders and mental abnormalities in drivers at fault for accidents. Our research did not support this finding. Rather, it seemed to contradict it.

Previous research suggests that many of the drinking drivers responsible for accidents have different kinds of psychopathology. Again, our research failed to support this notion but rather contradicted it.

Possible reasons for the discrepancies between our research and other researches are suggested.

As we study the implications of our own and other research, we shall devote time to the question: Is psychiatric treatment as an accident prevention measure valid?

How important is *mental illness* in the etiology of accident and, more specifically, automobile accident? If self-destruction is deemed a form of mental illness, we can make some responses to this question from the data of our research. We spe-

175

cifically studied suicide, depression, poor responses to stress and a number of other factors which lay some claim to being called "self-destructive."

In addition to our work, many other researchers have investigated the relationship of accident to mental illness and have answered that mental illness is present in many accident victims. Thus Chapter 1 of this book—Self-Destructive Factors in Accident—detailed the findings of suicide, increased alcoholic intake, "indirect self-destruction," character disorder, and many other types of "mental illness" which have been considered to be related to accident.

WHAT IS MENTAL ILLNESS?

We feel it pertinent at this point to dwell on the meaning of "mental illness." Of course, its first definition is some aberration of the mental functioning or mind. One can be mentally abnormal in one of at least two ways. One's mental activities or mind-related activities can be significantly different from those of most people. An example would be a severely depressed person who can hardly move or eat or speak and who is convinced he is worthless and about to die. A second way in which one can be mentally ill exists when one is *judged* to be functioning less happily, efficiently, morally, etc., than *someone* thinks is appropriate. "Judged" and "someone" are italicized in the last sentence because of their crucial place in the concept of "mental illness."

The essential question is *who* decides when one is mentally ill. Sometimes both the mentally ill person and others agree on the presence of mental illness. Sometimes they disagree. In the latter disputed cases, who makes the final decision? Very often society decides that an expert in mental affairs like a psychologist or psychiatrist is the final authority. After all, such a person's education and experience qualify him as a judge.

But questions can and have been raised about this way of deciding who among us is mentally ill. Signs of mental illness are not as clearly linked to difficulty as somatic signs of illness. Most people who have a body temperature that is much different from the usual one of 98.6 degrees F. are somatically ill. But things mental possess a greater variation than things somatic. Many people who are unusual or different seem to get as much done, get it done as well and are just as happy as those who do things in the more usual manner.

Thus, it may come to pass that a psychiatrist or a psychologist will deem someone "mentally ill." Often the "mentally ill" one will disagree, and often enough (if the case is tested in court), a new psychiatrist or psychologist will differ with the first one. Indeed, from such situations many authorities believe that "mental illness" is often *not* a diagnosis but a term of social opprobrium. It may be used to coerce people away from what they are doing (their mental illness) into some behavior which society deems more meritorious or at least tolerable.

For example, society may decide that inordinate alcoholic intake or intoxication is undesirable. It may subtly exert pressure on psychiatrists and psychologists to consider such intake or intoxication to be "mental illness." Under the judgment that they are mentally ill, people who drink may be persuaded in the direction of relinquishing their drinking. (We do not object to society's considering drinking "bad," but we raise questions as to the propriety and basis of its calling drinking a "mental illness.") Szasz[1] has discussed this issue—coercion through the term "mental illness"—at length.

We raise this issue because of its pertinence in the understanding of what produces "accidents" and in evaluating suggestions for preventing them. Some researchers have found "alcoholism" and "character disorder" in increased incidence in drivers responsible for accidents. Believing that these two entities are "mental illnesses," they have proposed psychologic or psychiatric treatment for them. If the "victims" of the "mental illnesses" would agree that they are mentally ill, there is a fighting chance for psychiatric treatment to relieve them of their illness. Thus, the accident rate might, indeed, be reduced. But if the mentally ill *do not see themselves* as mentally ill, they may be opposed to treatment. Then psychiatric treatment as an accident prevention measure may be fruitless. We will return to these issues as we discuss the implications of our own and other research.

SUICIDE AND SELF-DESTRUCTIVENESS
IN ACCIDENT

A central research question in this study has been, *Are suicide and suicide-like manifestations present in a significant number of automobile accidents?* As detailed in Chapter 1, a number of previous theorizations and researches point to this possibility. Let us recapitulate the work of some key contributors. Freud[2] and Menninger[3] utilize a "death instinct" theory. This theory postulated that human beings have an instinctual drive towards self-destructiveness. They further stated that this drive could manifest itself in suicide and that in some cases the suicide might be masked or unconscious. In these latter situations, the death instinct might manifest its strength through the occurrence of an "accident."

Mosely[4] presented anecdotal experiences of possible suicide in seeming accident situations. McDonald[5] pointed to an increased incidence of past automobile accidents among hospitalized psychiatric patients. He suggested that the increased accident rate in psychiatric patients was related to their higher incidence of suicide attempts. Selzer and Payne,[6] comparing suicidal and non-suicidal psychiatric patients, found a higher rate of accident occurrence in the suicidal group. Earlier work of our research group[7] identified a number of similarities in victims of suicide and in driver victims in one-car accidents.

In the present research, we attempted to answer the question: *Is suicidal activity a measurably higher factor in automobile accidents than in a suitable comparison group postulated to be non-self-destructive?* We chose as our target group driver victims in one-car automobile accidents. We believed that this group would reveal traits of suicide and self-destructiveness if such were present. By and large, we did *not* find evidence for accidents being manifestations of suicide attempts. In addition, we did not find increased evidence of suicidal history, communication of suicidal ideas or increased suicidal risk.

Now, let us integrate our research with the other work just described. Freud and Menninger[2, 3] were theorists who discussed a *possible* sequence of events. They also set forth anecdotal data which could substantiate their theory. However, it was at all times clear that the events they were explicating could be explained by alternative theories. Therefore it became the task of subsequent research to substantiate or replace that theory.

Mosely[4] gave case histories of accident-like situations which he judged to be suicides. Many of his histories were susceptible to other interpretations, but we do not suggest that this is a major objection to Mosely's work. Indeed, we would raise no significant objections to it in its own terms. In regard to the question of how many "accident" situations are due to suicide, however, Mosely's work does not provide an answer. There may well be a number of suicides which look like "accident." The question is, *Is such a group large or small?*

McDonald and Selzer and Payne, among other researchers already referred to, presented data which suggested that people who had been suicidal had *more* accidents than those who had not been suicidal.[5, 6, 13, 16] Methodological questions regarding their research are in order. For example, in Selzer's study the accident rate was apparently determined by the statements of the subjects. It is possible that people who make suicide attempts could remember self-injurious or traumatic accidents to a greater degree than those who are not suicidal. It is also possible that suicidal individuals would fantasize past automobile accidents to a greater degree than non-suicidal subjects.

There are other methodological issues. Interviewers might be biased to believe that suicidal individuals would have more accidents, and this might subtly influence the course of the interview so that such interpretations (that is, that there were more accidents in the suicide group) would be forthcoming. Finally, we will point out that an increased frequency of two life events (in this case, suicide and accident) suggests, but does not establish, that the accidents were suicide attempts or suicide equivalents. (These comments are not made in an attempt to depreciate Selzer and Payne's research which we consider good. They are made for the purpose of evaluating the conclusion of those investigators that accidents are masked or unconscious suicide attempts. We must do this, since our research points in an opposite direction.)

The present study indicates that suicidal and self-destructive factors do not play a significant role in the occurrence of most one-car automobile accidents and, perhaps, do not play a large role in the production of automobile accidents in general. (We except self-destructive factors of a psychological nature in pedestrians who are involved in automobile accidents. Our work, in our opinion, does not sufficiently deal with problems of pedestrian victims.)

Even though our overall statistical evaluation did not discriminate a suicidal or self-destructive accident group, it is still possible that such a group existed. The answers to the questions which were used to evaluate our hypotheses came from the sum of responses for *all* subjects in each of the three experimental groups. There might have been a small, self-destructive accident group whose presence was not noted in our statistical evaluation because it was masked by trends in opposite directions by the majority of subjects in the accident group.

Here is an example of how such a possibility might have worked. Several Data Sheet questions dealt with past suicidal ideation and activity. Our total accident group might have consisted of two subgroups. One subgroup might have been a depressed suicidal one in which the "yes" answers to the suicidal questions would, on average, have been higher than the average number of "yes" answers in the appendectomy group, which was presumably non-self-destructive. However, a second accident subgroup might have successfully and convincingly *denied* a past suicidal ideation and activity. Averaging the answers of these two subgroups might have produced a numerical figure for the entire accident group not statistically different from the figure for the entire appendectomy group.

Some support for this possibility is found in material from the narrative summaries. Of the 25 accident cases, there were four which were judged possibly self-destructive by the analysts. Of these, one was felt to be a case of suicide with possible conscious denial by the subject.

In addition, the narrative summaries revealed that five of the accident subjects fell into a "depressed" subgroup. They apparently were not so severely depressed as to affect the results of the Data Sheet (that is, the total accident group did not turn out to be significantly more depressed than the total appendectomy group in the Data Sheet evaluations). However, those five subjects represent 20 per cent of the total accident group. Thus there is, in our study, a suggestion that there exists a subgroup of self-destructive accident victims.

It should, however, be remembered that the 20 per cent depressed subgroup may have reflected a bias of the interviewers. The bias study (Chapter 9) shows that the investigators believed that self-destructive factors were present in the accident victims and the dynamic summaries were not subjected to any evaluation which could assess the effect of that bias.

There was one self-destructive hypothesis which was supported in our study. That was that the accident group showed high rates of drinking. (We will discuss this finding in detail further on in this chapter.)

CHARACTER DISORDERS AND MENTAL ABNORMALITIES IN ACCIDENT

A striking finding of our study was the absence of evidence for mental illness or "character" disorders in the accident subjects. Many previous studies of accident victims suggest that such characteristics are highly prevalent in this group. The accident prone formulations of Dunbar,[8] Alexander[9] and others pointed to an impulsive, antisocial individual who is non-introspective, active and adventurous in life style. Conger and his associates[10] identified a number of variables which discriminated between high and low accident groups. Findings relating to mental abnormalities in the accident group were poor control of hostility, low attention tolerance, higher separation anxiety, higher dependency needs, extremes of egocentricity or sociocentricity and fantasy preoccupations or unreflectiveness. Tillman and Hobbs[11] found evidence that individuals who had high accident rates came from homes marked by parental divorce and instability, had encountered difficulty with school authorities and juvenile courts, had frequent short term employments, had often been dismissed from jobs in adult life, had multiple item police records and had a personal life marked by social disregard. Finch and Smith,[12] who contrasted drivers who had been killed in accidents with a comparison group, found that the accident group had only 20 per cent of normal people. Seventy-six per cent of the group had personality disorders and 4 per cent were psychotic. This was contrasted with their comparison group in which there were 88 per cent normal people. Most of the personality disorders were diagnosed as *antisocial personality* and *alcoholic personality disorder*. Selzer[16] contrasted 96 drivers responsible for fatal vehicular accidents with a comparison group and found that the accident drivers demonstrated much more paranoid thinking and more evidence for suicide and depression than the comparison group.

Low Incidence of Psychopathology in Accident Group

There were many opportunities in our study to focus on the possible presence of psychopathology and character disorder. Although we were most importantly concerned with issues of suicidal behavior and self-destruction, we also looked for depression, counter-depression, risk-taking behavior, acting against medical advice, impulsive activity and unintegrated activity. Many Data Sheet items sought specific manifestations of these signs, symptoms and modes of behavior. Some signs of pathology such as depression, counter-depression and risk-taking behavior, were part of the central hypotheses of our study. The reader will recall that of the comparisons made between our three groups (utilizing the Data Sheet), none indicated that the accident group was more psychopathological than the control appendectomy group. (There was one important exception and that was in the area of drinking behavior.) In looking at the individual items from the Data Sheet, it is again difficult to find any indication of psychopathology in the accident group (cf. Chapter 7, Evaluation of Data Sheet Responses: Suggestions and Impressions). The narrative summary evaluation does suggest some significant differences between our three groups of subjects (cf. Chapter 8). It points to particular kinds of character reactions and particular types of preceding events which may be significantly linked to accident. However, we found it difficult to characterize these differences as examples of psychopathology. Rather, they seemed to represent types of personality organization and ways of coping with vicissitudes of life which fall within the nonpathological range.

What was the meaning of our inability to find psychopathology? Certainly it was not that we were biased against its presence. The members of the central research group thought it quite possible that accident victims might turn out to have many features in common with suicide victims. We know from our bias study that our clinical investigators believed that accidents were self-destructive. Thus, it is not likely that many of the researchers in our study screened out information which would point toward self-destructiveness.

However, our bias evaluations raise the possibility that investigators in *other* studies may have been biased in the direction of finding psychopathology in their accident groups. Their findings may have reflected that bias. In the bias evaluation which we performed, we found that, although our investigators developed data which contradicted their bias for self-destruction in accident, they still held to that bias after gathering data.

In pursuing this point, let us consider the interviewers who gathered data in various researches. In the researches that have just been quoted (as well as in many others which led to similar conclusions), interviewers with varying degrees of skill were utilized. Psychiatrists, psychologists, social workers and others have been interviewers. Our study was somewhat unusual in that we utilized psychoanalysts. Although we cannot prove it, we would suggest that psychoanalysts might be less likely than other interviewers to allow their biases to influence the data which they obtained. Much of psychoanalytic training is devoted to preparing analysts for the evaluation of their own biases and distortions. Also, analysts are usually individuals who have a much greater degree of experience in clinical interviewing than do interviewers in other groups. Thus, if the quality of the training and experience of the interviewers has anything to do with obtaining more accurate information, our study had certain advantages over many others.

In addition, our study utilized a stringent reliability testing for each case. This was not true of a number of the other studies and may constitute another support for our findings.

Finally, let us consider sources of erroneous conclusions stemming from the selection of subject and control groups in various studies.

In the studies we have cited, different "accident" groups and different "comparison" or "control" groups were utilized. This situation (that is, different studies using different target and control groups) may lead to the eliciting of conflicting or irrelevant data. Thus, a target group chosen because of supposedly possessing certain qualities may not in fact possess those qualities. Even if it does, it may not be able to reveal them under the conditions of the particular study. For example, a researcher may interview accident-producing drivers in order to learn something of their accident-linked psychology. If he studies them long after the accident, the psychological qualities which are connected with the accident may no longer be close enough to the surface so that they can be noted.

From this standpoint, let us evaluate some of the target and comparison groups which were utilized in various studies. In the Conger[10] and the Tillman and Hobbs[11] studies, groups of accident repeaters were compared with groups of nonaccident repeaters. The question must be asked, *Are accident repeaters a good group to study in order to find psychological accident-linked characteristics?* This may not, in fact, be so. We have already discussed the accident prone hypothesis and have shown how recent thinking tends to lend less and less credence to that hypothesis. Again, it is possible that studying drivers at some time *after* they have had their accident may not constitute an appropriate condition for discerning psychological characteristics linked to accident.

The Finch and Smith[12] study did not focus on one-car accident drivers. They (as far as we can tell from their report) chose drivers who were involved in traffic fatalities. Such a method of selection may have mixed so many drivers who were not responsible for accidents with those who were that the data which were forthcoming do not accurately reflect "accident" psychology.

The Selzer[13] study was the one that was closest to ours in that it selected in the target group drivers who were responsible for fatal accident. There is still a difference in that group and ours since we dealt with living drivers while Selzer and his associates, in many cases, could not interview the drivers since they were dead.

The comparison or control groups which were used in these studies are also different. For example, Selzer drew his control group from the general files of the state driver registration group, while Finch and Smith went to the neighborhood of each accident victim and going from door to door selected a driver who lived close to the victim.

And now to summarize this section. Our research failed to substantiate the presence of increased psychopathology in a group of drivers involved in one-car accidents. This was strikingly clear in the more objective, hypothesis-testing part of our study. The evaluation of the dynamic case histories raised the possibility of trends toward depression in a subgroup (about 20 per cent of the total accident group).

DRINKING AND PSYCHOPATHOLOGY IN ACCIDENT

Much research regarding automobile accident identifies high intake of alcohol as an important accompaniment of accident. The work which we report in this book is only an additional substantiation of this frequently found factor.

However, a question that was early raised in regard to the alcoholic intoxication linked to accidents has still not satisfactorily been settled (in our opinion). That question is, *What kinds of people do the drinking which is associated with automobile accident?* In earlier years it was felt that social drinkers might have contributed significantly to the population of drivers responsible for accidents. However, as research studies focused on various psychological and sociopsychological factors linked to accident, the importance of social drinking as a precursor to accident decreased. Psychopathological groups became relatively more important in the total drinking accident problem. In a recent article dealing with this issue,[14] Waller indicates that there are three groups which make up the overwhelming majority of persons in alcohol related crashes. They are problem drinkers, teenagers and heavy social drinkers. Note that in this theorizing, *social* drinking is only one of three important contributing groups, and that even though it is mentioned, a special subcategory *"heavy" social drinkers* is seen as making the contribution. Teenagers presumably enter the picture because of their lack of experience with automobiles and with other aspects of driving, although there may well be other pertinent psychological and sociopsychological factors which are significant in them.

The third group identified by Waller is "problem drinkers." We would now like to focus on the question, *Who are the problem drinkers?*

First, why is this an important question at all? The most significant reason is that measures which could be instituted to reduce the accident rate might vary depending on who the drivers are. For example, if it were true that social drinkers are responsible for most accidents, then educational measures might be quite valuable in reducing the accident rate. This is because social drinkers presumably are not addicted to alcohol and are free from significant other kinds of psychopathology. Also large numbers of this group would probably be amenable to educational measures which could prevent accidents.

However, much recent research concludes that those intoxicated drivers who are responsible for accidents do not come preponderantly from the "social drinker" group. This research indicates that high percentages of these drivers are victims of psychopathological conditions. Many of them are designated alcoholics.

We will now quote the work of two authorities in this area and also cite a well performed recent research study which documents this trend.

In 1967, Waller[15] reported a comparison between groups of drunken drivers, accident-involved drivers who had been driving but were not arrested, sober drivers involved in accidents, drivers with moving violations, drivers with citations plus arrest warrants and incident-free drivers. The purpose of the comparison was to identify the rates of problem drinking in the different groups. Problem drinkers were identified by the following criteria: two or more previous arrests involving the use of alcohol, or a "diagnosis" by the personnel of one or more of the community service agencies which had been in contact with the subjects, that the person had a problem with the use of alcohol. The diagnosis was based on criteria other than the mere presence of one or more arrests involving drinking. The actual rates of problem drinking in the groups were: drunken drivers, 63 per cent; drivers with an accident after drinking, 50 per cent; drivers with warrants, 30 per cent; nondrinking drivers with an accident, 14 per cent; persons with driving violations, 8 per cent; and drivers with no incidents, 3 per cent.

Another important support for this concept was supplied by Melvin Selzer. In 1968, Selzer[16] and his associates reported on the role of psychopathology and other psychosociological issues in the production of fatal accidents. The investigators interviewed the survivors and significant associates of drivers responsible for 96 fatal accidents as well as similar individuals in a 96 driver-matched control group. The researchers found that there was significantly more psychopathology in the fatality group. The psychopathology was found in three main categories: paranoid ideation, suicide proclivity, and clinical depression.

The more recent study which we cite is that of Finch and Smith.[12] Here are their findings in regard to psychopathology: In a group of drivers involved in traffic fatalities, 80 per cent were found to have significant psychopathology. The control group had only 12 per cent with psychopathology. The largest single group of psychopathological drivers involved in accidents were alcoholic personalities. They comprised almost half of the entire driver group.

If it is indeed true that a considerable number of those intoxicated drivers who produce accidents possess psychological illnesses, then, as we have already suggested, certain approaches to accident prevention seem feasible. Selzer,[18] for example, has suggested that those accident-producing drivers who have identified themselves through their alarming driving records and their excessive use of alcohol might be enjoined from driving until they have been "rehabilitated" or, if they are not amenable to treatment, that they be permanently barred from the road. Finch and Smith[12] indicate that alcoholism is a treatable disease and suggest that "alcoholic drivers" who, according to their research, make up an alarmingly large percentage of drivers involved in accidents, all be identified and subjected to psychiatric treatment.

Not all research, however, leads to a drinking-psychopathology linkage. In a recent report,[17] southern California researchers contrasted a sample of convicted drunk drivers with a subgroup of that sample who were involved in automobile fatalities. The comparisons were made in terms of violation records with the Department of Highway Safety and the police in regard to all possible traffic and nontraffic violations. There were *no* significant differences between the two groups. Although this is far from a conclusive study on psychopathology, it suggests that personality disorder and antisocial personality disorder are not closely linked to automobile accident.

Some Conclusions

Let us now consider some of the findings of our own research. We certainly found evidence of increased drinking in the accident group. This was manifested in two ways: There was increased drinking shortly before the accident, and there was a much higher rate of daily drinking in the accident group than in the other two groups.

However, as we have already detailed, we did not find evidence of increased psychopathology in our accident group. Not only was this true in a number of categories which were extensively examined (see the earlier parts of this chapter and Chapter 6), but we also asked whether there was any difference in terms of effects of drinking in regard to loss of consciousness or unusual social behavior. We found no differentiation among the three groups in this respect.

It thus may be inappropriate to think of many accident drivers as possessing psychopathology. Indeed, many current researchers[15, 18] prefer the term "problem drinkers" to "alcoholics" or "alcoholic personality disorders." This is because the latter designations are often terms of social opprobrium and little else. It also is abundantly clear from psychiatric experience that a label of psychiatric illness does not automatically imply that a person can be treated or is even willing to be treated.

Our research suggests that many drivers involved in one-car accidents are not psychologically ill, although they consume more alcohol than other subgroups of the population. Perhaps there may be certain groups of accident-producing drivers who are psychologically ill, but our work does not identify them. Our research suggests that the increased drinking done by the majority of our subjects represents a characteristic way of handling the tensions of their lives.

All people possess defense and coping mechanisms. The presence of these mechanisms does not constitute mental illness (unless all people who have psychological defenses and coping mechanisms are mentally ill). However, specific coping mechanisms carry with them particular disadvantages. In the case of drinkers, the increased possibility of accident is one of the disadvantages.

REFERENCES

1. Szasz, Thomas: *The Myth of Mental Illness.* New York, Hoeber and Harper, 1961.
2. Freud, Sigmund: *The Psychopathology of Everyday Life.* In the standard edition of *The Complete Psychological Works,* Vol. 6. London, Hogarth Press, Ltd., 1953-65.
3. Menninger, K. A.: Purposive accidents as an expression of self-destructive tendencies, *Int J Psychoanal, 17*:6-15, 1935.

4. Mosely, Alfred L.: *Research on Fatal Highway Collisions,* Harvard Medical School, 1962-65.
5. McDonald, J. M.: Suicide and homicide by automobile, *Am J Psychiatry, 121:*366-379, 1964.
6. Selzer, M. L. and Charles E. Payne: Automobile accidents, suicide and unconscious motivation, *Am J Psychiat, 119:*237-240, 1962.
7. Tabachnick, Norman, Robert E. Litman, Marvin Osman, Warren L. Jones, Jay Cohen, August Kasper and John Moffit: Comparative psychiatric study of accidental and suicidal death, *Arch Gen Psychiatry, 14:*60-68, Jan. 1966.
8. Dunbar, Flanders: *Psychosomatic Diagnosis.* New York, Paul B. Hoeber, Inc., 1943.
9. Alexander, Franz: The accident prone individual, *Public Health Reports, 64:*357-361, 1949.
10. Conger, John J., Herbert S. Gaskill, Donald D. Glad, Linda Hassel, Robert B. Rainey and William Sowrey: Psychological and psychophysiological factors in motor vehicle accidents, *JAMA, 9:*1581-1587, April 4, 1959. Reprinted in *Accident Research* (Hatton, Suchman and Klein, Editors). New York, Harper & Row, 1964.
11. Tillman, W. A. and G. W. Hobbs: The accident prone automobile driver, *Am J Psychiatry,* 105:321-331, Nov. 1949. Reprinted in *Accident Research* (Hatton, Suchman and Klein, Editors). New York, Harper & Row, 1964.
12. Finch, J. R. and J. P. Smith: *Psychiatric and Legal Aspects of Automobile Fatalities.* Springfield, Thomas, 1970.
13. Selzer, M. L.: Fatal accidents: The role of psychopathology, social stress and acute disturbance, *Am J Psychiatry, 124:*8, Feb. 1968.
14. Waller, J. A.: Truth, traps and tactics concerning alcohol, other drugs and highway safety, *California Medicine, 116:*10-15, Feb. 1972.
15. Waller, J. A.: Identification of problem drinking among drunken drivers, *JAMA, 200:*124-130, April 10, 1967.
16. Selzer, Melvin L.: Alcoholism, mental illness and stress in 96 drivers causing fatal accidents, *Behavioral Science,* Vol. 14, no. 1, p. 1, Jan. 1969.
17. U. S. C. (University of Southern California) Public Systems Research Institute (Seymour Pollock, M.D., Principal Investigator): The drinking driver and traffic safety. *Annual Report,* July 1970.
18. Cahalan, Don.: *Problem Drinkers.* San Francisco, Jossey-Bass, Inc., 1970.

CHAPTER 14

THEORETICAL ASPECTS OF ACCIDENT AND SUICIDE

Summary

The common feature of alcoholic intake in accident and suicidal people may be an increase in risk to life. However, the risk manifests itself in different ways in the two situations.

In the suicidal person, many impulses exist of which intention towards death is one. One of the safeguards to life is that life-preserving tendencies and impulses in the suicidal person alert him to the dangers of his self-destructive intentions. There is, thus, a constant struggle between life-ending and life-preservative impulses within him. Alcohol increases the possibility of death by decreasing the critical, realistic, life-evaluating actions of certain psychological apparatuses. It also increases the individual's belief that he can perform a self-destructive act and "get away with it"—that is, keep his life.

The situation in accident seems to be different. There the chances toward death are increased because the "accident" person is utilizing a mode of relief and adaptation, that is, drinking, which gravely impairs the quick and sharp use of his faculties in a life-threatening situation—driving. What may be added to this already dangerous situation is an increase in feelings of omnipotence which the accident person seeks and finds through the utilization of alcohol.

WHAT SUGGESTIONS for the psychological theory of accidents and suicides arise from our study? We began this research with the belief that there might be strong similarities in the psychologies of individuals who involve themselves (or become involved) in suicide and accident. We believed that an *intention* towards self-destruction was characteris-

191

tic of both modes of destruction, but, as we have seen, that belief was not borne out by the results of our research. Similarities of intention and similarities in other psychological areas were not found. However, our work gave us the opportunity to study in detail many aspects of the lives and personalities of accidental and suicidal individuals.

Now we will bring together certain positive and negative results of our research. We will comment on other work in these areas. Our aim: *to formulate concepts for understanding suicide and accident*—both as individual entities and in relationship to each other. The dimensions which we will stress in this discussion are risk, self-esteem, hope (and hopelessness), dependence, denial and values.

We do not hope to produce a comprehensive theory of accident and suicide. There are too many different types of suicidal and accidental situations for that, but we will attempt to identify some general characteristics of accidental and suicidal people. Also by focusing on these two types of destruction, we may add something to the general theory of self-destruction.

RISK

We begin this chapter with an evaluation of risk in man's life.

Every one of us lives with a number of risks. There are certain risks over which we have little or no control. For example, it is possible that some natural catastrophe such as lightning striking or a tidal wave may snuff out our lives. We take risks of this type by just being alive, and no person who accepts the value and responsibilities of living can avoid them. However, there are other situations involving death and destruction in which the risks are known and yet willingly taken.

What are some of these voluntary risks? People ingest and inhale certain substances which are known to have deleterious effects. We refer to the abuse of certain drugs which may have dangerous effects (such as the lowering of self-protective consciousness). In addition, these drugs may have addicting qualities which lead to a general decrease in health and to the necessity of engaging in certain dangerous life styles (such as crime). Next we note overeating which has well-documented, negative effects on health and longevity. Other types of risks are associated with athletic activities. Certain of them entail significant possibilities of death or injury (professional football and mountain climbing). However, even when the chance is less dangerous, people involve themselves in exertions which may cause continuing discomfort and poor health. Recently, a number of medical writers have commented on the craze for sports among middle-aged week-end athletes. As a result of this proclivity, physicians are seeing many needless cases of muscle and tendon sprains, joint pains, protruded intervertebral discs and other injuries.

An additional category of risk-taking activities involves the use of machines. Of course, the machine that comes first to mind is the automobile. There are many opportunities to reduce driving exposure. Yet few people take them and those who do cut down on driving rarely do it because of a concern over health or life. Most people refuse to drive because they don't wish to take the time or because a ride may be boring to them.

Why do people take all of these risks? The most obvious answer is that what they get by taking the risk is worth what they may lose. (We leave out of this discussion risks taken unknowingly.) There are at least three reasons why people do take risks.

First of all, some direct satisfactions result from risk-taking behaviors. For example, eating, smoking, drinking alcohol and taking drugs often induce a variety of physiological and psychological pleasant effects. People value these pleasant effects and are willing to take risks in order to get them.

Man's Love of Thrill

Another category of positive value has to do with man's love of thrill. There are experiences which are exhilarating in themselves. Sometimes they are especially exhilarating because they involve death-risking behavior. Consider someone climbing a mountain. First of all, that is a relatively rare experience. Certain pleasurable qualities are associated with it which are not readily found in other situations. Secondly, the pleasure is involved with arduous physical activity. One has a chance to test and be proud of one's own physical and mental capabilities. Finally, there may be great pleasure in knowing that one has done a dangerous thing. A heavy price may have to be paid for the pleasure, but an important reward awaits if one is successful. All of these conditions contribute to what can be called the pleasurable psychological experience of thrill.

Risk-Taking as a Defense Mechanism

Yet another kind of satisfaction associated with risk-taking behavior has to do with its use as a psychological defense. Every human being must endure and deal with frustrations, irritations and anxieties. Each person has his own group of defenses to cope with these situations. Certain defenses involve risk-taking behaviors. For example, in response to frustrations and irritations, some individuals feel weak and helpless. They, therefore, choose defenses which can counter those feelings by making them feel particularly strong. Certain drugs, alcohol, for example, can produce such a feeling. However, using these drugs means taking a risk. There are many other psychological defenses which likewise involve risk-taking.

Now, what about suicide and accident as risk-taking situations? A certain number of people participate in a particular risk-taking situation called suicide attempts. We emphasize the factor of risk because no one can *know* when making a suicide attempt whether or not he will die. An even larger group of people take a risk with accidents. There is an (at least semantic) point of similarity between accident and suicide. Every time a person makes an attempt upon his own life, he is doing something which involves a certain risk. In a similar way, every time a person drives he is making an accident attempt, that is, putting himself in a position of risk in regard to well-being and life.

Now, a difference may be that the suicide attempt is "intentional," while the accident situation does not involve an intention towards death. There is support for this differentiation since suicidal people have a conscious desire to do away with themselves while accident people do not.

However, research has shown that the psychological factors involved in suicide are quite complex and do not hinge entirely or even mainly upon intention. In the first place, intention itself is not simple. The suicidal person has intentions to die, but he also has conscious and unconscious intentions to live. In addition, the actual severity of the suicide attempt will depend on such factors as the desire to use the suicidal act as a communicative modality, the response of significant others to the suicide attempt, the type of suicidal weapon used, the making of a suicidal plan and the total number of positive and negative experiences existing in the suicidal individual's life.

In a similar way, research suggests that psychological characteristics of accident people and situations are complex. A small group of accident victims has been identified (with some degree of tentativeness) as having features in common with suicidal attempts. In our present group of accident victims, perhaps one person (that is 4 per cent of the total group) had marked suicidal features, while perhaps as many as 25 per cent had some elements of depression which made them closer to a suicidal group than the remaining 75 per cent. In other studies, relatively small groups of depressive or suicidal people have also been identified (see Chapters 1 and 13). However, many other psychological features have been identified in accident—action orientation, impulsiveness, disregard for the law, etc. (see Chapter 1).

Risk-Taking: Some Conclusions

In addition to psychological issues, many other features contribute to risk in accident. Certain factors involve the individual. His state of responsiveness, his motor integration and other aspects of his psychophysiological intactness are important. Then, too, aspects relating to the automobile and the environment through which the driver and the automobile move are significant.

To summarize: All people live with risk and all people take risks, but people are different in the particular categories of risk-taking they become involved in. Two special categories are the "suicidal state" and driving which is the "accident state," or at least an early precursor of it. At first glance, suicide and accidents seem to be quite different because conscious intention is usually high in suicide, usually low in accident. However, when all intentions are considered—intentions to live and to die, conscious and unconscious intentions—it is then noted that accidents and suicides are less dissimilar. For in suicides usually intentions to live are present, while in at least some accidents intentions to die are present. Also in both suicides and accidents, a great number of factors (both psychological and otherwise) affect the possibility of the actual occurrence of a suicide or accident.

LOSS IN SUICIDE AND ACCIDENT

In the previous section we pointed to the prominent role of conscious intention in suicide. What is connected to the intention to kill oneself? In suicide, it seems quite clear that feelings of loss are important precedents of the suicidal intention. Most often there are *external losses* which enter the picture. Sometimes they are recent ones. A person has lost a loved one or his good health or a great deal of money—something that means a lot to him. Sometimes—and this seems to be true of the more lethal suicide attempts—the loss has not been an acute one but is rather an accumulation of losses that have occurred over a long period of time. For example, an older person focuses increasingly on the loss of his physical and mental abilities. Then he has to leave his business which may have been a most important source of sustenance to him (and in many ways more than merely financial). Finally, he has lost many of his friends and family through death. Eventually he may come to feel that he himself should be dead.

Hinted at in the above description is the second important loss which exists in suicide, that is, an *internal loss*. It can be variously categorized as a loss of drive, as a loss of feeling of purpose, as a loss of feeling of worth. These attitudes are all characteristics of the depressive state. As is well known, depression and suicide are quite closely linked, but there is one additional feature that is characteristic of suicide. The suicidal person feels that he has completely lost his *self-esteem,* that there is no chance of his ever returning to the actuality or the feeling of being a significant person, and that therefore he would be better off dead.

These losses (external and internal), so recurrent in attempted suicide, are simply not found to a large extent in accident. Our data, as well as much previous study of accident victims, strongly suggest that those victims have *not* given up. On the contrary, they seem to be fairly well involved in life. Also in general, it does not seem to be true that their involvement in life has decreased prior to the accident. In our psychodynamic studies, we characterized the accident group as having *a strong involvement in life.* They seem to be interested in finishing things. It is true that many studies point to a lack of regard for others and a kind of antisocial quality. That finding (although not repeated in our study) is not incompatible with the point we now make. We believe that what we noted in the accident victims was a sense of interest in and commitment to life. One might think that there was an aversion to the feeling that they were not able to deal with life. Perhaps they were sensitive to an accusation that might be made by themselves or others that they were giving in to the frustrations of life and losing hope. But however it is understood, their feeling of involvement seemed to contrast strongly with the helpless, hopeless attitude of the suicidal people.

DRINKING: SOME PSYCHOLOGICAL ASPECTS

Now we will review some important psychological aspects of increased alcohol intake. We focus on this issue because it is one of the most prominent findings in our study, as well as many others involving accident. *Over half* of the people involved in *accidents* and *about half* of the people who are involved in *serious suicide attempts* have ingested a large amount of alcohol. We should try to understand the meaning of drinking in these two life situations.

A most frequently observed psychological value of drinking is its tendency to assuage the dependent needs of individuals. When people feel "down," when they are irritated or frustrated, when they feel tense and would like to get more from life, they take a drink. Sometimes the drink in itself is a kind of indulgent reward; sometimes the drink helps them move on to the gratification of other needs. Both everyday experience and many research and theoretical studies support the notion that alcohol is one of the great relaxers and indulgences of mankind.

When we drink we take care of our dependent needs. Very often drinking is a way of dealing with general feelings of being low. Sometimes it is a way of dealing with very strong feelings of inferiority. But before we go too far in this direction, let us state our impression that *not all* people who drink have strong feelings of inferiority.

A specific consequence of alcoholic intake is the production of feelings of increasing strength or omnipotence. There are differing ideas (which do not necessarily conflict with each other) as to how this occurs. Many people react with a feeling of pleasantness and euphoria to alcoholic intake. It is not known exactly what mediates this transmission from an external substance to an internal feeling, but there seems little question that it is a common experience. In addition to direct physiological effects, alcohol helps bring on feelings of increasing strength because we have quickly done something that has changed our mood. This is a relatively unusual and rapid change. Thus, we may feel that we are stronger and more powerful.

So far we may venture to say that both suicidal people and accidental people drink a good deal. Let us consider, however, that the needs for drinking and/or the intensity of concern that leads to it may be different in the two groups.

Dependence, Denial and Drinking

Let us next consider the issue of dependence in suicide and accident. Our finding (which is not at variance with a great deal of other research on people making suicidal attempts) is that suicidal attempters are quite closely involved with other individuals. For example, in our interviews they welcome the change to talk. They want to tell their troubles. As a matter of fact, they are so "clutching" that people often don't like them. Our interviewers, for example, although feeling somewhat uncomfortable about it, often wanted to terminate their work with the suicidal subjects and were happy when they had finished it.

Contrast these findings with those in the accident group. The accident subjects tend to be more independent and do not like to turn to others. They shy away from the interviewers when they are asked about their problems. They seem to say that they would like to take care of things all by themselves.

Drinking in the Suicide Group

Consider also the situation of hope (or hopelessness). The suicidal person says that he has given up or given in. He considers himself an inadequate person who has lost. He wants a release from responsibility and his intention to suicide is one way of achieving it.

Related to helplessness in suicide is the symbol and reality of death. It is possible that death enters the picture in at least two ways. First of all, the suicidal person feels bad. He feels that he has not taken care of his responsibilities and that he is unable to do so. He believes that people may be angry at him. Part of the difficulty which he encounters in interpersonal transactions has to do with his assuming that other people do not like him. Then he treats them *as if* they do not like him. What is implicit about this situation is that the suicidal person is reacting to his own superego, his own aspirations which he has failed to achieve. As a result, he probably feels that he *deserves* to be punished. Death, of course, is an extreme type of punishment which may be suited to his extreme failure. Sometimes he is caught between feeling that death is deserved and should be imposed and also feeling that he does not wish to leave life.

Death is additionally seen as a one-way ticket out of a life which has become increasingly depressing and unsatisfying. Furthermore, the suicidal attempter is not only convinced that he has little chance of future success but is also quite ashamed of his track record.

The accident person in contrast does not seem to be a loser nor, and this is more important, does he seem to *feel* like a loser.

The finding is that he does not consciously contemplate suicide (in a majority of cases) nor does he unconsciously have feelings of wanting to die. As we have already indicated, he seems to be working hard to show that he can cope, that he can make it, that the frustrations and difficulties of his life are not overwhelming. Life has not put him down.

In the light of these considerations, what can we now make of the high rate of drinking in accident and suicide? For suicidal people, drinking is probably a great gratification. They are feeling quite low and, although they may be considering suicide, they may not have actually come to the conclusion that they will attempt it. We note that suicidal acts are often a long time in coming to fruition. Even when suicide has been decided on, certain plans must be set up so that it can be successful.

However, as we have already indicated, impulses toward suicide are not the only ones that exist in suicide attempters. There are conflicting countersuicidal impulses. During the periods when conflict over whether a suicide attempt should be made is going on, feelings are tense. Drinking is an easily available way of dealing with that tension. (To put it another way, it is a method of dealing with dependent needs stimulated by the suicidal person's sense of loss.)

Along these lines, a little studied issue has been the effect of drinking on aborting suicidal situations. If the theory which has just been presented (particularly that part of it which deals with drinking as a way of relieving dependent gratifications and that part which talks about how needy and hopeless suicidal people feel) is true, then drinking may actually be helpful in reducing tendencies towards suicide. We do not know how many cases of suicide have been aborted by drinking because we have not considered that hypothesis a good one to research. We have in the past observed that those people who do make suicide attempts or who succeed in killing themselves drink a lot. We have assumed in many cases that the drinking can only have deleterious effects. That may not be so.

It is not that we maintain that drinking is *only* a positive feature in suicidal situations. In some cases, the alcohol may sufficiently take care of dependent needs so that feelings of self-esteem increase (and the tendency towards death decreases). Even if the suicidal intention is aborted partially, the person is still at risk because of alcohol's tendency to impair many of the usual, rational, life-preserving ways of thinking (and acting). This cutoff of rationality can be a risk to life because there may be a lack of appreciation of the danger to life of certain acts. (Here there is an important similarity to the drinking driver who gets into an accident. He also has life-preserving, perceptual, motor and integrative processes impaired by the effects of drinking.) These peculiarities of suicidal logic (which may also be true of "accidental" logic) have been discussed by Schneidman.[1] Another theoretical understanding of them has been provided by psychoanalysts who postulate "splitting" in the mind. This splitting is a psychological mechanism which allows an individual to separate one possible aspect of his action or thinking from others which are significantly related to it.

Drinking in the Accident Group

Now, what is the situation in people who have accidents? These people do not suffer from intense feelings of loss nor are they convinced that they are incapable. However, they do have their share of daily frustration, not enough money, disappointments at work, and conflicts with friends and relatives—in short, an entire panoply of small hurts, disappointments of large ideals and the necessity to deal with people who are not all they could be. One might argue that "accident people" are on their way to suicide as a reaction to the frustrations, disappointments and irritations of their life. However, the point is that although they may be on their way to suicidal states, they are still some distance from them. But in regard to the frustrations of these people, drinking is probably also used as a restorative or as a way of dealing with unsatisfied dependent needs.

We have already characterized the accident person as one who may not pay enough attention to his dependent needs. He has to be strong, manly and self-reliant, but such a facade may not hold up indefinitely or it may need some additional props. At times, the accident person must find certain release and gratification for his dependent needs. Now it is that drinking comes into play. For alcohol has that wonderful property of healing small hurts. A disagreement with a friend or relative could result in a fight that would have unpleasant short or long term effects. Continued disappointments are bad for self-esteem and too much dwelling on them leads to depression. How valuable at such times to give a little gift of ease to one's self! It feels "good" and it helps avoid the "bad."

In addition, human beings have strong needs for social contact. It is important to talk with new people or old friends and to meet members of the opposite sex for sexual gratification. One of the institutions which our society provides for all of these needs is the neighborhood bar, and in that bar alcohol flows freely.

Thus drinking may serve many valuable needs for those people who utilize it. However, there is an important risk which accompanies it, and that is that the danger the drinker incurs if he is also a driver. This is because driving is a highly complicated task requiring the utmost attention to the external world and also the ability to react quickly to it.

Drinking interferes with the explicit pattern of perception, integration and execution of motoric abilities necessary for driving. It dulls the portions of the nervous system which mediate these functions.

It is also possible that a psychological risk is added to the physiological one. We have already characterized the accident person as someone who is strongly involved in carrying out certain activities in his life. A feeling of great strength, something approaching omnipotence, might be very acceptable to him—particularly if he has to deny dependent needs. The "accident" person may like to drink because his feelings of omnipotence are enhanced by alcohol.

THE RELATIONSHIP OF RISK-TAKING TO VALUES

We originally talked about risk and framed our theoretical discussion in terms of it. Now let us return to that issue. We have seen that accident people take a risk when they drink. An outsider looking at drinking accident persons might say, "They are self-destructive and should stop it." This makes very good sense if one considers that the maintenance of life and of basic health is an important issue. There is little doubt that most people, including most accident victims, favor health. However, when the situation is looked at from the inside of the accident person, another value becomes apparent, that is, the value that comes from being able to maintain one's aplomb, the value that inheres in being able to take care of the frustrations and disappointments of everyday life through good and effective coping mechanisms.

The accident person has found such a coping mechanism. He maintains a feeling that he is doing well and he uses alcohol to help him achieve it. If he happens to be introspective and wishes to evaluate if less dangerous coping mechanisms are possible for him, he might be willing to look more seriously at the "self-destructive" implications of his drinking. Our evidence suggests that most accident people are not introspective in this way. The reason is that drinking is part of a successful set of psychological defenses. "Successful" means that anxiety is kept relatively well-handled and does not disturb. These people are thus probably unwilling even to consider that they are self-destructive.

Under the above conditions, then, the accident person may be quite willing to accept the risk that accompanies his drinking (just as many or most of us are willing to accept the risk that accompanies our driving at all). The reason for both the accident people and ourselves accepting these risks is the same. We are making it—there is a (generally) satisfying mix of pleasure and absence of anxiety in our lives.

So in the last analysis, it becomes a question of *who* decides *which* values are more important. It seems quite understandable that someone, having suffered through the vicissitudes of life and having come to an acceptable way of fighting his anxiety, should choose to hold onto that way. In fact, that he should resist suggestions to the effect that there is something wrong with this hard won and valued attitude, is likewise understandable.

All of this does not imply that society should do nothing about the drinking-accident situation. It does, however, constitute an attempt to understand how much energy and value is attached to drinking so that, if we do wish to alter the situation, we will know what we are up against.

REFERENCE

1. Schneidman, E. S.: *Logical Content Analysis in Analysis of Communicative Content* (George Gerbner et al., Eds.). New York, John Wiley, 1969.

Chapter 15

REDUCING THE ACCIDENT TOLL
Summary

A significant subgroup of accident drivers is characterized by depressive and possibly suicidal features. Depressed people seek and come into contact with "helpers." These "helpers" can then act in a number of ways to reduce behavior which could lead to accidents.

The largest group of drivers who become "at fault" in accidents are not depressed or suicidal. Most of them have been drinking and the accident toll can be reduced if the effects of drinking on driving can be minimized or drastically reduced.

There are a number of ways to achieve this end:

1. Drinking drivers can be barred from the road.

2. Educational measures which take into account the specific psychology of "accident-producing" drivers may be instituted.

3. The increased use of caffeine and/or other stimulants after drinking can be encouraged.

4. Research on safe "driving after drinking" techniques should be conducted.

5. There should be continuing emphasis on the development of safety features for automobiles and the environment through which they pass.

WHAT SUGGESTIONS for a decrease in the accident toll emerge from our research? At the beginning we reiterate that psychological factors (the focus of our work) constitute only one part of a complex picture. Many other issues contribute to accident, and effective anti-accident measures will emerge from consideration of *all* of them. However, the psychological findings of our study, both in themselves and in relationship to other significant factors linked to accident, suggest certain positive and negative preventative paths.

Averting Depression and Suicidal Tendencies

First, we will consider depression and suicide. Previous studies by Selzer,[1] Finch and Smith,[2] and the Los Angeles Suicide Prevention Center[3] pointed to a significant subgroup of accident drivers at fault who were depressed (and to some degree suicidal). The new research we report in this book points to a significant subgroup (between 20 and 25 per cent) of accident drivers which is likewise characterized by self-destructive and/or depressed features. These features reveal themselves in different ways in our studies. We do not find great evidence for suicide, although we do feel that a particular subgroup shows depression. However, this depression does not become evident in the most objective part of our research (Chapter 6).

(In our dynamic evaluations we characterized the subjects in the "depressed group" as manifesting less depression than that which would make them appear pathological to psychiatrists or psychologists. We thought that they might seem more like the "normally" depressed people who are always with us.)

In terms of drinking behavior, there is, however, an increase in drinking in both the suicide and accident groups in about 25 per cent of the subjects. This suggests that there is increasing tension in these two groups and, together with other evidence accumulated by ourselves and others, it strengthens the possibility of increased depression and/or self-destructive states.

There are many ways in which depressed and suicidal people put themselves in touch with potential helpers. They turn to friends who may often note their depression. Acquaintances and business associates likewise sense the "trouble" in these people. Depressed individuals often go to physicians because they feel physically ill or run-down; to the physicians they often mention depression. Finally, they seek the help of mental health professionals and call crisis and suicide prevention centers. All these contacts of depressed people provide pathways to helping them. The contacts, of course, must deal with the depression, the crisis, and other problems which bring the depressed people to them.

To that valuable work can now be added the task of accident prevention. If these contacts can be educated as to the relationship between depression, suicidal and self-destructive states, and accident, they will then be in a position to implement a reduction in the accident rate.

Particularly must they focus in this group on the relationship between alcohol and accident. As we have already suggested (and shall presently reaffirm), many who are likely to have accidents may not be amenable to suggestions to curtail their drinking. However, *individuals in the depressed subgroup of potential accident victims are acutely aware of inner distress and seek out and respond to the intervention of helpers.* Thus, any emphasis on the avoidance of combined driving and drinking during depressed phases may well bear fruit in terms of a lowered accident rate. This is a relatively new area of clinical work. There should now ensue a period of clinical trial with the subsequent development of particular approaches suited to the prevention of accident. In our opinion, this clinical research should be pursued immediately.

The total number of drivers who would also fall into a depressed or self-destructive subgroup probably amounts to no more than 25 per cent of all accident drivers at fault. That however is a significant group and deserves a great deal of effort. However, what will help prevent the other 75 per cent of accidents?

Keeping Drinking Drivers Off the Road

Many previous workers in the field have suggested that accident prevention must center around the problem of increased drinking. This suggestion seems quite reasonable since alcoholic intoxication is the largest factor linked to automobile accident. Finch and Smith[2] argue for the identification, barring from the road and bringing into treatment of alcoholic drivers. Selzer[1] has urged a similar course emphasizing the dangerousness of this group of individuals when they drive.

The proposal to bar drinking drivers from the road seems to us worth exploring and implementing. However, it must be realized that a number of technical, legal and value choice problems arise in considering this course. In addition, the reaction of certain industries to this proposal must be considered.

From a technical standpoint, criteria for evaluating which drivers to identify, the implementation of identifying procedures, and the specific technical and legal methods to bar the identified drivers from the road must be developed.

These problems, however, would be the least of the lot. More important would be the citizenry's feeling about relinquishing certain activities. Will the people of this country tolerate a severe sanction upon their drinking? We should remember that the Nineteenth Amendment attempted to do away with drinking but there was a great popular outcry against it. Eventually that amendment was repealed. Although it is true that we are not discussing a complete prohibition of drinking, we are considering a partial one. Again, what would citizens feel about the restriction of their privilege to drive? Driving is so integral a part of this country's way of life that a considerable furor might be put up by driver groups who would not wish to have their driving restricted.

Economic interests which have frequently acted (and in a most forceful way) to preserve themselves would possibly come into play. What would the reaction of the alcohol industry be to a measure which would significantly reduce its profits? If statutes such as those we are now considering should come into existence, there would possibly be a marked decrease in the number of drivers and presumably in the number of automobiles that would be sold. Would the automobile industry stand still for this? Added to that group's possible displeasure at such a turn of events would be the similar feelings of related industries. In the evaluations of suggestions to bar drinking drivers from the road, these issues must be dealt with.

Is Psychiatric Intervention Feasible?

An additional suggestion relating to drinking drivers and the reduction of accident has been that such drivers receive medical and psychiatric treatment to rid them of their drinking habit. Is such a course likely to bring about the desired result?

Our research suggests that many (perhaps most) accident drivers cannot easily be said to possess "mental illness." Moreover (and this is most to the point), they do not consider themselves to be psychologically in need of help. That faces us with the possibility that not only would they be unresponsive to psychological therapy, but might indeed react with indignation and anger to attempts to force it on them.

As we have previously described (Chapter 14), most accident drivers are utilizing a group of coping mechanisms and defense mechanisms which includes drinking. They are presumably willing to pay the price in terms of greater risk of accidental injury or death. In addition, many drivers who become at fault in accidents seem to *need to deny* problems and vulnerabilities. Under these conditions, the likelihood of their responding positively to psychiatric intervention is quite limited.

Apart, then, from the "depressive" group of accident-producing drivers, we may not have much to expect from psychological "treatment." Short of barring drinking drivers from the road, are there other techniques for lessening the possibility of their producing accidents?

It is our belief that many accident-producing drivers do not wish to look upon themselves as mentally ill. (In fact, they do not care to believe that they are limited in any way.) Educational measures should stress increased mastery and competence through following good driving procedures. This would take into account the specific sensitivities of accident-producing drivers. The general educational approach should be *how to drive more safely and effectively* rather than *how to avoid getting yourself into an accident.*

Some Positive Suggestions

What kind of education does the accident problem call for?

As we have indicated, many accidents occur when people are on their way home from parties or bars. Therefore, a series of educational measures might be focused on those drivers who attend private parties and public bars and drink.

1. Many accidents take place when the driver falls asleep. Large amounts of caffeine would probably help avoid sleeping with its concommitant accidents. In addition, it seems likely that caffeine would counteract drowsiness and increase safe driving

for many drivers who do not completely fall asleep. We, therefore, suggest an increase in the practice of drinking coffee after
alcoholic intake. This program exists to a limited degree today,
but it could be vastly expanded. Here are some suggestions
which could lead to increased caffeine or stimulant intake.

   a. An advertising campaign—it could include posters, person-
      al urging by bartenders and waitresses and messages on
      cocktail napkins such as, "Make the last drink a cup of
      coffee."
   b. An educational effort aimed at the general public with par-
      ticular emphasis on coffee drinking at the conclusion of
      private parties.
   c. The attractive packaging of caffeine containing candy or
      wafers under such slogans as "Power Pills." Another possi-
      bility—bowls of "power pretzels" containing caffeine or
      other suitable stimulants. These could be utilized at bars
      and private parties.

   2. People who drink should be encouraged to drive home with
someone who has not been drinking. In many cases this should
be easy to achieve. As we have indicated, much of the drinking
that results in accidents takes place in bars and parties. It is probable that most of this drinking, as well as most other drinking,
takes place within a fairly close radius of the drinker's home. If
a determined effort were made to have nondrinkers drive home
after parties, a decrease in the accident toll might result.

   Pursuing this safety measure, it is possible that specific groups
of people (which might be sponsored by Alcoholics Anonymous
or safety-minded groups) could be designated "Safety Squads."
These "Squads" would be on call to anyone requesting a ride
home. Perhaps local organization of these "Safety Squads"
would expedite their efficiency.

   3. We should plan research on safe driving techniques to be
used after drinking. Are there certain speed patterns which are
safer than others? Are there certain techniques of braking or ac-
celerating which can be learned? Once such techniques are discovered, they should be taught. We do not know much about
possibilities in this area because we have not looked for them.

Additional anti-accident measures must focus on safety aspects of the automobile and the environment. Much work has been done on the "packaging" aspects of human beings in automobiles. There are a number of ways to make that "package" a less destructive one. To safety belts and padded interiors, we may soon be adding air bags.

Returning to the tendency of drivers who have accidents to fall asleep, it may be worth while to build alarm devices into cars. These alarm systems might be keyed to increased alcohol vapors in the automobile or to erratic driving patterns.

Research along this line should continue, and whatever other devices safety engineers can fashion should be utilized. We should also increase experimentation with traffic regulating devices. Also, we can focus on safer design of transportation pathways and the relationship of automobiles to pedestrians.

All these suggestions will not *eliminate* the problem of automobile accident (although we believe that they can significantly reduce the rate).

In the related field of suicide, it has been suggested that a certain rate must always be with us. That rate represents the essential human right to decide whether one should live or not. Perhaps a certain accident rate is indicative of society's high valuation of risk-taking.

However, there are other societal and human values besides risk-taking. One of the most important is *the preservation of life*. These recommendations stemming from a consideration of psychological factors in accident are offered in support of that particular value.

REFERENCES

1. Selzer, Melvin L.: Alcoholism, mental illness and stress in 96 drivers causing fatal accidents, *Behavioral Science*, Vol. 14, no. 1, p. 1, Jan. 1969.
2. Finch, J. R. and J. P. Smith: *Psychiatric and Legal Aspects of Automobile Fatalities.* Springfield, Thomas, 1970.
3. Tabachnick, Norman, Robert E. Litman, Marvin Osman, Warren L. Jones, Jay Cohen, August Kasper and John Moffit: Comparative psychiatric study of accidental and suicidal death, *Archives of General Psychiatry, 14*:60-68, Jan. 1966.

APPENDICES

DATA SHEET
The Accident Study

PRELIMINARY INFORMATION

SUBJECT: .... P.F. NO.: ....
INTERVIEWER: ....
INTERVIEW DATES: 1 ....
                     2 ....
                     3 ....
                     4 ....
                     Other ......
WARD AND ROOM NO.: .... SERVICE: ....
MEDICAL STATUS AND ADMITTING PROBLEM: ....
....
....
AGE: .... OCCUPATION: .... MARITAL STATUS: ....
HIGHEST SCHOOL GRADE COMPLETED: ....
HOME ADDRESS: .... HOME PHONE: ....
.... BUSINESS PHONE: ......
If accident or suicide attempt subject, give brief description of the occurrence: ....
....
....
....
....

SECTION A—SUICIDAL ACTS AND COMMUNICATIONS

1. Hospitalization resulted from a deliberate suicide attempt.
   1. Yes
   2. No
   3. NI*

2. In the seven days prior to the accident, suicide attempt or appendicitis, there was a suicide attempt.
   1. Yes
   2. No
   3. NI

3. Seven days to six months prior to the accident, suicide attempt or appendicitis, there was a deliberate suicide attempt.
   1. Yes
   2. No
   3. NI

---

* No information.

4. Six months to one year prior to the accident, suicide attempt or appendicitis, there was a deliberate suicide attempt.
1. Yes
2. No
3. NI

5. One year or longer prior to the accident, suicide attempt or appendicitis, there was a deliberate suicide attempt.
1. Yes
2. No
3. NI

6. In the seven days prior to the accident, suicide attempt or appendicitis, subject had suicidal thoughts.
1. Yes
2. No
3. NI

7. Seven days to six months prior to the accident, suicide attempt or appendicitis, subject had suicidal thoughts.
1. Yes
2. No
3. NI

8. Six months to one year prior to the accident, suicide attempt or appendicitis, subject had suicidal thoughts.
1. Yes
2. No
3. NI

9. One year or longer prior to the accident, suicide attempt or appendicitis, subject had suicidal thoughts.
1. Yes
2. No
3. NI

10. In the seven days prior to the accident, suicide attempt or appendicitis, subject communicated suicidal ideas.
1. Yes
2. No
3. NI

11. Seven days to six months prior to the accident, suicide attempt or appendicitis, subject communicated suicidal ideas.
1. Yes
2. No
3. NI

12. Six months to one year prior to the accident, suicide attempt or appendicitis, subject communicated suicidal ideas.
1. Yes
2. No
3. NI

13. One year or longer prior to the accident, suicide attempt or appendicitis, subject communicated suicidal ideas.
1. Yes
2. No
3. NI

14. Subjects thinks about death:
1. Never
2. Once a year
3. Once a month
4. Once a week
5. Every day
6. NI

15. Subject thinks abut his own death:
1. Never
2. Once a year
3. Once a month
4. Once a week
5. Every day
6. NI

SECTION B—ACCIDENT HISTORY

16. Traffic Acidents

    A. During the last month, how many traffic accidents did the subject have?

        1. None
        2. One
        3. More than one
        4. NI

    B. During the last six months, how many traffic accidents did the subject have?

        1. None
        2. One
        3. More than one
        4. NI

    C. During the last three years, how many traffic accidents did the subject have?

        1. None
        2. 1-3
        3. More than 3
        4. NI

    D. During his entire lifetime, how many traffic accidents did the subject have?

        1. None
        2. One
        3. 1-5
        4. More than 5
        5. NI

17. Other Accidents Requiring Hospitalization

    A. During the last month, how many other accidents requiring hospitalization did the subject have?

        1. None
        2. One
        3. More than one
        4. NI

    B. During the last year, how many other accidents requiring hospitalization did the subject have?

        1. None
        2. One
        3. More than one
        4. NI

    C. During the last three years, how many other accidents requiring hospitalization did the subject have?

        1. None
        2. One
        3. More than one
        4. NI

    D. During his entire lifetime, how many other accidents requiring hospitalization did the subject have?

        1. None
        2. One
        3. 1-5
        4. More than 5
        5. NI

18. Traffic Violations

    A. Status of Driver's License:

        1. In Effect
        2. Suspended
        3. Revoked

                4. Never had one
                5. NI

B. Non-Moving Violations during the Last Year:
  1. 0-1
  2. 2-5
  3. 6-10
  4. 11-20
  5. Over 20
  6. NI

C. Moving Violations during the Last Year:
  1. 0-1
  2. 2-3
  3. 4-5
  4. Over 5
  5. NI

D. Attitudes toward Driving Violations:
  1. Much concern
  2. Moderate concern
  3. Little or no concern
  4. NI

SECTION C—DEPRESSION

19. In the seven days prior to the accident, suicide attempt or appendicitis, to what degree did the subject manifest the following systoms:

A. Sleep disorder—early morning waking?
  1. Not at all
  2. Mild
  3. Moderate
  4. Severe
  5. NI

B. Sleep disorder—difficulty in going to sleep?
  1. Not at all
  2. Mild
  3. Moderate
  4. Severe
  5. NI

C. Fatigue?
  1. Not at all
  2. Mild
  3. Moderate
  4. Severe
  5. NI

D. Despondency?
  1. Not at all
  2. Mild
  3. Moderate
  4. Severe
  5. NI

E. Social withdrawal?
  1. Not at all
  2. Mild
  3. Moderate

4. Severe

5. NI

F. Disorganization, confusion and difficulty in concentration?

1. Not at all

2. Mild

3. Moderate

4. Severe

5. NI

G. Diminished sexual activity?

1. Not at all

2. Mild

3. Moderate

4. Severe

5. NI

H. Other symptoms of depression?

1. Not at all

2. Mild

3. Moderate

4. Severe

5. NI

20. Seven days to six months prior to the accident, suicide attempt or appendicitis, to what degree did subject manifest the following symptoms:

A. Sleep disorder—early morning waking?

1. Not at all

2. Mild

3. Moderate

4. Severe

5. NI

B. Sleep disorder—difficulty in going to sleep?

1. Not at all

2. Mild

3. Moderate

4. Severe

5. NI

C. Fatigue?

1. Not at all

2. Mild

3. Moderate

4. Severe

5. NI

D. Despondency?

1. Not at all

2. Mild

3. Moderate

4. Severe

5. NI

E. Social withdrawal?

1. Not at all

2. Mild

3. Moderate

4. Severe

5. NI

F. Disorganization, confusion and difficulty in concentration?

1. Not at all
2. Mild
3. Moderate
4. Severe
5. NI

G. Diminished sexual activity?

1. Not at all
2. Mild
3. Moderate
4. Severe
5. NI

H. Other symptoms of depression?

1. Not at all
2. Mild
3. Moderate
4. Severe
5. NI

21. Six months to one year prior to the accident, suicide attempt or appendicitis, to what degree did subject manifest the following symptoms:

A. Sleep disorder—early morning waking?

1. Not at all
2. Mild
3. Moderate
4. Severe
5. NI

B. Sleep disorder—difficulty in going to sleep?

1. Not at all
2. Mild
3. Moderate
4. Severe
5. NI

C. Fatigue?

1. Not at all
2. Mild
3. Moderate
4. Severe
5. NI

D. Despondency?

1. Not at all
2. Mild
3. Moderate
4. Severe
5. NI

E. Social withdrawal?

1. Not at all
2. Mild
3. Moderate
4. Severe
5. NI

F. Disorganization, confusion and difficulty in concentration?

1. Not at all
2. Mild

	3. Moderate
	4. Severe
	5. NI
G. Diminished sexual activity?	1. Not at all
	2. Mild
	3. Moderate
	4. Severe
	5. NI
H. Other symptoms of depression?	1. Not at all
	2. Mild
	3. Moderate
	4. Severe
	5. NI

22. One year or longer prior to the accident, suicide attempt or appendicitis, to what degree did subject manifest the following symptoms:

A. Sleep disorder—early morning waking?	1. Not at all
	2. Mild
	3. Moderate
	4. Severe
	5. NI
B. Sleep disorder—difficulty in going to sleep?	1. Not at all
	2. Mild
	3. Moderate
	4. Severe
	5. NI
C. Fatigue?	1. Not at all
	2. Mild
	3. Moderate
	4. Severe
	5. NI
D. Despondency?	1. Not at all
	2. Mild
	3. Moderate
	4. Severe
	5. NI
E. Social withdrawal?	1. Not at all
	2. Mild
	3. Moderate
	4. Severe
	5. NI
F. Disorganization, confusion and difficulty in concentration?	1. Not at all
	2. Mild
	3. Moderate

	4. Severe
	5. NI
G. Diminished sexual activity?	1. Not at all
	2. Mild
	3. Moderate
	4. Severe
	5. NI
H. Other symptoms of depression?	1. Not at all
	2. Mild
	3. Moderate
	4. Severe
	5. NI

SECTION D—EMOTIONAL PROBLEMS

23. Has the subject had contact with a mental health professional?

1. Yes
2. No
3. NI

    A. If yes, the most extensive contact was:

1. 1 interview
2. Brief therapy
3. Less than one year
4. More than one year
5. Repeated unsuccess-ful therapies
6. NI

    B. If yes, the contact was:

1. In-patient
2. Out-patient
3. Both in- and out-patient
4. NI

    C. If yes, subject was in contact:

1. At time of accident, suicide attempt or appendicitis
2. Within last year
3. Within last five years
4. More than five years ago
5. NI

24 Did the subject experience the early loss of his mother?

1. Yes
2. No
3. NI

    A. If yes, choose one:

1. Before age 6
2. Between 6-12
3. Between 12-18
4. NI

B. If yes, how?

1. Natural death
2. Accidental death
3. Suicidal death
4. Homicidal death
5. Chronic illness
6. Divorce
7. Abandonment
8. NI

25. Did the subject experience the early loss of his father?

1. Yes
2. No
3. NI

    A. If yes, choose one:

1. Before age 6
2. Between 6-12
3. Between 12-18
4. NI

    B. If yes, how?

1. Natural death
2. Accidental death
3. Suicidal death
4. Homicidal death
5. Chronic illness
6. Divorce
7. Abandonment
8. NI

26. Did the subject experience the early loss of another important figure?

1. Yes
2. No
3. NI

    A. If yes, choose one:

1. Before age 6
2. Between 6-12
3. Between 12-18
4. NI

    B. If yes, how?

1. Natural death
2. Accidental death
3. Suicidal death
4. Homicidal death
5. Chronic illness
6. Divorce
7. Abandonment
8. NI

27. In the seven days prior to the accident, suicide attempt or appendicitis, did the subject manifest:

    A. Frequent bursts of increased activity (in work, hobbies, sex or sports)?

1. Yes
2. No
3. NI

    B. Restless irritability with others?

1. Yes

			2. No
			3. NI
	C.	Episodes of excessive time spent driving?	1. Yes
			2. No
			3. NI
	D.	Episodes of using driving to work off steam?	1. Yes
			2. No
			3. NI
	E.	Great denial?	1. Yes
			2. No
			3. NI
	F.	Specific fears or phobias?	1. Yes
			2. No
			3. NI
	G.	Significant increase in smoking?	1. Yes
			2. No
			3. NI

28. In the seven days to six months prior to the accident, suicide attempt or appendicitis, did the subject manifest:

	A.	Frequent bursts of increased activity (in work, hobbies, sex or sports)?	1. Yes
			2. No
			3. NI
	B.	Restless irritability with others?	1. Yes
			2. No
			3. NI
	C.	Episodes of excessive time spent driving?	1. Yes
			2. No
			3. NI
	D.	Episodes of using driving to work off steam?	1. Yes
			2. No
			3. NI
	E.	Great denial?	1. Yes
			2. No
			3. NI
	F.	Specific fears or phobias?	1. Yes
			2. No
			3. NI
	G.	Significant increase in smoking?	1. Yes
			2. No
			3. NI

29. Six months to one year prior to the accident, suicide attempt or appendicitis, did the subject manifest:

	A.	Frequent bursts of increased activity	1. Yes

(in work, hobbies, sex or sports)?	2. No
	3. NI
B. Restless irritability with others?	1. Yes
	2. No
	3. NI
C. Episodes of excessive time spent driving?	1. Yes
	2. No
	3. NI
D. Episodes of using driving to work off steam?	1. Yes
	2. No
	3. NI
E. Great denial?	1. Yes
	2. No
	3. NI
F. Specific fears or phobias?	1. Yes
	2. No
	3. NI
G. Significant increase in smoking?	1. Yes
	2. No
	3. NI

30. One year or longer prior to the accident, suicide attempt or appendicitis, did the subject manifest:

A. Frequent bursts of increased activity (in work, hobbies, sex or sports)?	1. Yes
	2. No
	3. NI
B. Restless irritability with others?	1. Yes
	2. No
	3. NI
C. Episodes of excessive time spent driving?	1. Yes
	2. No
	3. NI
D. Episodes of using driving to work off steam?	1. Yes
	2. No
	3. NI
E. Great denial?	1. Yes
	2. No
	3. NI
F. Specific fears or phobias?	1. Yes
	2. No
	3. NI
G. Significant increase in smoking?	1. Yes
	2. No
	3. NI

31. When exposed to some disappointment, loss or being "put down," does the subject manifest:

    A. Frequent bursts of increased activity   1. Yes
       (in work, hobbies, sex or sports)?   2. No
                                     3. NI

    B. Restless irritability with others?   1. Yes
                                     2. No
                                     3. NI

    C. Episodes of excessive time spent driving?   1. Yes
                                     2. No
                                     3. NI

    D. Episodes of using driving to work off   1. Yes
       steam?   2. No
                                     3. NI

    E. Great denial?   1. Yes
                                     2. No
                                     3. NI

    F. Specific fears or phobias?   1. Yes
                                     2. No
                                     3. NI

    G. Significant increase in smoking?   1. Yes
                                     2. No
                                     3. NI

SECTION E—ALCOHOLIC HISTORY

32. Customarily, the subject drinks daily: 1. Never
                                     2. One drink
                                     3. 2-4 drinks
                                     4. 5 or more
                                     5. NI

33. Does the subject ever drink to the point   1. Yes
where his state of consciousness is moderately   2. No
impaired (does not respond to auditory, visual or   3. NI
tactile stimuli as well as he usually does)?

    A. If yes, how often?   1. Every day
                                     2. 2-6 times a week
                                     3. Once a week
                                     4. 2-5 times a month
                                     5. Once a month
                                     6. 2-11 times a year
                                     7. Once a year or less
                                     8. NI

34. Does the subject ever drink to the point   1. Yes
where his state of consciousness is severely im-   2. No

paired (loss of consciousness) or there is extreme   3. NI
change in social behavior?
    A. If yes, how often?

1. Every day
2. 2-6 times a week
3. Once a week
4. 2-5 times a month
5. Once a month
6. 2-11 times a year
7. Once a year or less
8. NI

35. Has drinking increased in the two days   1. Yes
before the accident, suicide attempt or appendi-   2. No
citis?   3. NI

36. Has drinking increased in the six months   1. Yes
before the accident, suicide attempt or appendi-   2. No
citis?   3. NI

SECTION F—DRUG INGESTION

"Drugs" are defined as mood changers. They include narcotics, sedatives, hypnotics, tranquilizers, stimulants and psychedelic or "mood-expanding" drugs.

37. In the seven days prior to the accident,   1. Never
suicide attempt or appendicitis, was the subject   2. Occasionally
taking drugs?   3. Moderately
    4. Heavily
    5. NI

    A. If yes, they were primarily obtained   1. A physician
    from: 2. Other legal source
    3. Extra-legal source
    4. NI

38. Seven days to six months prior to the acci-   1. Never
dent, suicide attempt or appendicitis, was the   2. Occasionally
subject taking drugs?   3. Moderately
    4. Heavily
    5. NI

    A. If yes, they were primarily obtained   1. A physician
    from: 2. Other legal source
    3. Extra-legal source
    4. NI

39. Six months to one year prior to the acci-   1. Never
dent, suicide attempt or appendicitis, was the   2. Occasionally
subject taking drugs?   3. Moderately
    4. Heavily
    5. NI

A. If yes, they were primarily obtained from:
1. A physician
2. Other legal source
3. Extra-legal source
4. NI

40. One year or longer prior to the accident, suicide attempt or appendicitis, was the subject taking drugs?
1. Never
2. Occasionally
3. Moderately
4. Heavily

A. If yes, they were primarily obtained from:
1. A physician
2. Other legal source
3. Extra-legal source
4. NI

SECTION G—SELF-DESTRUCTIVELY NOT SEEKING OR FOLLOWING MEDICAL ADVICE

41. In the seven days prior to the accident, suicide attempt or appendicitis, did the subject visit a physician?
1. Yes
2. No
3. NI

42. Seven days to six months before the accident, suicide attempt or appendicitis, did the subject visit a physician?
1. Yes
2. No
3. NI

43. Six months to one year prior to the accident, suicide attempt or appendicitis, did the subject visit a physician?
1. Yes
2. No
3. NI

44. Customarily, did the subject visit a physician when he thought he should?
1. Rarely
2. About half the time
3. Usually
4. NI

45. In the seven days prior to the accident, suicide attempt or appendicitis, did the subject follow any medical advice which was prescribed for him?
1. Yes
2. No
3. NI

46. Seven days to six months prior to the accident, suicide attempt or appendicitis, did the subject follow any medical advice which was prescribed for him?
1. Yes
2. No
3. NI

47. Six months to one year prior to the accident, suicide attempt or appendicitis, did the subject follow any medical advice which was prescribed for him?
1. Yes
2. No
3. NI

48. One year or longer prior to the accident, suicide attempt or appendicitis, did the subject follow any medical advice which was prescribed for him?
1. Yes
2. No
3. NI

49. Customarily, how often does the subject follow prescribed medical advice?
1. Rarely
2. About half the time
3. Usually
4. NI

50. Did the subject ever sign out of a hospital against medical advice?
1. Yes
2. No
3. NI

51. Did the subject ever refuse hospital treatment when suggested by a physician?
1. Yes
2. No
3. NI

SECTION H—INCREASED RISK TAKING

52. In the seven days prior to the accident, suicide attempt or appendicitis, approximately how many times did the subject injure himself and/or have a "narrow escape" from injuring himself or killing himself by taking some unnecessary risk?
1. None
2. 1-2 times
3. 3-10 times
4. Over 10 times
5. NI

53. Seven days to six months prior to the accident, suicide attempt or appendicitis, approximately how many times did the subject injure himself and/or have a "narrow escape" from injuring himself or killing himself by taking some unnecessary risk?
1. None
2. 1-2 times
3. 3-10 times
4. Over 10 times
5. NI

54. Six months to one year prior to the accident, suicide attempt or appendicitis, how many times did the subject injure himself and/or have a "narrow escape" from injuring himself or killing himself by taking some unnecessary risk?
1. None
2. 1-2 times
3. 3-10 times
4. Over 10 times
5. NI

55. One year or longer prior to the accident, suicide attempt or appendicitis, approximately how many times did the subject injure himself and/or have a "narrow escape" from injuring or killing himself by taking some unnecessary risk?
1. None
2. 1-2 times
3. 3-10 times
4. Over 10 times
5. NI

SECTION I—ADJUSTMENT TO CHANGE

56. New Responsibilities
    A. Advance at work, school or financially:
1. Yes
2. No
3. NI

   1. If yes, subject reports his feelings predominately:
1. Positive (Pleasant)
2. Mixed
3. Negative (Unpleasant)
4. NI

2. If yes, interviewer (or rater) evaluates advance for the subject as predominately:

1. Positive (Pleasant)
2. Mixed
3. Negative (Unpleasant)
4. NI

3. If yes, the most recent occurred:

1. 7 days to one month earlier
2. One month to six months
3. Six months to one year
4. One year or longer
5. NI

B. Marriage or engagement:

1. Yes
2. No
3. NI

1. If yes, subject reports his feelings predominately:

1. Positive (Pleasant)
2. Mixed
3. Negative (Unpleasant)
4. NI

2. If yes, interviewer (or rater) evaluates advance for the subject as predominately:

1. Positive (Pleasant)
2. Mixed
3. Negative (Unpleasant)
4. NI

3. If yes, the most recent occurred:

1. 7 days to one month earlier
2. One month to six months
3. Six months to one year
4. One year or longer
5. NI

C. New baby or pregnancy:

1. Yes
2. No
3. NI

1. If yes, subject reports his feelings predominately:

1. Positive (Pleasant)
2. Mixed
3. Negative (Unpleasant)
4. NI

2. If yes, interviewer (or rater) evalu-

1. Positive (Pleasant)

ates advance for subject as predominately:

   2. Mixed
   3. Negative (Unpleasant)
   4. NI

3. If yes, the most recent occurred:

   1. 7 days to one month earlier
   2. One month to six months
   3. Six months to one year
   4. One year or longer
   5. NI

57. Transitions
   A. Death of a loved one:

   1. Yes
   2. No
   3. NI

   1. If yes, subject reports his feelings predominately:

   1. Positive (Pleasant)
   2. Mixed
   3. Negative (Unpleasant)
   4. NI

   2. If yes, interviewer (or rater) evaluates transition for subject as predominately:

   1. Positive (Pleasant)
   2. Mixed
   3. Negative (Unpleasant)
   4. NI

   3. If yes, the most recent occurred:

   1. 7 days to one month earlier
   2. One month to six months
   3. Six months to one year
   4. One year or longer
   5. NI

   B. Divorce, separation or break-up of a close interpersonal relationship:

   1. Yes
   2. No
   3. NI

   1. If yes, subject reports his feelings as predominately:

   1. Positive (Pleasant)
   2. Mixed
   3. Negative (Unpleasant)
   4. NI

   2. If yes, interviewer (or rater) evalu-

   1. Positive (Pleasant)

ates transition for subject as pre-dominately:

    2. Mixed
    3. Negative (Unpleasant)
    4. NI

3. If yes, the most recent occurred:

    1. 7 days to one month earlier
    2. One month to six months
    3. Six months to one year
    4. One year or longer
    5. NI

C. Change of job:

    1. Yes
    2. No
    3. NI

1. If yes, subject reports his feelings predominately:

    1. Positive (Pleasant)
    2. Mixed
    3. Negative (Unpleasant)
    4. NI

2. If yes, interviewer (or rater) evaluates transition for subject as pre-dominately:

    1. Positive (Pleasant)
    2. Mixed
    3. Negative (Unpleasant)
    4. NI

3. If yes, the most recent occurred:

    1. 7 days to one month earlier
    2. One month to six months
    3. Six months to one year
    4. One year or longer
    5. NI

D. Change of residence:

    1. Yes
    2. No
    3. NI

1. If yes, subject reports his feelings predominately:

    1. Positive (Pleasant)
    2. Mixed
    3. Negative (Unpleasant)
    4. NI

2. If yes, interviewer (or rater) evalu-

    1. Positive (Pleasant)

ates transition for subject as predominately:

   2. Mixed
   3. Negative
     (Unpleasant)
   4. NI

3. If yes, the most recent occurred:

   1. 7 days to one month
     earlier
   2. One month to six
     months
   3. Six months to one
     year
   4. One year or longer
   5. NI

E. Addition of family member: (relative,
roommate, domestic help, etc.)

   1. Yes
   2. No
   3. NI

  1. If yes, subject reports his feelings
     predominately:

   1. Positive (Pleasant)
   2. Mixed
   3. Negative
     (Unpleasant)
   4. NI

  2. If yes, interviewer (or rater) evalu-
     ulates transition for subject as pre-
     dominately:

   1. Positive (Pleasant)
   2. Mixed
   3. Negative
     (Unpleasant)
   4. NI

  3. If yes, the most recent occurred:

   1. 7 days to one month
     earlier
   2. One month to six
     months
   3. Six months to one
     year
   4. One year or longer
   5. NI

F. Work, school or financial setback:

   1. Yes
   2. No
   3. NI

  1. If yes, subject reports his feelings
     predominately:

   1. Positive (Pleasant)
   2. Mixed
   3. Negative
     (Unpleasant)
   4. NI

  2. If yes, interviewer (or rater) evalu-

   1. Positive (Pleasant)

ates transition for subject as predominately:

    2. Mixed
    3. Negative
       (Unpleasant)
    4. NI

3. If yes, the most recent occurred:

    1. 7 days to one month
       earlier
    2. One month to six
       months
    3. Six months to one
       year
    4. One year or longer
    5. NI

G. Trouble with the law:

    1. Yes
    2. No
    3. NI

1. If yes, subject reports his feelings
predominately:

    1. Positive (Pleasant)
    2. Mixed
    3. Negative
       (Unpleasant)
    4. NI

2. If yes, interviewer (or rater) evaluates transition for subject as predominately:

    1. Positive (Pleasant)
    2. Mixed
    3. Negative
       (Unpleasant)
    4. NI

3. If yes, the most recent occurred:

    1. 7 days to one month
       earlier
    2. One month to six
       months
    3. Six months to one
       year
    4. One year or longer
    5. NI

H. Vacation:

    1. Yes
    2. No
    3. NI

1. If yes, subject reports his feelings
predominately:

    1. Positive (Pleasant)
    2. Mixed
    3. Negative
       (Unpleasant)
    4. NI

2. If yes, interviewer (or rater) evalu-

    1. Positive (Pleasant)

ates transition for subject as predominately:

   3. If yes, the most recent occurred:

2. Mixed
3. Negative
(Unpleasant)
4. NI
1. 7 days to one month earlier
2. One month to six months
3. Six months to one year
4. One year or longer
5. NI

SECTION J—VIOLENCE

58. How often does subject act in an impulsive (sudden, unpredicted) way which results in some destruction of physical objects?

1. Never
2. Twice a year or less
3. 3-12 times a year
4. 13-52 times a year
5. More than 52 times a year
6. NI

59. How often does subject act in an impulsive (sudden, unpredicted) way which results in some physical injury to himself?

1. Never
2. Twice a year or less
3. 3-12 times a year
4. 13-52 times a year
5. More than 52 times a year
6. NI

60. How often does subject act in an impulsive (sudden, unpredicted) way which results in physical injury to other people?

1. Never
2. Twice a year or less
3. 3-12 times a year
4. 13-52 times a year
5. More than 52 times a year
6. NI

SECTION K—LACK OF INTEGRATION BETWEEN DEPRESSIVE AND COUNTER-DEPRESSIVE STYLES OF LIFE

61. Many (perhaps all) people tend to change from mood states which, on the one hand, are quiet, orderly, deliberate, thoughtful, serious and perhaps slightly depressed, to mood states which are more active and noisy, unplanned, impulsive

1. Never
2. Less than once a month
3. Once a month
4. Once a day

and happy. How often does the subject make such changes in either direction?

5. Several times a day
6. NI

SECTION L—LOSS OF SELF ESTEEM

62. In the week before the accident, suicide attempt or appendicitis, was the subject thinking poorly about himself in regard to not having done well and/or having others indicate that he was not doing well in regard to some issue (work, school, approval of others, etc.) which was important to him?

1. Yes
2. No
3. NI

SECTION M—DRIVING HISTORY

63. Years driving:

1. 0-5
2. 6-10
3. 11-15
4. 16-20
5. 21-25
6. 26-30
7. 31-40
8. 41-50
9. 50 or more
10. NI

64. Driving exposure—average miles to work:

1. 0-10
2. 11-50
3. 51-150
4. 151-500
5. 500 or more
6. NI

65. Attitude toward car and driving:

1. Very important for self-esteem
2. Moderate interest and concern
3. Just transportation
4. NI

SECTION N—THE ACCIDENT WHICH LED TO THIS HOSPITALIZATION

66. Other occupants of the automobile:

1. Wife
2. Children
3. Wife and children
4. Girl friend
5. Friend(s)
6. Other
7. NI

67. Time of day:
1. Morning
2. Afternoon
3. Early evening
4. Late evening or early morning
5. NI

68. Drinking within twelve hours prior to the accident:
1. One drink or several beers
2. 2-3 drinks or 3-4 beers
3. 4-5 drinks or 6-pack of beer
4. 6-9 drinks or over six beers
5. NI

69. Reason for the trip (during which the accident occurred):
1. To or from work
2. On a date
3. Just driving around
4. Dragging
5. Vacation
6. To or from party, bar or other entertainment
7. Other
8. NI

70. How subject says accident happened:
1. Fell asleep
2. Precipitated by another car
3. Lapse of attention
4. Don't remember
5. Mechanical failure
6. NI

71. What happened?
1. Left the road
2. Left road and hit stationary object
3. Other
4. NI

SECTON O—DYNAMICS OF THE INTERVIEW

72. Initial attitude of the patient:
1. Cooperative
2. Moderately cooperatively
3. Uncooperative
4. NI

73. Later attitude of the patient:

    1. Cooperative
    2. Moderately cooperative
    3. Uncooperative
    4. NI

74. Resistances of the patient:

    A. Amnesia?

        1. Yes
        2. No
        3. NI

    B. Other physical handicap?

        1. Yes
        2. No
        3. NI

    C. Medicated state?

        1. Yes
        2. No
        3. NI

    D. Legal difficulties?

        1. Yes
        2. No
        3. NI

    E. Family interference?

        1. Yes
        2. No
        3. NI

    F. False information?

        1. Yes
        2. No
        3. NI

    G. Refusal to answer?

        1. Yes
        2. No
        3. NI

    H. Severe evasiveness?

        1. Yes
        2. No
        3. NI

Interviewer: Please check following on ALL ACCIDENT CASES:

1. Was patient wearing seatbelts?

    1. Yes
    2. No

2. If patient wears glasses, was he wearing them at the time of the accident?

    1. Yes
    2. No
    3. NA†

74	75	76	77	78	79	

† Not applicable.

DATA SHEET QUESTIONS USED TO TEST HYPOTHESES*

	Direct Test	*Indirect Test*
Hypothesis A	1	—
Deliberate Suicide Attempt		
Hypothesis B	2	6
Suicide Attempts and Preoccupation	3	7
	4	8
	5	9
	10	1
	11	14
	12	15
	13	19A-22H
Hypothesis C	2	
Depressive Symptoms	3	
	4	
	5	
	6	
	7	
	8	
	9	
	10	
	11	
	12	
	13	
	14	
	15	
	19A-H	
	20A-H	
	21A-H	
	22A-H	

* The Hypotheses are listed at the end of Chapter 3, Development and Identification of the Hypotheses, p. 49. They are then evaluated in Chapter 6, Evaluation of Data Sheet Responses: The Hypotheses, p. 75. Letters and numbers refer to specific questions in Appendix I.

	Direct Test	Indirect Test
Hypothesis D	27A	27B-D
Counter-Depressive Attitude	28A	28B-D
	29A	29B-D
	30A	30B-D
	31A	31B-D
Hypothesis E¹	36	—
Recent Drinking—Onset last six months		
Hypothesis E²	32	—
Chronic, Excessive Drinking	33A	
	34A	
Hypothesis E³	37	—
Recent Drug Abuse		
Hypothesis E⁴	38	—
History of drug abuse	39	
	40	
Hypothesis F¹	45	—
Not following medical advice, recent		
Hypothesis F²	46	
Not following medical advice, chronic	47	
	48	
	49	
	50	
	51	
	44	
Hypothesis G¹	52	27C
Risky behavior—recent		
Hypothesis G²	53	28C
History of risky behavior	54	29C
	55	30C
		31C
		59
Hypothesis H	56A	57C
New responsibility, last six months	56A-3	57C-3
	56B	57D
	56B-3	57D-3
	56C	57E
	56C-3	57E-3
Hypothesis I	58	—
Impulsive Actions	59	
	60	
Hypothesis J	61	—
Lack of integration between depression and counter-depression		

	Direct Test	Indirect Test
Hypothesis K Recent loss of self-esteem	62	57A
		57A-3
		57B
		57B-3
		57F
		57F-3
		57G
		57G-3
Hypothesis M Recent life change	56A	
	56A-3	
	56B	
	56B-3	
	56C	
	56C-3	
	57A	
	57A-3	
	57B	
	57B-3	
	57C	
	57C-3	
	57D	
	57D-3	
	57E	
	57E-3	
	57F	
	57F-3	
	57G	
	57G-3	
	57H	
	57H-3	

THE SIGNIFICANT OTHER STUDY

Interviewer Guide—Data Sheet

I. Description of Event (Accident, Suicide or Appendectomy)

A. Informant will describe details of the event resulting in subject's hospitalization: e.g., how it happened, what led up to it, and other supplementary information centering around the event itself.

....
....
....
....
....
....

B. In the opinion of the informant, what could have been done by the informant, subject, or anyone else, to avoid the event which led to the hospitalization?

....
....
....
....

II. Health and Medical Information

A. How has the subject's general health been in the last year?
Good .... Poor .... NI ....
1. If poor, what has been wrong? ....
....
....

B. Have there been any changes in the subject's health in the last six weeks? (Last six weeks here always means six weeks prior to hospitalization, not from time of interview.)
Yes .... No .... NI ....
1. If yes, please describe these changes: ....
....
....

C. How has the informant's health been in the last year?
Good .... Poor .... NI ....
1. If poor, what problems has he had? ....
....

242

2. Have there been any changes in his health in the last six weeks?
Yes .... No .... NI ....
   a. If yes, please describe: ....

D. Has the subject had any contact with a physician in the last year?
Yes .... No .... NI ....
1. If yes, for what reason? ....

E. Has the subject had contact with a physician in the last six weeks?
Yes .... No .... NI ....
1. If yes, for what reason? ....

F. Has the informant had contact with a physician in the last year?
Yes .... No .... NI ....
1. If yes, for what reason? ....

G. Has the informant had contact with a physician in the last six weeks?
Yes .... No .... NI ....
1. If yes, for what reason? ....

H. Has the health or changes in the health of either the subject or the informant affected the relationship between the two?
Yes .... No .... NI ....
1. If yes, how? Please describe: ....

I. Has the subject had contact with a mental health professional in the last year?
Yes .... No .... NI ....
1. If yes, for what reason? ....

2. If yes, how many contacts were there? ....
J. Has the subject had contact with a mental health professional in the last six weeks?
Yes .... No .... NI ....
1. If yes, for what reason? ....

2. If yes, how many contacts? ....

K. Did either the subject or informant's contact with the mental health professional affect the relationship?
Yes .... No .... NI ....
1. If yes, how? Please describe: ....
....
....

III. Occupational Information
A. Has the subject been working in the last year?
Yes .... No .... NI ....
1. If yes, what kind of work has he done? ....
....
2. How long has he held a job? ....
3. What was the previous job and how long did he have it? ....
....
....

B. In the last six weeks, have there been any changes in his work?
Yes .... No .... NI ....
1. If yes, has there been a promotion?
Yes .... No .... NI ....
2. If yes, has he lost his job?
Yes .... No .... NI ....
3. If yes, has he been demoted?
Yes .... No .... NI ....
C. Has he had any specific problems with other workers or with his employer?
Yes .... No .... NI ....
D. Have there been any other changes or anticipated changes?
Please specify: ....
....
....

E. Has the informant been working in the last year?
Yes .... No .... NI ....
1. What kind of work has he been doing? ....
....
....
2. How long has he held a job? ....
3. What was the informant's previous job? ....
....
....

F. Have there been any changes in the informant's working in the last six weeks?
Yes .... No .... NI ....
1. If yes, has there been a promotion?
Yes .... No .... NI ....

2. If yes, has he lost his job?
Yes .... No .... NI ....
3. If yes, has he been demoted?
Yes .... No .... NI ....
G. Has the informant had any specific problems with other workers or with his employer?
Yes .... No .... NI ....
H. Any other changes or anticipated changes in the informant's work?
Yes .... No .... NI ....
If yes, please specify: ....
....

I. Have any recent changes, either by the subject or informant, affected the relationship between the two?
Yes .... No .... NI ....
1. If so, how? ....
....
....

IV. General Financial Matters

A. In general, over the last year, has the subject managed his money adequately?
Yes .... No .... NI ....
B. Has the informant managed his money adequately?
Yes .... No .... NI ....
1. If no for either, have there been major debts?
Yes .... No .... NI ....
2. If yes, who has incurred them? ....
....

C. Have debts or money mismanagement ever caused disagreement between subject and informant?
Yes .... No .... NI ....
1. If yes, please describe: ....
....

D. Has there been a change in the last six weeks in the subject's debts or money management?
Yes .... No .... NI ....
1. If yes, please describe: ....
....

E. Has there been a change in the last six weeks in the informant's debts or money management?
Yes .... No .... NI ....
1. If yes, please describe: ....
....

F. How have these changes affected the relationship? Please describe:
....

. . . .
. . . .

V. *Transitions*

A. In the last six weeks has the subject experienced the death of any friend or relative?

Yes . . . . No . . . . NI . . . .

1. If yes, who? . . . .

B. Has someone related to or close to the subject been ill?

Yes . . . . No . . . . NI . . . .

1. If yes, who? . . . .

C. Has the relationship between the subject and the informant been affected by this?

Yes . . . . No . . . . NI . . . .

1. If yes, please, describe in which way this had occurred: . . . .
. . . .
. . . .

D. In the last six weeks, has anyone close to the subject had a child?

Yes . . . . No . . . . NI . . . .

1. If yes, who? What is the relationship? . . . .
. . . .

E. In the last six weeks, has anyone close to the subject become pregnant?

Yes . . . . No . . . . NI . . . .

1. If yes, who? What is the relationship? . . . .
. . . .

F. Has the relationship between the subject and the informant been affected by this?

Yes . . . . No . . . . NI . . . .

1. If yes, in what way? Please describe: . . . .
. . . .
. . . .

G. Has the subject moved in the last six weeks?

Yes . . . . No . . . . NI . . . .

H. Has the subject planned any changes in living arrangements in the last six weeks?

Yes . . . . No . . . . NI . . . .

I. Has the subject taken a trip in the last six weeks?

Yes . . . . No . . . . NI . . . .

J. Has the subject planned a trip in the last six weeks?

Yes . . . . No . . . . NI . . . .

K. Has the informant moved in the last six weeks?

Yes . . . . No . . . . NI . . . .

L. In the last six weeks has the informant experienced the death of any friend or relative?

Yes . . . . No . . . . NI . . . .

1. If yes, who? ....

M. Has someone related to or close to the informant been ill?

Yes .... No .... NI ....

1. If yes, who? ....

N. Has the relationship between the informant and the subject been affected by this?

Yes .... No .... NI ....

1. If yes, please describe in which way this has occurred: ....

....

....

O. In the last six weeks, has anyone close to the informant had a child?

Yes .... No .... NI ....

1. If yes? What is the relationship? ....

....

P. In the last six weeks, has anyone close to the informant become pregnant?

Yes .... No .... NI ....

1. If yes, who? What is the relationship? ....

....

Q. Has the relationship between the informant and the subject been affected by this?

Yes .... No .... NI ....

1. If yes, in what way? Please describe: ....

....

....

R. Has the informant moved in the last six weeks?

Yes .... No .... NI ....

S. Has the informant planned any changes in living arrangements in the last six weeks?

Yes .... No .... NI ....

T. Has the informant taken a trip in the last six weeks?

Yes .... No .... NI ....

U. Has the informant planned a trip in the last six weeks?

Yes .... No .... NI ....

V. Has the relationship between the subject and the informant been affected by any of this?

Yes .... No .... NI ....

1. If yes, which of the above seemed to contribute to this, and how? ...

....

....

....

W. Has the subject been in trouble with the law in the last six weeks?

Yes .... No .... NI ....

1. If yes, what happened? ....

....

2. If yes, is this the first time that the subject has been in trouble with the law?
Yes .... No .... NI ....
X. Has the relationship between the subject and the informant been affected by this?
Yes .... No .... NI ....
1. If yes, please describe in which way: ....
....
Y. In the last six weeks, has the informant been in trouble with the law?
Yes .... No .... NI ....
1. If yes, what happened? ....
....
2. Is this the first time that the informant has been in trouble with the law?
Yes .... No .... NI ....
Z. Has the relationship between the subject and the informant been affected by this?
Yes .... No .... NI ....
1. If yes, please describe in which way: ....
....

VI. Mood Information

A. Most of the time, the subject is a moody person? (That is, he has definite highs and lows, frequently changing.)
Yes .... No .... NI ....
B. Most of the time, the informant is a moody person?
Yes .... No .... NI ....
C. Have you known the subject to be depressed? (Depression can be characterized to the informant as sleeplessness, loss of appetite, despondency, withdrawal, and a loss of interest in activities.)
Yes .... No .... NI ....
D. Have you known the informant to be depressed?
Yes .... No .... NI ....
E. Any changes in the last six weeks in mood or depression in the subject?
Yes .... No .... NI ....
F. Any changes in the last six weeks in mood or depression in the informant?
Yes .... No .... NI ....
1. If yes, please describe changes in the subject: ....
....
....
2. If yes, please describe changes in the informant: ....
....
....

G. Have any of these changes affected the relationship between subject and informant?
Yes .... No .... NI ....
1. If yes, please describe: ....
....
....

H. Has the subject ever made a deliberate suicide attempt?
Yes .... No .... NI ....
1. If yes, when? ....
....
2. What did he do? ....
....
3. Did this have any affect on the informant?
Yes .... No .... NI ....
   a. If yes, please describe: ....
....
4. How did this affect the relationship between subject and informant?
Please describe: ....
....
5. Has the informant ever made a deliberate suicide attempt?
Yes .... No .... NI ....
1. If yes, when? ....
....
2. What did he do? ....
....
....
3. If yes, how did this affect the relationship between the subject and the informant? ....
....

I. Has the subject ever indicated any other evidence of being "suicidal" (e.g. talking about suicide?)
Yes .... No .... NI ....
1. If yes, please describe: ....
....

J. Has the informant ever felt suicidal?
Yes .... No .... NI ....
1. If yes, please describe: ....
....

K. Any recent changes in the suicidal behavior or feelings of the subject or informant in the last six weeks?
Yes .... No .... NI ....
1. If yes, please describe: ....
....
....

2. If yes, how has this affected the relationship between subject and informant? ....

....

....

....

L. Has the subject ever had an automobile accident?

1. If yes, please describe each (Were there injuries? How severe?): ...

....

....

....

2. When did they occur? ....

....

M. Has the informant ever had an automobile accident?

Yes .... No .... NI ....

1. If yes, describe each: ....

....

....

2. When did they occur? ....

....

N. Has any of the accidents affected the relationship between subject and informant?

Yes .... No .... NI ....

1. If yes, please describe: ....

....

....

(*Note to Interviewer:* The accident and suicide behavior of the subject referred to in this interview does not include the recent hospitalization event.)

VII. Information about Usage of Alcohol and Drugs

A. Has the subject used alcohol regularly?

Yes .... No .... NI ....

B. Has the subject used alcohol excessively (to point of drunkenness) in the past?

Yes .... No .... NI ....

C. Has subject's drinking behavior changed in the last six weeks?

Yes .... No .... NI ....

1. If yes, how? Please describe: ....

....

....

D. Has the informant used alcohol regularly?

Yes .... No .... NI ....

E. Has the informant used alcohol excessively (to point of drunkenness) in the past?

Yes .... No .... NI ....

F. Has drinking behavior changed, for the informant, in the last six weeks?
Yes .... No .... NI ....
1. If yes, how? ....
....

G. How have the changes in drinking behavior of either the subject or the informant affected the relationship between subject and informant? ...
....
....
....

H. Has the subject in the last year, used medication prescribed by the physician?
Yes .... No .... NI ....
1. If yes, what medications were used, and how often did he use them?
....

I. Has the subject, in the last year, used drugs which were not prescribed?
Yes .... No .... NI ....
1. What drugs? ....
2. How often were they used? ....
J. Any changes in drug use in the last six weeks for the subject?
Yes .... No .... NI ....
1. Please describe this: ....
....

K. How have these changes affected the relationship between the subject and the informant? ....
....
....

L. Has the informant, in the last year, used medication prescribed by a physician?
Yes .... No .... NI ....
1. What medication was used and how often was it used? ....
....
....

M. Has the informant, in the last year, used drugs which were not prescribed?
Yes .... No .... NI ....
1. What drugs were used? ....
2. How often were they used? ....
....

N. Have there been any changes in the informant's drug usage in the last six weeks?
Yes .... No .... NI ....
1. Please describe: ....
....

O. How have these changes affected the relationship between the subject and the informant? . . . .
. . . .
. . . .
. . . .

VIII. *Information about Sexual Behavior*
A. Has the subject had regular sexual activity in the last year?
Yes . . . . No . . . . NI . . . .
B. Has the subject apparently been satisfied or pleased sexually?
Yes . . . . No . . . . NI . . . .
C. With whom has the subject had sexual activities? . . . .
. . . .
. . . .

D. Have there been any changes in the subject's sexual behavior in the last six weeks?
Yes . . . . No . . . . NI . . . .
1. If yes, how have these changes affected the relationship between the subject and the informant? . . . .
. . . .
. . . .

E. Has the informant had regular sexual activity in the last year?
Yes . . . . No . . . . NI . . . .
F. Has the informant been satisfied or pleased sexually?
Yes . . . . No . . . . NI . . . .
G. With whom has the informant had sexual contacts? . . . .
. . . .
. . . .

H. Have there been any changes in the informant's sexual behavior in the last six weeks?
Yes . . . . No . . . . NI . . . .
1. If yes, how have these changes affected the relationship between subject and informant?
. . . .
. . . .

IX. *General Friendships*
A. Does subject have several close friends?
Yes . . . . No . . . . NI . . . .
B. Does he have any friends?
Yes . . . . No . . . . NI . . . .
C. Would the subject generally be regarded as a loner?
Yes . . . . No . . . . NI . . . .

D. Does the informant have several close friends?
Yes .... No .... NI ....
E. Does the informant have any close friends?
Yes .... No .... NI ....
F. Would the informant generally be regarded as a loner?
Yes .... No .... NI ....
G. Has the subject, in the last six weeks, experienced problems with any friends?
Yes .... No .... NI ....
H. Has the informant, for the last six weeks experienced problems with friends?
Yes .... No .... NI ....
I. Has this affected the relationship between subject and informant?
Yes .... No .... NI ....
1. If yes, please describe: ....
....
J. Has the subject, in the last six weeks, acquired or sought out any new friends?
Yes .... No .... NI ....
K. Has the informant, in the last six weeks, acquired or sought out any new friends?
Yes .... No .... NI ....
L. Has this affected the relationship between subject and informant?
Yes .... No .... NI ....
1. If yes, please describe: ....
....
....

X. *Character of the Relationship between Subject and Informant*
A. How long have subject and informant known each other? ....
B. At what point did the relationship become close? ....
....
1. In last six weeks, has there been a change in this closeness?
Yes .... No .... NI ....
C. During the relationship, have there been separations?
Yes .... No .... NI ....
1. How often? ....
2. When? ....
D. Do religious beliefs or conflicts influence your relationship?
Yes .... No .... NI ....
1. If yes, any recent changes?
Yes .... No .... NI ....
E. Have subject and informant argued in past?
Yes .... No .... NI ....

1. How often, on average? ....
2. Any physical fights?
Yes .... No .... NI ....
3. What are arguments about? ....
   ....
   ....

F. Has there been a change in the last six weeks?
Yes .... No .... NI ....
Describe: ....
....
....

INDEX OF NAMES

SUBJECT INDEX

257